The
Happy
Sleeper

JEREMY P. TARCHER/PENGUIN

a member of Penguin Group (USA)

New York

The
Happy
Sleeper

The Science-Backed Guide to Helping

Your Baby Get a Good Night's Sleep—

Newborn to School Age

HEATHER TURGEON, MFT, AND

JULIE WRIGHT, MFT

ILLUSTRATIONS BY JACK SHEEHY

JEREMY P. TARCHER/PENGUIN
Published by the Penguin Group
Penguin Group (USA) LLC
375 Hudson Street
New York, New York 10014

USA · Canada · UK · Ireland · Australia
New Zealand · India · South Africa · China

penguin.com
A Penguin Random House Company

Most Tarcher/Penguin books are available at special quantity discounts for bulk purchase
for sales promotions, premiums, fund-raising, and educational needs. Special books
or book excerpts also can be created to fit specific needs. For details, write:
Special.Markets@us.penguingroup.com.

Library of Congress Cataloging-in-Publication Data

Turgeon, Heather.
The happy sleeper : the science-backed guide to helping your baby get a good night's
sleep—newborn to school age / Heather Turgeon, Julie Wright ; illustrations by Jack Sheehy.
p.   cm.
Includes bibliographical references and index.
ISBN 978-0-399-16602-0
1. Infants—Sleep.   2. Children—Sleep.   3. Child rearing.   I. Wright, Julie (Julie
Theresa).   II. Title.
BF723.S45T87   2014   2014035240
649'.1—dc23

Printed in the United States of America
17   19   20   18

Book design by Gretchen Achilles

Contents

Foreword

Compassionate, courageous, and creative, *The Happy Sleeper* is a book for every parent of a young child to savor in its magnificent exploration of effective strategies for helping children get to bed smoothly and sleep well through the night. Heather Turgeon and Julie Wright have written a user-friendly, scientifically informed, practical guide that provides the information and intention you need to cultivate healthy sleeping habits not only for your child but for yourself as well!

Why is sleep so important? It is during sleep that we secrete the growth hormones our bodies need to grow and replenish themselves well. Sleep also allows our body and brain to rest and recover from the day's activities. Recent studies have revealed, too, that during sleep our brains in effect clean themselves up—removing unhelpful by-products of the day's neural activity—so that we can function well when we're awake. Given all of this, it's no surprise that babies and children need so many hours of sleep as they grow. Infants and toddlers sleep half their day or more! In childhood the amount of optimal sleep gradually decreases, but school-age children still need roughly 10 hours of sleep. Even as adults, we should spend about a third of our time sleeping!

Without the proper amount and quality of sleep, science reveals, we will have difficulty focusing, remembering, and calming our emotions. When we haven't slept well we don't learn or operate as effectively because our brain hasn't had the necessary sleep time to optimize its functioning. Even more, without proper sleep, our immune system does not function well, and so we can become vulnerable to infectious diseases. And our metabolic system doesn't function optimally, so we can be prone to overeat and not process food well, putting us at risk for obesity and diabetes. For each of these reasons, sleep is one of the most important "activities" we humans participate in. And as parents, helping our children develop good sleep hygiene is one of the most important contributions we can make to their well-being.

In this fabulous guide, you'll learn to take important findings from sleep research and combine them with a crucial working knowledge of attachment research so that you'll optimize not only your children's sleep habits, but also their attachment to you. Attachment is all about providing security for your children through anticipating their inner needs, making them feel safe, and communicating with them in a soothing manner. Heather Turgeon and Julie Wright are brilliant sleep whisperers with decades of experience helping parents cultivate secure attachment while simultaneously shaping healthy sleep habits. That's exactly the combination studies suggest is the win-win-win of effective parenting: give your children the relationship security they need while also providing them the structure they require to sleep well and thrive. And all this while you, too, get some important rest.

You'll learn in these pages what science and clinical wisdom have to tell us about how to keep the relationship with your child filled with compassionate communication while also structuring healthy sleep strategies. You'll discover how you can nurture emotional understanding between you and your child while at the same time implementing behavioral strategies that ensure they get the sleep they need. The authors provide you with a framework that will leave you feeling confident in the positive outcome of your approach. This is a plan that works.

Parenting is one of the most challenging roles one can play in life. It's tricky to know when to hold our children close and when to let them venture out on their own to learn important skills, such as the self-soothing techniques that will help them be Happy Sleepers for the rest of their lives. Having this book as your companion, you will gain the clarity and conviction necessary to build a secure relationship with your child and, in turn, to help them build a secure relationship with themselves and their broader community. Read on, connect with compassion, creativity, and courage, and sleep well!

—DANIEL J. SIEGEL, MD

Introduction

Your baby already knows how to sleep.

Our clients are always shocked when they hear this. They've been breaking a sweat rocking their baby into a deep slumber, waking up every 2 hours to feed throughout the night, or wringing their hands in frustration with a wide-eyed, nap-resistant toddler.

But it's true. Sleep is a basic action that babies are naturally born to do. Their bodies crave healthy sleep, and their brains are wired for it. By 5 or 6 months of age, almost all babies are capable of sleeping well without much assistance from Mom or Dad.

So why do so many families struggle at night? The answer is that most parents do what works today, don't notice when it's no longer needed tomorrow, and then keep pushing even harder when it's become a hindrance the day after that. They work overtime with all kinds of fanfare and tricks to put their babies to bed. We've heard it all: parents feeding, rocking, and bouncing on a yoga ball for 45 minutes every night, lying down with kids, re-tucking, and refilling water glasses endlessly—one couple even told us they found themselves putting on a full music show with guitars, singing, and lights every night before bedtime.

Over time, parents' "helping ways" overshadow their baby's natural sleep abilities. Children get confused as to whether *they* or *their parents* are doing the soothing, and parents aren't sure when and how much to back off so their little ones can take over the job.

The Happy Sleeper is the guide to doing just that. We will give you a clear, easy-to-follow system for transferring the role of independent sleep to your baby or child, as we've done for thousands of families in our practice. If you're consistent in how you apply the methods in this book, your baby or child's sleep will improve dramatically within one to two weeks.

Good Sleep Is in Their Genes

Kids don't need to be *trained* to sleep; they're *built* to sleep. Think about it: sleep is like other areas of development, and you know how quickly your baby learns. Within a year, a baby can sit, pull to stand, and maybe take her first steps. She understands language and soon she'll speak in sentences. Almost overnight, she's a master in all realms.

So why should sleep be any different?

SKILL DEVELOPMENT OVER TIME

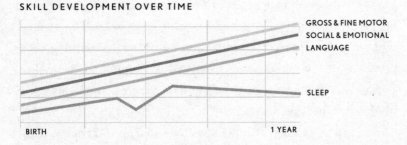

For many babies, skills in other domains grow and improve, but sleep skills stall or regress.

But over and over in our practice, we see that it is. Children take off in their motor, social, cognitive, and language skills, while sleep skills stall and even decline as the months go on. It's a common course for little kids—they show robust, thriving development in all other domains but actually *regress* in their ability to sleep.

In the early months, this happens when a soothing technique like nursing or rocking to sleep works and becomes your go-to habit (and we don't blame you!). The problem is that while newborns often *need* these soothing devices, they outgrow this need quickly as their natural self-soothing abilities grow—sometimes within a matter of days or weeks. With toddlers and kids, the same idea applies. We know that they can sleep, but milestones and life transitions (learning to climb out of the crib, starting preschool, or having nightmares) rock the boat just enough to warrant a new trick (like lying down with them until they doze off) that kids quickly become reliant on.

As parents get stuck in a habit of soothing their little one to sleep, it masks the child's natural abilities and makes it look as if she *can't* sleep on her own.

Imagine your child was capable of walking, but you still carried her everywhere instead of letting her practice this new skill! This overhelping is the crux of family sleep problems. Eventually parents become exasperated, while baby's sleep potential has actually been stifled.

Why We Wrote This Book

We wrote this book to help solve a dilemma. Over and over in our parenting groups, we've seen moms and dads work diligently to be responsive and nurturing around sleep, only to become frustrated, exhausted, and confused as their baby's sleep gets worse instead of better. These parents feel stuck, and many reach the end of their rope and turn to a harsh, shut-the-door-and-don't-go-in approach.

We know that sleep is a natural, hardwired function that shouldn't be so difficult. As clinicians who follow science and new thinking on child development, we realized why sleep was stumping so many families—it's the same overhelping or "helicopter parenting" dilemma that parents find themselves in elsewhere. Logic tells us (and research confirms) that overhelping doesn't work: When we do things for our babies and kids that they are capable of doing for themselves, it keeps them from developing to their potential (in this case, their sleep potential). The problem is that, as parents, we don't know how to stop overhelping, while still being warm and supportive to our kids.

The topic of baby sleep needs a fresh perspective. It's been bogged down in old-school notions like "training" and misunderstandings of basic concepts like attachment. In this book, we take an integrated approach that is sensitive, simple, and truly effective. We don't want anyone suffering sleep deprivation unnecessarily, nor do we ever want a baby to feel alone or fearful. Happily, neither of these ever needs to happen.

Our methods are based on two logical, research-based ideas. One: babies and little kids need warmth, sensitivity, and a sense that the world is a safe place. Two: they thrive best (and sleep best) when they have structure, routine, and clear expectations. When we work with parents to fix a sleep issue, we always locate the solution in one of these two places. If one of these is missing, a child's sleep ends up falling short of what she's developmentally capable of:

a 10-month-old baby waking every 1 to 2 hours at night (you'd be surprised how many we've met!), an 18-month-old who only naps in a stroller, or a child refusing to fall asleep unless Mom or Dad snuggles up too.

These parents swear that their child's not capable or is just a bad sleeper. But when we craft a sleep plan together (as we'll do in this book), within a week or two their baby is sleeping eleven hours straight, their toddler is taking a beautiful 2-hour nap in her crib, or their child is kissing them good night, grabbing his stuffed animal, rolling over, and falling asleep on his own.

Sleep affects virtually every part of your child's life. Well-rested babies and kids are emotionally balanced, flexible, and creative; they're healthier; they think clearly and retain information better. When your child sleeps well, she (and you) feel the ripples of this everywhere. It's amazing to see how good sleep transforms a family.

How to Use This Book

Chapter 1 is an introduction to childhood sleep issues, including information about how much sleep your baby or child needs.

Chapter 2 outlines the Happy Sleeper approach to good sleep for all ages (babies, toddlers, preschoolers, and young school-age kids). This chapter explains the underlying ideas that all of our methods are based on.

Chapters 3 to 5 have all the practical information, steps, and methods you need for your child's particular age, and for any issue or goal you have with sleep.

Chapter 3 is for babies 0 to 4 months old.

Chapter 4 is for babies 5 to 24 months old.

Chapter 5 is for children 2 to 6 years old.

Chapters 3 to 5 are organized this way:

1. HEALTHY SLEEP HABITS ☼

   This is the foundation for good sleep. If you put these hab-its in place, your child will have the best chance of sleeping well, both now and in the long run. Even if you're looking for the answer to a specific problem, don't skip over this section—these habits strongly influence the quality of your child's sleep.

2. SLEEP SOLUTIONS ☽

   For every sleep issue in your child's age range, we have a solution that is responsive and supportive *and* keeps your baby or child in charge of soothing and independent sleep (with the exception of little babies ages 0 to 4 months, who are gradually growing into this capacity).

3. TROUBLESHOOTING ☆

   What to do about teething, motor milestones, potty train-ing, sleep regressions, and more? The last section of each chapter answers common questions that arise for your child's age.

Chapter 6 addresses special situations like bed sharing, travel-ing, and other arrangements and circumstances that can change the way your child sleeps.

Chapter 7 will help you, the parent, sleep well. We see too many parents sacrificing their own sleep needs. We want to help you make sleep a priority for you, not just your child.

Chapter 8 explains the science of sleep and how sleep develops over the first years of life.

The Appendix has tools for creating your child's schedule, tracking progress on your sleep plan, and more. You'll find more helpful tools on our website, www.thehappysleeper.com.

The
Happy
Sleeper

1.

The Happy Sleeper

Do any of these scenarios sound familiar?

You feed or rock your baby until she's fast asleep, lower her gently into her crib, and tiptoe out of the room. Two hours later, she's awake and calling for you.

It's past bedtime, but your toddler runs when you try to put pj's on him, breaks down in tears over brushing teeth, and summons you back into the room repeatedly for more water, another song, and different stuffed animal configurations.

You have to lie down with your little one until he falls asleep, which can take up to 45 minutes and, sometimes, you doze off, too.

Your baby will only nap in the stroller, car, or with you carrying her.

Your child stays up too late and you suspect he's not getting enough sleep, but you can't figure out how to get him into bed earlier.

Your child calls out to you at night and needs you to sleep with her, or to join you in your bed.

You and your partner are so exhausted you can barely function, much less be present or happy with your baby during waking hours.

Sleep is a basic building block of your family's health and happiness—just like good food and regular exercise. Sleep is about as natural as it comes; in fact, kids are literally *built* to do it. Their brains are programmed to develop good sleep from the time they're babies.

Your child wants to sleep; and with the right patterns in place, her natural abilities will surprise you. Naptime, bedtime, and sleeping through the night—they don't have to be a big struggle or a source of anxiety. As easy as it is to disrupt sleep and create unhealthy sleep habits, it's achievable and often quick to get back on the right track. Consider this scene:

You help your baby wind down after her last feeding. You give her a bath and put on her pjs. After a few stories, a few cuddles, and a song, you kiss her good night, lower her into her crib, and leave the room. Your happy sleeper rolls over, grabs her lovey, moves into a comfortable sleep position, and drifts off until the next morning. You have time to yourself to eat dinner, read a book, or spend time with your partner before going to bed and getting a full night's sleep.

If your baby is at least 5 months and you follow our approach consistently, you can go from one of the cumbersome patterns mentioned above, to this happy sleeper scene in roughly *one to two weeks* (if your baby is under 5 months, we'll show you how to move in this direction). And if you read and adopt our fundamental concepts, your family will have a solid sleep foundation for years to come. It's a myth that sleep is always a struggle and that changing sleep patterns is very hard. If you have a clear plan, your family's sleep can improve quickly.

Good sleep not only makes life more peaceful and enjoyable, it's a basic need that affects your child's happiness, success, and health. Insufficient sleep is like having a big piece of your life's foundation missing; it's like walking around while your body starves for food or water.

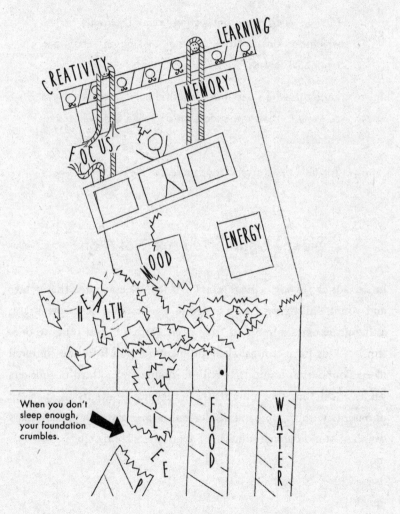

Sleep is part of your foundation. When it's off, the rest starts to crumble!

DID YOU KNOW . . .

- Napping helps babies learn and remember language.

- Missing sleep compromises the brain's prefrontal cortex, which our kids need for decision-making, attention, and emotional control.

- Little kids who sleep fewer than 10 hours a night are twice as likely to have low scores on cognitive tests when they enter school.

- Too little sleep in childhood increases the risk of obesity.

Sleepy Nation: You Are Not Alone

Little kids are losing critical hours of sleep. It's estimated that babies and young children get an average of 9½ hours of sleep per night, although experts agree that they need 11 to 12, and roughly one-third of kids have clinical sleep problems. A poll from the National Sleep Foundation found that half of infants and a third of toddlers get less sleep than their parents think they need. Seventy-five percent of parents with infants and 82 percent of parents with preschoolers say they would change something about their child's sleep.

Caffeinated drinks are consumed by lots of sleepy adults and, if you can believe it, kids! The American Academy of Pediatrics notes that children ages 6 to 10 drink caffeinated beverages eight out of ten days. One study found that two-thirds of children ages 2 to 5 consumed drinks like soda and tea.

Why don't kids sleep enough? There are lots of answers to this question, but here are two of the most common:

- We get confusing messages about sleep: cry-it-out, tough love, feed-on-demand, co-sleep . . . parenting approaches seem to contradict one another and leave many families puzzled and sleepless.

ATTACHMENT PARENTING
FEED ON DEMAND
CO-SLEEP

CRY IT OUT
TOUGH LOVE
DON'T SPOIL

- We're busy: life is bursting at the seams! Especially for families with older children, homework, technology, activities, and work schedules make it hard to protect aspects of healthy sleep like early, consistent bedtimes. Artificial lights and electronics delay sleep for children and adults, keeping us all up past our optimal bedtimes. Even though sleep should come naturally, our modern lives easily disrupt it.

Kids don't necessarily grow out of sleep issues either; in fact, research suggests that a significant percentage of young children with sleep disruptions still have them years later. On the other hand, when you develop healthy sleep habits early, they grow with your child. Imagine that your baby, who is a self-soother, turns into a happy preschooler who feels confident and knows what to do when the lights go out, a school-age child who can have a sleepover at a friend's house, and eventually a well-rested and sharp teen who's set up for success. It's not an overstatement to say that the positive sleep foundation you establish for your young child will be the one he has throughout his life.

HOW MUCH SLEEP DO YOU REALLY NEED?

AGE	SLEEP NEEDS
Newborns (0–2 months)	12 to 18 hours
Infants (3–11 months)	14 to 15 hours
Toddlers (1–3 years)	12 to 14 hours
Preschoolers (3–5 years)	11 to 13 hours
School-age children (5–10 years)	10 to 11 hours
Teens (10–17)	8.5 to 9.25 hours
Adults	7 to 9 hours

Source: National Sleep Foundation

Take a look at sleep recommendations for every member of your family, including yourself. Just as with adults, children vary in how much sleep they need to function at their best, which is why there's a range instead of a magic number. But almost all children consistently need this amount of sleep in a 24-hour period. It's a lot of sleep—roughly half your child's life or more! A very small percentage of people are thought to be "short sleepers," or those who require less sleep than the rest of us. If your child seems fine with less than the recommended amount of sleep, you might be surprised that she does even better with 30 to 60 minutes more. Think about the fact that your goal is not just a child who is *functioning*, but one who is optimally alert, creative, and balanced.

How to Tell If Your Child Is Getting Enough Sleep

It can be tricky to tell whether your child is well rested, because kids rarely communicate this clearly. Insufficient sleep in children is hard to spot for two reasons:

- **Babies and little kids don't wind down when they're tired—they wind up.** Anyone who's watched overtired kids run circles around a bouncy house, or throw a tantrum insisting on more television before bed will tell you this is true. Babies get overstimulated and fussy when they're tired (as you'll see in Chapter 3, that's a big reason for the early evening "witching hour"). Sleep loss in older children is linked with symptoms of attention-deficit/hyperactivity disorder (ADHD).

- **Kids aren't good judges of their own sleepiness.** In one well-known set of children's sleep studies at Stanford, when kids' sleep was restricted to just 4 hours a night, they still didn't say they were sleepy. You really can't count on your child to tell you when he's tired—he needs *you* to help him wind down and sleep.

Overt sleepiness is especially hard to detect when little ones are on the move; sometimes it's only obvious when they finally sit still— for example, riding in a car or sitting on the couch reading a book. This is when you'll see signals of drowsiness, like your child rubbing his eyes or staring into space.

Here's how you can tell whether you have a well-rested or sleepy child on your hands. Check the ones that apply to your child.

SIGNS OF A SLEEP-DEPRIVED CHILD

- ☐ Needs to be woken up in the morning
- ☐ Hyperactive, inattentive, moody, impulsive, or aggressive
- ☐ Falls asleep before scheduled naps if taken on a walk or car ride
- ☐ Sleeps in on the weekends
- ☐ Falls asleep in school
- ☐ Becomes clumsy, irritable, easily frustrated

SIGNS OF A WELL-RESTED CHILD

- ☐ Wakes up naturally
- ☐ Alert most of the day or until naptime

☐ Doesn't fall asleep in the stroller or car during the day (in between naptimes)

☐ Has more or less the same sleep schedule on weekdays and weekends

☐ Has the same nap habits at home and day care or preschool

What if your child does get enough sleep overall, but it happens in a way that isn't working for the family—for example, your baby needs to be rocked and bounced for 30 minutes, or your toddler's bedtime is a dragged-out affair of requests for extra water, bonus potty trips, and "just one more story." Maybe your baby will fall asleep only with you in the bed, or will only nap in the stroller. In this case, your child might get enough hours of sleep *total*, but the manner in which he does it is disruptive or challenging, and it involves you overhelping, so he isn't accessing his self-soothing abilities. These are important issues to address; good sleep isn't just about hitting the numbers, it's about setting up habits and routines in your house that feel good for everyone.

Throughout this book we'll not only help you achieve long and consistent sleep for your baby or child, we'll also walk you through how to make healthy sleep *easy and pleasant* (yes, you heard that right) for the whole family.

Good Sleep = Successful, Happy, Healthy

Watch your child sleep—eyes fluttering, arms limp, legs tucked up. It's a beautiful and peaceful thing. We tend to think of falling asleep as shutting down (and feel incredible relief as parents when our kids finally do) but, actually, sleep is not your child's "off mode." Transitioning to sleep turns on a whole host of vital activities in your child's brain and body. For example, when your child enters deep sleep, growth hormones are secreted that allow cells to divide and tissues to repair and regenerate. During sleep, memories are consolidated and your child processes information learned during the day.

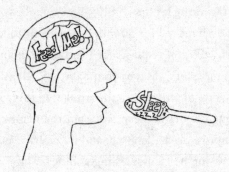

Sleep is like nutrition for your child's brain.

Even if you think you know the value of good sleep, you'll probably be surprised to find out just how much sleep affects different areas of your child's mental and physical health.

Learning and Academic Success

It's a simple fact at any age—newborn, preschool, or teenager—good sleep makes for a higher-achieving child.

In one well-known experiment, researchers restricted or extended the sleep of school-age kids by 30 minutes and found that it had a significant impact on their reaction time, attention, and memory. In fact, *the difference of 1 hour between the two groups made an impact that was equivalent to two years of academic level.*

One of the best predictors of a child's success in school is her level of "executive function," or the ability to manage emotions, behaviors, and thinking—and this skill set is very sensitive to sleep loss. Many studies have shown that even after a modest decrease in sleep, the brain's prefrontal cortex (the hub of executive function) becomes less active. Sleepy kids can still do the basics—talk, eat, run around, play—but sophisticated thinking, impulse control, and creativity go steadily downhill.

When your child sleeps, certain connections between brain cells are strengthened while others are "pruned" or lost (this is an important part of development because the brain is refining its circuits and prioritizing what it needs the most). This essentially remodels the brain and consolidates the information learned while awake. Babies have an intense need for sleep, which is probably because they have so much to learn. Infants learn language better after a nap, and preschool children's spatial learning is boosted by a midday nap. From the ages of 2½ to 6 years, short sleep (fewer than 10 hours per night) has been linked to lower vocabulary and nonverbal intellectual skills, and this is true even of kids who later catch up to their peers in sleep duration. In other words, missing sleep early in life may have a lasting effect.

Behavior and Emotions

As an adult, how do you feel and act when you're tired? You probably think and move slowly. You want to curl up, power down, and recharge. Your bed calls to you.

Sleepy kids don't respond this way to being tired, or necessarily even *know* that they're tired. Instead, they become stressed, wind up, and get a second wind.

Psychologists continue to find connections between sleep and ADHD. Children with sleep issues have a higher prevalence of hyperactivity and attention problems (and vice versa, kids with ADHD-like symptoms are at higher risk for sleep problems). Kids with ADHD also tend to be sleepier during the day, which might explain why stimulant medications seem to help. In fact, studies also suggest that treating sleep problems may be enough to eliminate hyperactivity and attention issues for some children. This benefit applies to kids without any diagnosed attention or behavior problems, too. One experiment showed that adding just 30 minutes more sleep per night made a significant improvement (for kids without any history of behavioral issues) in how restless, impulsive, and moody children were. Reducing sleep by 50 minutes had the opposite effect.

Health

Too little sleep is linked to weight gain in both kids and adults, and children who have short sleep durations are at higher risk for obesity when they grow up. Sleep loss disrupts chemicals in the body that regulate appetite and metabolism. Insufficient sleep also raises the risk of hypertension and can affect the immune system, which may make kids more likely to get sick.

Parents' Life

Parents lose about 350 hours of nighttime sleep in the first year of their baby's life. In a National Sleep Foundation poll, almost two-thirds of parents (even those with toddlers and preschoolers) reported getting less sleep than they need.

To some extent, this is just how it goes—a baby naturally turns your sleep schedule upside-down for a few months. Thankfully, parents can adapt; we seem to be biologically capable of flexing around a newborn's every-2-hour waking pattern, being alert enough to tend to our babies at night, and still managing to go about our daily lives.

HERE'S HOW PARENTS DESCRIBE SLEEP DEPRIVATION

"I feel underwater and blurry, panicked and overwhelmed."

"On edge. Easily angered. Forgetful."

"In a fog and emotional."

"Grumpy and hungry."

"Disoriented and 'off.' Everything is harder on those days, especially remembering to smile."

"Cranky, depleted, foggy, impatient, and unavailable!"

"Dread and nervousness as evening sets in."

"Like a piece is missing."

The problem is that for some parents, the initial sleep loss in the first few months becomes the new normal in the months and years that follow. These parents end up carrying a significant "sleep debt" because they accumulate missed hours of sleep over time without ever getting the chance to fully pay it back. People with children of all ages are roughly twice as likely as those without kids to say that they're not sleeping enough and that they're unable to do activities like exercise because they're too sleepy. Subpar sleep also makes parents irritable, impatient, and less productive. It can make small tasks seem insurmountable and, even worse, keep us from enjoying and connecting with our kids.

10-MONTH-OLD EVAN AND
HIS EXHAUSTED PARENTS

Joanna: When Evan was 10 months old, his sleep regressed dramatically and I found myself nursing him to sleep each night (even though we had cut this out of our routine 5 months prior). This put him to sleep for an initial 5-hour stretch, but after that, he was waking up hourly! My husband and I felt like we were in a dark cloud of exhaustion. The hardest part was that we started to feel resentment toward him and were enjoying him less. Once we carried out our sleep plan, the whole family started sleeping well and we went back to enjoying and finding so much pleasure in each other's company.

Think about it this way: working on your child's sleep is important for you and, in turn, your healthy sleep is important to your child, so you can feel available, patient, and energetic.

If that's not enough, consider that poor sleep also poses a serious safety risk to your family. People with children in the house are significantly more likely to drive drowsy than those without kids. Drowsy driving is a major safety hazard: incredibly, 37 percent of adults say they've fallen asleep at the wheel (and 13 percent of those say they do so approximately once each month). It's conservatively estimated that 100,000 police-reported crashes every year are a direct result of driver fatigue—resulting in 1,550 deaths and 71,000 injuries.

The Happy Sleeper

HERE'S WHAT MAKES A GOOD SLEEPER

· A warm, attuned parent

· A pattern of self-soothing

· Clear family sleep habits

· A regular schedule that supports natural, biological sleep mechanisms

Whether you're coming to us in a blurry, sleep-deprived crisis, or you're simply trying to optimize your baby's sleep, with this book you'll have all of these in place. Using our techniques, you'll be able to fix immediate sleep issues and set up habits that support optimal sleep as your child grows.

If you're conflicted about imposing a structured and harsh program to improve your child's sleep, you can stop worrying. Warm, supportive parenting and a full night of independent sleep are not mutually exclusive—we're going to show you how they work together naturally and seamlessly.

So now that we know the urgency of good sleep and elements you need to get it, let's look at the Happy Sleeper approach to getting there!

2.

The Happy Sleeper Approach

"Cry It Out" Versus "Attachment Parenting" Sleep Methods

If you've reached out for sleep help before, you know that it can sound polarized into methods of "crying it out" and "attachment parenting." The first emphasizes structure and independent sleep; the second tells you to be flexible and responsive to your baby's needs. These approaches *seem* to contradict each other.

But this is a false, unhelpful divide. It makes parents unduly upset and confused because independent sleep and a loving, secure attachment are pitted against each other—as if they are at odds. In psychological terms, "attachment" involves being there to support your little one, *while also encouraging her to learn, develop, and move toward independence* (you can read more about attachment on page 22). When you change a pattern to improve your baby or child's sleep, there is usually protesting involved—you're doing things differently and re-shaping a well-entrenched habit! This is okay. If you are careful, thoughtful, and consistent in how you do this, your baby will feel supported (even though she may express big feelings about the change), and eventually she'll learn a new pattern that helps her sleep well. Passing the job of soothing to your capable baby or child is very much in line with attachment theory.

For the best sleep, you need both the consistency of structured sleep training programs and the responsiveness (or as we will call it here, the "attunement") of attachment-friendly ideas.

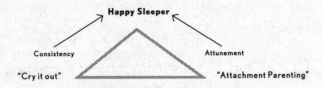

The Happy Sleeper Approach

Consistency and Attunement for Good Sleep

In this section we'll look at two important aspects of healthy sleep—consistency and attunement—and how they work together to produce great little sleepers.

Consistency: Your Tiny Scientist

You know that consistency is important in all realms of parenting, but do you know it's because your child's brain, even as a newborn, is set up to detect and understand patterns? Newborns acquire knowledge and skills at a breathtaking pace and they are capable of associative learning (linking and remembering objects and events in their environment) right from the start.

THE PATTERN-SEEKING BRAIN

Baby brains already have the machinery to learn and remember patterns. Your baby needs only basic, lower regions of the brain, which she already has up and running, for associative learning. A 2-month-old can remember an event for a day or two. A 3-month-old can remember an event for roughly a week—but if babies are given reminders, the memory lasts far longer than this. At 6 months, development of areas like the visual cortex and the hippocampus are thought to make babies more particular and specific when it comes to associations. At this age, you might notice that if you try to change something about your routine or habits even slightly, your baby protests!

This is why even the smallest babies learn patterns and habits so quickly, and why they can easily become reliant on the sights, sounds, feels, and even tastes (like a bottle before bed) in their environment when it comes to sleep. Over the first 6 months of life, babies become better and better at associative learning and are capable of remembering and linking events more strongly and specifically.

The key is to *use* your child's natural tendency to detect patterns and form habits, rather than being hampered by it. Babies and children are pattern-seekers, but they also forget old patterns more quickly than adults—making space in their inner laboratories for new behaviors. This is a huge advantage when you're working on sleep. Later in this book, when you establish a pattern of your baby's self-soothing, by using techniques like the Soothing Ladder or the Sleep Wave, your baby will detect and trust this pattern, let go of the old, unhelpful pattern, and then turn inward to feel calm. Not only do babies and kids look for patterns, they *relax* when they find them (and we don't need to tell you how important relaxing is to sleep).

Example of Consistency: Make It Work for You

Here is a 6-month-old baby who has detected a pattern that, over time, *disrupts* sleep:

- Your baby sleeps on a stroller walk. After a few weeks, she associates the motion of the stroller, curve of the seat, and the sounds of street noise with falling asleep. Now she seems unable to fall asleep in her flat, still, quiet crib.

Here's the same baby, but now she has a pattern that *helps* sleep:

- You put your baby in her crib for naps. She associates the motion of turning her head back and forth, the feel of her lovey, and the sounds of a fan in her room with falling asleep. Her room, her crib, and her body movements give her the cues that help her sleep.

Every technique we will teach you (especially for children over 5 months) requires the core element of consistency. It's not just a tip; it's a powerful fact about the way your child's brain operates. Lots of parents tell us that they've tried and tried to get their child to sleep, but when we probe for more information, we almost always find a spot of inconsistency (even a small one) that confuses the child and disrupts sleep progress. If you harness this idea when you put a sleep plan in place, you're likely to see old, unhelpful patterns fade and new, helpful ones take over within one to two weeks.

Consistency in the First 3 to 4 Months: A Special Case

The first months of life are unique in how unstructured they are—this is a time when you shouldn't feel pressured to schedule your baby's feeding and sleep. Following your baby's cues in these early months allows for the natural development of her biological sleep rhythms. It's also key to early attachment and the success of breast-feeding. Little babies need time for their nervous systems and growing bodies to mature before falling into structured routines.

This time is like a "honeymoon" period when you can use whatever soothing methods work for you. When you respond with sensitivity to your baby's cues, she internalizes a feeling of trust and a sense that the world is a good place. In these first few months, err on the side of meeting your baby's needs. In Chapter 3 we give you specific techniques for doing this, while steering clear of unhelpful sleep habits.

As your baby nears 4 months, she becomes very aware and surprisingly sensitive to a predictable and regular routine. By 5 to 6 months, most babies are capable of sleeping through the night and beginning to develop a regular nap schedule. This is why we have separate chapters for babies 0 to 4 months old and those who are 5 months to 2 years—the approach you take to helping your younger baby sleep is very different from the one you can take with an older baby or toddler.

Attachment and Attunement: How to Avoid Nighttime Helicopter Parenting

Babies and children need our warmth, touch, and love. When we soothe our little ones and meet their needs, it builds a sense of trust and allows them to feel comfortable exploring the world. This innate, biologically programmed system is present not just in humans but in many animals (baby monkeys stay close to their mom and use her as a base for exploration, too). This is the basis of attachment theory—one of the most important models for understanding child development.

Unfortunately, in many parenting books and in the media, the term "attachment" is translated and misinterpreted as a stick-like-glue, attached-at-the-hip idea. A lot of parents are missing the other half of the equation: a secure attachment comes from warmth and responsiveness, *and* it includes seeing when your child doesn't need your help and is ready for the challenges that are part of developing and learning. This is how you encourage your child to grow and become more independent over time.

When it comes to sleep, parents who take the term "attachment"

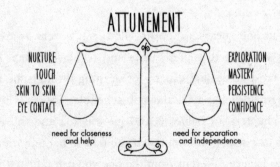

There are two sides to a healthy, balanced attachment.

literally end up swooping in too quickly and overhelping their child—becoming like a helicopter parent at night. No wonder people think attachment parenting is exhausting and so many who follow it end up in a sleep crisis! Parents with a *balanced* understanding of attachment often avoid sleep problems down the road because their baby has room to practice his sleeping abilities.

MOM EXHAUSTED AND STUMPED BY "ATTACHMENT PARENTING"

One day, a dear mom of a 6-month-old blurted out, "I just can't do this attachment parenting thing anymore." We asked her what she meant and she said, "This 24/7 responding to every peep and wake up. I'm spending so much time every night getting my baby back to sleep, over and over, and her sleep is not improving, it's getting worse. We're both so tired we can barely function." We see this a lot—parents aren't given the full story about what secure attachment really means, and that it includes having an eye toward your baby's growing independence, learning, and, sometimes, struggle. They're diligent about helping, but over time the baby is overly reliant on the parents and hasn't practiced her own abilities.

You probably do this balancing act in other realms of parenting without even thinking about it. Imagine that your 15-month-old is working hard on a shape sorter. Her chubby little hand is jamming the pieces in just slightly askew. You're dying to nudge the piece for her but you know she needs to struggle if she's going to learn. You might offer a word or two of encouragement, but if you swipe the circle and pop it through the designated hole, she's sure to hand the next piece right to you and ask you to do it for her again. When it comes to sleep, the same idea applies. When you do something for your child that she is able to do herself, you take away her chance to struggle and ultimately learn.

This is why we use the term "attunement" instead of "attachment"—so we can be clear about the goal. To be attuned is to be present and curious, so you can watch your baby and know when to help *and also when to give her space.* Attuned parents are responsive, while also having clear expectations. They send the message, *I'm here with you, and I'm watching, but I know you can do it.* You don't underhelp (by shutting the door and never responding) or overhelp (lying down with your child, rocking or nursing your baby to sleep after she has outgrown this need). When you respond to your child this way, it's amazing how you'll see her sleep skills flourish. It's not because you've trained her or tricked her into sleeping well, it's because she's able to practice and develop her natural, innate ability to sleep. Pause, observe, and allow your child to find her own way. It can be tough to do, but this is how your baby grows.

> An attuned stance is curious, not knee-jerk. It gives children the reassurance that they have a loving, nurturing parent nearby, but it also gives them credit for what they're capable of and allows them to practice. Babies change and grow so rapidly; attunement allows parents to maximize (instead of stifle) sleep development because it gives their little one enough room to flex those budding skills. In the Appendix, you'll see exercises to help parents build attunement and mindfulness.

Sounds logical, right? But over and over, we see that parents either skew toward overhelping, or they overhelp, get fed up, and feel that they have no choice but to resort to a harsh, underhelping stance. Each of the methods in these chapters gives you concrete directions for how to be responsive, but to also allow your child to stay in charge of his own self-soothing (after the age of 5 months) so that he can sleep happily and independently.

Example of Attunement: Toddler Sleep Troubles

Here's a scenario of a toddler who's having a very common and normal fear of the dark. Night after night, he won't fall asleep alone in his room and you're all exhausted.

Underhelping: You get frustrated and snap at him, "There's nothing to be afraid of!" You close the door and don't go back in, even when he cries.

Overhelping: You immediately lie down with your child until he falls asleep, and continue to do this every time he goes to bed.

Attuned plan: You and your child practice making the room dark during the day. You talk about how light and dark work and use a flashlight to play and teach about shadows. When it's time for bed, you give your child's stuffed animal 10 hugs and kisses and tell him he can get these in the night if he needs them. You say good night and set up 5-minute "check-ons" (see Chapter 5 for the Reverse Sleep Wave).

YOUR BABY'S "INTERNAL ATTUNEMENT"
Feeling Good on Her Own

You know how certain people seem to feel fundamentally *okay* when they're alone—just themselves? They're confident and comfortable in their own skin. Other people feel uneasy without distraction or company at all times.

The idea of comfort and trust in *oneself* (known as "internal attunement") is something that isn't usually communicated to parents, but it's really important. This capacity grows slowly over your child's development. It builds in the moments your baby is separate from you, when she can practice exploring and building self-confidence in her inner world; and it applies to daytime but also nighttime patterns. In fact, when we meet teens and adults who can't sleep well (or be alone in general), we wonder if this critical piece of confidence and internal attunement is underdeveloped. Instead of only sending the message, "you need me," to your child, we want to help you give her the chance to feel secure by herself and able to sleep peacefully (knowing Mom or Dad is nearby). When our babies gradually become conscious of the feeling of comfort and trust in themselves—solving some of their own dilemmas and being okay on their own—they start to develop the inner world of their mind and a growing awareness of their unique self. This "awareness of awareness" or relationship with self is part of what makes us uniquely human and able to move through the world with kindness and compassion.

EXERCISE: WAIT, WATCH, AND WONDER (ALSO KNOWN AS LET HIM BE!)

This exercise is a great way to watch your baby's process of internal attunement. See your baby staring at his hands, at the tree branches swaying outside the window, or the light dancing across the ceiling? Wait, don't do anything. Watch, notice everything you can about what your baby is up to. Wonder, how long will he continue and what will he do next? If your baby is happy and/or focused in his own little world, let him be! Don't feel as though he needs your constant stimulation and input. How about times when your baby is struggling, persisting, maybe even getting a little frustrated? Maybe he's reaching for a toy or trying to roll or crawl. Again, despite our impulse to help and rescue, the attuned response is to wait, watch, and wonder. When babies gain this confidence during the day, it strengthens their ability to access it at night.

Note About Attunement in the First 3 to 4 Months

In the first 3 to 4 months of life, your baby's needs and patterns are unpredictable and require lots of flexibility and constant shifting on your part. Parents of newborns have a lot of wiggle room to try new things and do whatever works for their baby.

During this time, you initially weigh more heavily on the responsiveness side of the equation, but over time you will fade your help and let your baby take over. Your goal is to be curious and watch for signs that your baby can self-soothe, as every baby develops at a different pace. In Chapter 3, we will show you how to do this with tips for encouraging self-soothing and the Soothing Ladder. When your baby calls out, don't automatically rush in and assume that he needs to be fed. Hesitate, watch, and listen with curiosity—this gives your baby the opportunity to show you his ever-growing abilities. Yesterday, his fussing may have escalated to the point where he needed your help, but today is a new day, and if you pause, you may notice him start to suck his fingers or stroke his lovey to soothe himself. If you didn't wait a moment and watch, you would never know about this new ability. It would be like picking your baby up and carrying him every time he was about to pull to a stand and work on cruising.

Note About Attunement for Older Children

Older babies and little kids are already capable of sleeping well (even if it doesn't seem so in your house quite yet). At this point, you will still be responsive, but you will focus on "passing the baton" of soothing to your child, and creating predictable responses and clear expectations around sleep. Attunement with older children is always loving and nurturing, but when sleep time comes, you hand over responsibility to your very capable child and allow her the space she needs to feel confident and secure in her sleep world.

Keep these principles in mind as you read the chapter for your baby or child's age. Remember that good sleep goes beyond a quick fix (although we'll give you plenty of those, too)—it's part of your family philosophy and will last over the years and through many twists and turns in your child's development.

3.

Baby (0 to 4 Months)

TROUBLESHOOTING SLEEP ☆

Baby getting own room, to schedule or not, rolling to tummy, teething, swings and other devices, illness, catnaps, napping on the go,
waking up shortly after bedtime, reflux.

☀ HEALTHY SLEEP HABITS ☀

Your Baby's Sleep: The Goal of the First 4 Months

Sleep is something that new moms and dads think about, ask about,
crave, and compare notes on constantly. Newborn schedules are so
erratic and the quest for a full night's rest so pressing, it makes sense
that sleep is the most popular topic of conversation (it probably
doesn't help that *How's she sleeping?* is every friend, family member,
and stranger's favorite question).

In the first 4 months of your baby's life, she may not sleep through
the night (Chapter 4 outlines the path to sleeping through the night
for babies 5 months and older), but we'll show you how to set the

stage and encourage your baby's sleep to gradually grow longer and longer.

THE GOALS OF THIS CHAPTER ARE TO:

- Establish good sleep patterns and the right sleeping environment in your home.

- Give you tools to support your newborn's growing self-soothing skills, and explain how to strike a balance between *soothing* and encouraging *self-soothing*.

- Avoid common pitfalls (like repeating habits automatically) that interrupt your baby's natural sleep progression.

A key idea in this chapter is the "curious stance." Very young babies need a lot of help from parents to calm their developing little nervous systems—that's why we naturally rock and sway as we hold them in our arms. But over time, they gradually become able to take over this role of soothing (*self*-soothing) to fall asleep. The problem is that when a parent gets in the habit of automatically repeating soothing actions over and over (like bouncing and rocking to sleep), as time goes on, it begins to mask the baby's budding abilities. On the other hand, a curious parent watches closely and notices moments when the baby is okay on her own and doesn't need help. The curious stance is the path to knowing when to soothe your baby, while gradually, over time, stepping back to give her space so she can show you what she's capable of.

Whether you have a newborn who sleeps 5 hours at a stretch, or one who wakes up every 2 hours around the clock, we guarantee that soon your baby can sleep well. We're going to help you build a good foundation for healthy sleep no matter what your baby's starting point.

Your Baby's Sleep Timeline: What to Expect

Newborn: *Sleep off and on; irregular pattern*

8 weeks: *One 4- to 8-hour stretch of sleep at night; frequent and unpredictable daytime naps*

3 months: *Most baby sleep has shifted to night; more awake during the day*

5 to 6 months: *Circadian system matures. Most babies able to sleep 11 to 12 hours at night.*

Newborns typically sleep 16 to 18 hours a day, made up of frequent naps and stretches of nighttime sleep. A newborn's sleep is naturally erratic, because her nervous system and internal clock are immature (see Chapter 8). In other words, new babies are *supposed* to sleep in fits and spurts. This can truly be a shock to the system for parents, who are used to being in control of when and how long they sleep. We know from firsthand experience how grueling this is, and how painful it can be (some would say it feels like torture!) to rise from a deep sleep to feed and soothe a newborn. When you're in the midst of it, it feels like it will never end—like your deep craving for sleep will never be satisfied.

It will. As the newborn months pass, your baby's sleep skills grow and the family will eventually sleep well again and have a consistent routine. Every baby's sleep development is different, though—some tuck into long stretches of sleep within a few weeks of birth, while others continue to wake up every few hours for months. If your baby is premature, sleep can take more time to unfold, but your baby's sleep will catch up, as the effects of her adjusted age fade. It's important to know that you can't expect a very young baby to adhere to a schedule (nor do you want her to, because feeding on demand is the way to establish successful breast-feeding). It's best to follow her lead and allow her body time to mature into a regular sleeping pattern.

Day-Night Confusion

When you bring your tiny bundle home from the hospital, she may sleep for periods off and on around the clock, without any distinguished pattern of day and night. This is typically referred to as "day-night confusion"—the result of your baby's undeveloped circadian system. When she was nestled tightly in the womb, your baby got signals about the time of day from you, because chemicals like melatonin were rising and falling with *your* circadian rhythms. But after birth, and without these chemical signals coming from Mom, a newborn's biological clock on its own is very immature—that fact makes for unpredictable sleep and restless nights.

It takes months for your baby's internal clock to mature. This is a normal developmental process—it will happen, it just takes time. You can encourage your baby's grasp of day and night by:

• Exposing your baby to indirect sunlight during the day. To best signal his internal clock, venture out early in the day.

Try for a 10:00 a.m. walk, or sit on the porch at this time. Just remember not to keep your newborn in direct sunlight.

- Letting him know it's morning. When your baby wakes up for the day, sing him a song and open the shades to let in sunlight.

- Gently waking your baby during the day to feed at least every 3 hours.

- Keeping him in the living areas and activity during the day, and in a dark, quiet room at night.

- Lowering the lights in the house at night (even if your baby is awake).

A particularly challenging time for many parents can be **4 to 6 weeks**, as babies begin to "wake up" from their sleepy newborn state. This new alertness (which you can also see in baby's ability to smile, for example), combined with an as-yet still immature nervous system, can make sleep elusive. Your baby might seem extra fussy around this period. Some parents feel like during the first four weeks of their baby's life, they run on adrenaline, and after it wears off and their baby's sleep is still erratic, they feel truly sleep deprived.

Around **8 weeks**, many babies begin to sleep for one long stretch at night (this could be 4 to 8 hours). This usually happens in the beginning of the night, while babies often continue to wake up every 2 to 4 hours for the rest of the night and take frequent daytime naps.

Most 3- or 4-month-olds are capable of sleeping at least 8 hours continuously, but some still wake up every 2 to 4 hours, and some who were sleeping long stretches actually start to wake up more frequently (see "Sleep Regression," page 83). At this point, fussiness can be a sign that your baby is tired (see "Naps and the 90-Minute Awake Window," page 73).

By roughly **5 months**, your baby is capable of sleeping 11 to 12 hours at night (as you'll learn in the next chapter, this may include feedings). Most doctors agree that by 6 months of age, babies are capable of sleeping 11 to 12 hours without eating. Some parents choose to wean all feedings at this point, while others keep feedings in place. If your baby is still eating at night beyond 5 or 6 months, these feedings can be brief, and (with our help), he can return directly to sleep so that his sleep and yours will be almost continuous.

The Magical 7:00 p.m. Bedtime

It's common in the first weeks of life for newborns to be out in the living room with their parents until late in the evening. But somewhere around 6 to 8 weeks, you may notice that your baby tucks into a longer stretch of sleep starting at around 6:00 or 7:00 p.m. This is because her circadian system is maturing and beginning to send her little body signals to fall asleep roughly with sunset. If you see this stretch of sleep in the early evening, it means that your baby is ready to call it a day roughly around sunset. In Chapter 8, you can read about circadian rhythms and how your baby's internal clock matures.

In fact, the "witching hour" (a period of fussiness and crying— see page 79) that so many parents see in the late afternoon/early evening is often a sign of overtiredness. During the day, and especially in the evening, you'll start to notice that your baby's discontent is a

signal that she'd rather be sleeping (even though it can still be difficult to get her to sleep, because her body is dysregulated).

Seven p.m. is a magic time. If you try to keep baby up, it can backfire because she becomes overtired and less likely to sleep well. On
the other hand, an earlier bedtime often begets a longer and longer
stretch of sleep over time. As your baby's internal clock matures, she
is likely to start waking up very early. Given this natural tendency for
early rising, putting her down at 7:00 p.m. gives her the best chance
of getting the 11 to 12 hours of sleep she needs. Your baby may not
seem tired, but that's okay. The optimal time to put your baby down
is not when she's yawning and fussing, but before this, when she's
quietly cooing or playing.

MADELINE'S EARLIER BEDTIME
MAKES FOR LONGER SLEEP

*Liz: Madeline started trying to nap from 6:00 to 7:00 p.m. each
night, so when she was 3 months, I was able to convince my husband to put her to bed earlier. We also made her room more cave-
like. The first night she slept 11 hours! I heard her a few times on
the monitor and watched her move around to get comfortable and
once saw her bring her hands to her mouth to self-soothe, but
each time she quickly went back to sleep on her own. It worked so
well for us, I wish I had tried it even earlier. Before the change,
she was going to bed pretty late (10:00 p.m. or later some nights)
and only sleeping 7 to 8 hours.*

Start moving toward this bedtime at least by the time your baby
is around 10 weeks old. If your baby is going to bed later than 7:00

p.m., you can move bedtime back 15 minutes or less every night, or simply put her to sleep at this time right away—after several nights, she will likely adjust. While you're thinking about bedtime schedules, keep in mind that after the first 8 weeks or so your baby will be ready to sleep approximately 90 minutes to 2 hours after waking up from her last nap, so take her final naptime into consideration. You can gently wake your baby in anticipation of her needing a 90-minute awake period before bedtime. Up to about 3 months or so, many babies can occasionally nap until 6:00 p.m., be gently roused for their bedtime routine, and go right back down at 7:00 p.m. This is good to remember because at this age, naps are very erratic.

Does this mean you're homebound after 6:00 p.m. from now on? No! Lots of parents can easily tote a sleeping newborn baby into a bustling restaurant. Just be aware that your child's internal clock is developing, and an early bedtime is a good idea. By 4 months, she'll probably do best with her own sleeping place at home for a consistent bedtime.

3-MONTH-OLD LEO MOVES
FROM 9:00 TO 7:00 P.M. BEDTIME

Stephanie: When I first learned about the 7:00 p.m. bedtime, Leo was about 3 months old and going to bed at about 9:00 or 9:30 p.m. We tried moving bedtime to 7:00 p.m. right away, but he wasn't ready yet. A week later, though, I started to see him naturally wanting to go to bed earlier and earlier. Now, he goes to bed at 7:00 p.m. and sometimes a bit earlier if it's been a busy day. He is a happy 7:00 p.m. to 7:00 a.m. sleeper with usually one feeding per night.

BABY BEDTIME: THE CASE FOR WATCHING THE CLOCK

Establishing a set bedtime enlists the forces of your baby's powerful internal clock. Even a small, nightly fluctuation in bedtime can lessen this effect. When you keep to a regular schedule, your baby's ability to self-soothe, fall asleep, and stay asleep is greatly enhanced. Bedtime is an aspect of sleep with which we urge you to be very consistent. It might feel like a mechanical adherence to the clock, but remember that your baby has an internal clock that *wants* things to come at predictable times.

Bedtime Routines

Remember from Chapter 2 that babies are natural pattern seekers, and they learn routines very quickly. One of the best ways to harness this pattern-seeking power is with the right bedtime routine. The consistent, soothing motions that you go through right before bed will become a potent cue for your baby to wind down and shift into sleep mode. Put your bedtime routine in place before you think your baby needs it (6 to 8 weeks is a good time to start) because the predictability helps set the stage for her growing ability to self-soothe.

Sample Bedtime Routines

These are just examples. You will find your own special steps (for example, some parents include baby massage—others have their own rituals); just be sure you choose soothing rather than activating ones, and keep the same order, with a calm tone.

0 TO 2 MONTHS	3 TO 5 MONTHS	5 TO 7 MONTHS
Bath	Bath	Bath
Massage	Pjs	Massage
Pjs	Feed	Pjs
Feed	Baby-led play	Feed
Songs while you sway	Book(s)	Book(s)
Bed	Songs while you sway	Say good night to objects in the room
	Bed	Song while you sway
		Bed

The Soothing, Repetitive Routine

Your bedtime routine should be 30 to 45 minutes long at this age and consist of things like a bath, infant massage (see "Baby Massage Basics," page 43), pajamas, books, feeding, songs, and bed. If your tone is *warm and calm*, the steps of the routine are *predictable*, and the end of the routine is *clear*, your baby will learn this and her body will expect the transition to sleep. We like to say that you can stand on your head as the last step of your bedtime routine—it really doesn't matter, as long as you do it the same way every night! Always end with the same song and keep your last words to your baby, like "Night, night, I love you," consistent as well.

Separate Feeding from Sleep

Try not to feed your baby as the very last part of your routine, because it can quickly create a strong association between drinking milk and falling asleep. This sleep association is one of the most likely to interrupt the process of your baby turning inward to soothe herself to sleep. If you look for opportunities to loosen this association now, it will create more space for your baby's growing ability to self-soothe down the road. Singing a song (the same one every night) between feeding and putting your baby in bed is a great way to end the routine instead.

Try putting your baby down and then shushing and patting her a little as she falls asleep instead of lowering her into her sleeping place already asleep. This way, when she wakes during the night, she won't be surprised to find herself in bed. As you know, all babies are different; at this age, some will still need to be fed to sleep. Just remember to stay curious and be willing to try putting your baby down a little awake. You can read more about putting your baby down awake on page 57. If your little one still relies on being fed to sleep when she's 5 months old, we'll show you how to change this pattern in Chapter 4.

Slow Down, Your Baby Is a Sponge

Your baby has an astounding ability to pick up on your mood and energy level. The more centered and relaxed you are, the easier it will be for your baby to feel exactly the same way. It doesn't mean that you have to keep everything completely quiet (we don't want you tiptoeing around for the next five years); just imagine sending a signal of calm, rather than the disquieting cue, "Please, just fall asleep!" Take some deep breaths yourself—a good way to slow your nervous system down. What you do in your routine doesn't matter as much as how you do it.

When we lead parenting groups, we often have parents share their routines with each other. One day, a mom described how she spread a swaddle blanket on the bed as she began her routine. As she demonstrated it for the group, her voice got soft as her arms smoothly spread the blanket out. There was a collective deep breath and sigh in the room—some moms started to yawn!

Don't underestimate the power of your baby's "sponge neurons" or "mirror neurons" (brain cells that are affected by the mood and behaviors of those around us). Babies are exquisitely attuned to our intentions and internal states (meaning whether we are activated or relaxed), so slowing down can help enormously. In fact, studies show that when caregivers holding their babies have heart and respiratory rate changes, babies' rates change right along with them.

Baby-Led Play

By 3 months of age, babies really like 10 to 15 minutes of quiet, baby-led play as part of their routine. During this time, get down on the floor with your baby and just watch and follow her play. It's a chance to shift from *you doing things to* your baby (the way the daytime often goes while you're feeding, bathing, carrying her, and so forth), to your baby being in charge and showing you what she is interested in. As your baby feels your attention, her brain becomes primed for self-regulation, which will help her sleep. In the first 4 months, baby-led play is very simple; it might just mean mirroring her expressions and following her gaze. Try, and see if your baby likes it.

Do the Last Steps in the Room Where Your Baby Sleeps

Move into the room where your baby is sleeping for the last steps of the routine, dim the lights, slow down your voice and movements, and keep things quiet. Light—both natural and artificial—affects sleep for people of all ages (see page 120), so dimming lights for an hour before bed (including avoiding TV, computers, and all screens) is helpful to all of us.

Your Individual Baby

The ingredients of your bedtime routine will depend on your baby. Some babies will clearly indicate at a certain point that they no longer want to lie still for massage or want to get into their bed sooner and get comfortable while you sing the last song or say good night. Some parents sing the last verse as they're walking out of the room.

> *Julie: When Jack was a baby, he loved to be sung to right before sleep. By that time, I was so tired that I would lie on the floor and put my feet up on the edge of his mattress and I would "sing to my toes." I don't really know how we ended up with that zany ritual, but it's a good example of coming up with your own! He knew which was our last song, after which I got up, said "Night night,*

sleep tight, see you in the morning light," and quietly left the room.

BABY MASSAGE BASICS

A little soothing massage gives your baby's body and nervous system a fabulous path to falling asleep. Massage reduces stress levels, supports well-being and bonding, boosts immune function, and promotes brain development.

- Lay your baby down on a warm, flat, safe surface where you are also comfortable.

- Put a little pure vegetable oil, such as sweet almond oil, into your palms and rub your hands together to warm the oil.

- Make eye contact with your baby and let him know you are starting the massage.

- Wrap your hands around one of his thighs and pull down, one hand following the other. Use a gentle "milking" motion to massage down the length of both legs.

- When you get to the little feet, use your thumbs and trace circles all over the soles and then gently pull on each toe as you slide your fingers off the end.

- Place your hands flat over baby's chest and stroke outward in big, slow circles.

- With one hand flat across baby's chest, stroke downward to his thighs on both sides.

- Take up each little arm and repeat the milking motion from shoulder to hand, rotating the wrists a few times in each direction.

- Trace circles on baby's palm with your thumbs and gently pull on each finger, sliding off the end.

- Gently roll baby to tummy and trace circles on either side of his spine, moving up and down from neck to waist.

- Finish with long, firm strokes all the way from shoulders to feet.

- Babies generally like a gentle but firm touch, rather than a super-light, ticklish touch.

Follow your baby's cues and stop if he's had enough. It's normal for babies to begin to resist massage as they become more mobile and active; you can build it into another part of your day if and when it no longer helps him wind down at bedtime.

Your Baby's Environment and Soothing Tips

Your baby's environment can support or interfere with sleep. Along with his physical environment, your baby's feeling of being connected with you is key. It's good to know that you cannot *spoil* your baby—not only does his nervous system need your responsiveness and soothing, he is naturally geared to monitor whether he's cared for and safe. Hold, comfort, and make a lot of physical contact with your baby—this helps him internalize a sense that he's loved and that the world is a good place.

QUICK LIST: ENVIRONMENT AND SOOTHING

White noise	Swaddling
Light	The need for sucking
Walking, rocking, carrying	Your nighttime station

White Noise

Your baby is used to the muffled sounds he heard in the womb, and may be soothed and calmed by white noise that emulates it. Instead of using constant, loud, and monotone static white noise, use nature sounds like waves or rain, which have slight variations. You can also use a fan (a little moving air is also consistent with safe sleeping recommendations) on a low or moderate volume. Keep the noise going all night rather than using a timer or a device that shuts off. Once your baby is about 4 months old, white noise is no longer needed for soothing, but you can certainly keep it as a way to mask noises from inside and outside the house.

Light

Light is an important cue to help your baby sleep and wake, so use light to your advantage. Put up shades or curtains in your bedroom (or wherever your baby is sleeping) to mask early morning light. Even the first hints of sunrise can send alerting signals to your baby, so a very dark room gives him the best chance of sleeping longer. You can achieve this by installing blackout shades, putting up temporary darkening shades, using blackout fabric, or even just taping dark garbage bags over the windows.

When your baby wakes up for the day, make sure that his brain and body know it's daytime. Gently pull back the shades, sit on the porch in indirect sunlight, or go for a walk in the morning to help his developing internal clock. Talk to him and sing a good morning song!

Walking, Rocking, and Carrying

Your baby feels soothed by your warmth, the feel of your skin, and the motion as you carry him. Tote him around, wear him in a sling, and allow him a lot of time in contact with you. Walking outside is often very calming to babies because of the motion, change of environment, light, and fresh air.

Swaddling

Newborns have a startle reflex that regularly sends their legs and arms flying. For safety reasons, we put our little ones on their backs for naps and bedtime, but this means that the jerking motion can really disrupt their sleep. Snug swaddles keep limbs hugged toward the body and many babies sleep better this way. Most babies do well being swaddled until they are 2 to 4 months old. There are also some babies who never like being swaddled and do just fine without it.

SWADDLING HOW-TOS

· Remember to always put babies down on their backs to sleep.

· Keep the room cool—65 to 68 degrees Fahrenheit.

· Use breathable fabrics and don't overdress baby for sleep.

· Keep the sleeping surface free of any loose blankets, pillows, or positioners.

· Stop swaddling when your baby can roll over at all, in either direction, since it can pose a suffocation risk.

· Stop swaddling when your baby can kick out of the swaddle, but make sure he didn't just kick out of the swaddle because it was put on too loosely. You can now use a blanket sleeper, sleep sack, or simple cotton pj's.

· In order to keep baby's hips healthy, leave plenty of room for baby's knees to spread apart, bend up, and move around in the swaddle. Just as in the womb, this position allows the hip joints to develop naturally, preventing loosening or damage to the soft cartilage of the socket. It's fine for the upper part of the swaddle around the arms to be a little snugger.

· Swaddle with your baby's elbows bent and arms folded on the chest. This mimics their position in the womb, ensures healthy joint development, and is calming and regulating. Babies have a natural instinct to work their fingers and thumbs toward their face for self-soothing; this swaddling position gives them every opportunity to do that.

When your baby is ready for un-swaddling, you can go cold turkey, or start by leaving one or both arms out for a few nights. The transition will be a little bumpy, whether you do it right away or wait a few weeks. It's better to err on the side of safety and un-swaddle as soon as baby can roll.

Some parents find it hard to let go of swaddling because they've always linked it to better sleep, but coming out of the swaddle is a logical step in sleep development. The end goal is for your baby to find his own comfortable sleeping positions, so having freedom of movement is key. It may disorient him at first, but trust us, this is a step in the right direction. Everything you can do to encourage movement and agility will have a positive effect on sleep, because when your baby chooses his own body positions, he'll sleep better. It may be on his tummy, with an arm outstretched, knees tucked under, bum up in the air . . . you won't know until he has the chance to practice.

This is why we like to see babies graduate into long-sleeved, long-legged cotton onesies with feet (with a similar "blanket sleeper" as a second layer during cold seasons) instead of sleep sacks, which can get twisted or hamper movement. Do everything you can to ensure that, once your baby can roll, he's free and can move at will around the crib. Now he can shift around and resettle during the night, just like the rest of us.

Many babies have a brief period of wild rolling and traveling around the crib when this ability first emerges. As with all sleep regressions and developmental surges, it's temporary and will subside as the novelty wears off.

3½-MONTH-OLD'S SLEEP IMPROVES POST-SWADDLE

Carla: Cece struggled to get her arm free of her swaddle at 3½ months. We considered wrapping her even snugger, but she seemed to want the opposite. We tried un-swaddling and, almost immediately, she started to suck her thumb to soothe herself to sleep. Her sleep improved dramatically, even though she wasn't rolling yet—she'd figured out her own soothing technique.

The Need for Sucking

Many babies have a strong need for sucking (which is separate from their need for nourishment), so you can encourage either thumb or pacifier use to satisfy this need and improve the capacity to self-soothe. The current American Academy of Pediatrics recommendation is to use a pacifier for bedtime and naps, but you don't need to reinsert it if it falls out during the night (see "Safe Sleeping Practices," page 51). Which is better, pacifier or thumb? Truly, they each have their pros and cons:

Pacifiers

Pacifiers take a lot longer for your baby to be able to insert solo, but they are much easier to take away when the time is right. Some moms worry that this will interfere with breast-feeding but research does not support this idea—babies know the difference!

Thumbs

Thumbs are readily available, easier to insert (once they learn how), and don't get lost in the crib. The downside can be that it's trickier to stop thumb sucking down the road (although most children will naturally stop thumb sucking if it isn't given any attention or judgment).

Your Nighttime Station

It will help both you and your baby if you can prepare the items you'll need overnight and put them in a convenient place before bed so you don't need to do any extra work when your baby wakes up. Put diapers, wipes, an extra set of pajamas, a glass of water, your feeding pillow, and anything else you might need for nighttime awakenings right next to your bed. Have a dim nightlight next to you and keep your feedings as unstimulating as possible (try to resist chatting with your adorable bundle at this hour of the night). If your baby is within arm's reach, you may not even have to get out of bed to take care of him and put him back down again.

Safe Sleeping Practices

Here is a summary of the American Academy of Pediatrics (AAP) guidelines for safe sleeping. These are best practices for lowering the risk of sudden infant death syndrome (SIDS), as well as suffocation and other sleep-related deaths.

- Always put your baby on her back to sleep for naps and nighttime.

- Room sharing, without bed sharing, is recommended for these early months. Sleeping in the same room with parents has been shown to lower the risk of SIDS.

- Always use a firm sleeping surface: your baby's mattress should be firm—avoid a sagging or soft mattress or one that has been handed down, heavily used, or old. Car seats and other sitting devices are not recommended for routine sleep.

- Keep soft objects and loose bedding out of the bed. This includes bumper pads and any kind of wedges or position-ers, which can up the risk of suffocation since babies can scoot and position their faces against them. Your baby's sleep surface should be a simple fitted sheet without stuffed animals, pillows, or blankets.

- Once baby can roll even a little bit in either direction, it's time to stop swaddling.

- Don't put a hat on baby during sleep due to risk of overheating.

- Breast-feeding, for moms who are able, is associated with a reduced risk of SIDS. Exclusive breast-feeding for at least the first 6 months is recommended.

- Offer a pacifier at naptime and bedtime. Having a pacifier while falling asleep has been shown to reduce SIDS risk. You don't need to go in and reinsert your baby's pacifier after it falls out, however.

- Avoid overheating: keep the room temperature cool (around 65 to 68 degrees Fahrenheit is ideal) and do not overbundle your baby.

- Have a little moving air in baby's room right around the level of their face. An air purifier or low fan works well for this.

- Avoid smoke exposure, alcohol, and drugs during pregnancy and after birth.

- Do not use home cardiorespiratory monitors (home monitors) as a strategy to reduce SIDS risk.

- Infants should be immunized in accordance with AAP/CDC (Centers for Disease Control and Prevention) recommendations.

- Supervised, awake tummy time is recommended to facilitate development and minimize the occurrence of flat head (see page 68).

☽ SLEEP SOLUTIONS ☽
Encouraging Self-Soothing

Self-soothing is the number one skill your baby needs for good sleep, both now and in the future. Many sleep problems for children of all ages have to do with trouble self-soothing, so it's great to understand and support this ability early on.

As you know, newborns need a lot of soothing from us—remember they have been nestled, carried, and bounced naturally for 9 months. In fact, the "vestibular" sense, or the sense of motion, is one of the very first senses a fetus develops (at just 10 weeks after conception—when baby is still smaller than a fig—she begins to perceive movement), so she has spent almost all of her precious little life feeling the rise and fall of your footsteps and other behaviors throughout the day. Human babies are born in a very immature state, with nervous systems that require a lot of input from caregivers. This is why we wrap small babies in our arms or hold them over our shoulder while we walk around the house, rock them in gliders, and tuck them into slings. The first few months are also the time when soothing and responding to baby's cues are essential. As you do this, your baby builds trust in you; as she builds trust, she will naturally feel more relaxed. This is secure attachment. Babies who feel this security will explore more, develop naturally, and become more independent over time.

Babies who are responded to with sensitivity during the early months are gradually able to turn to their *self*-soothing abilities. Being able to self-soothe to sleep means feeling confident in your own sleeping place and able to get comfortable and drift off. In the first months of life, your baby will go from needing a lot of external soothing (shushing, rocking, and so forth), to gradually being able to take over this job herself. When she starts to self-soothe, she might do this by tucking her arms under her chin, moving her head from side to side, or making little noises to get comfortable—whatever she figures out as her own personal technique. It's really sweet to see babies find their special ways of self-soothing.

As the parent of a newborn, you get to watch this process unfold. As you nestle with her, pat, feed, and bounce her, you can also look for chances to let her flex her budding sleep skills. The following tips will help you with this goal.

QUICK LIST: ENCOURAGE SELF-SOOTHING

1. **Put your baby down awake.** Look for opportunities to put your baby down awake at least once a day. A major reason babies wake up and cry is because they find themselves in a sleeping place they didn't go into knowingly.

2. **Loosen the feeding-sleep association.** Gently remove breast or bottle at the end of a feeding *before* baby falls asleep.

3. **Discern your baby's sounds.** If baby is fussing, whining, grunting, squawking, babbling, or making any other such noise, resist the urge to swoop in! Babies can be very noisy on their way to self-soothing.

4. **Use the Soothing Ladder to avoid overhelping.** If your baby wakes up at night and cries for about a minute, be curious about the least intrusive thing you can do to settle her.

5. **Don't let your baby cry for more than a minute.** As you're encouraging self-soothing, don't let your baby cry for more than a minute during the first 4 months.

6. **Daytime independence.** Look for moments during the day when your baby is happy to hang out solo. What better way to nurture confidence and self-regulation.

7. **Transitional object.** Also known as a lovey or blankie, this is a soft, special object your baby can use to help her self-soothe.

8. **Tummy time.** Tummy time is important for your baby's sleep. Once she can roll and move (usually around 4 months), your baby has skills for getting comfy and sleeping well.

Did you know that babies, children, and adults *all* wake periodically during the night as we go through our sleep cycles? When you compare babies who are "good" sleepers with those who are "bad" sleepers, which ones do you think wake more often? The answer is, both groups wake with the same frequency—it's just that the "good" sleepers are practiced at self-soothing, so we don't realize how often they wake up. Babies' sleep cycles are about 60 minutes (compared to an adult's 90-minute cycle), so those who can't soothe back to sleep have many times during the night when they may potentially call out for help.

SCAFFOLDING AND SLEEP

As you read the following list of strategies, keep this idea of "scaffolding" in mind.

Scaffolding is a concept used in child psychology that helps parents know how much to help, versus how much to back off and allow their baby or child to struggle a little while practicing a new skill.

Imagine you, the parent, are the scaffolding and your child is the building. You know that scaffolding around a growing

building gives just enough support to allow the building to grow, and is gradually taken down as the building gets stronger. In the same way, you are ready to give your baby just enough support to grow and progress, while allowing her to struggle a little as she gets stronger and shows her new, budding skills.

1. Put Your Baby Down Awake

There's nothing more natural than your baby dozing off in your arms. As moms ourselves, we both remember it as one of the sweetest experiences of new parenthood. And let's face it, especially if you're breast-feeding, your newborn baby falling asleep in your lap is practically an unstoppable force. Soak up this beautiful time.

The hitch is that, as your baby reaches 3 months of age, the learned association between feeding, rocking, bouncing, or swinging and falling asleep becomes stronger, and your baby becomes very aware of, and reliant on, that pattern. Gradually fading these sleep associations in the early months, when a baby's awareness is lower, can be very effective and easier than doing it later. For this reason, we recommend that you look for opportunities to put your baby down drowsy but awake. Do this as often as it works for you, so that your baby has the space to fall asleep by himself if he can.

Going to bed slightly awake also helps your baby sleep much better through the night, because he won't need as much help from you to settle back to sleep every time he briefly wakes (which all babies, children, and adults do throughout the night as they cycle through stages of sleep). Imagine, from your baby's perspective, what it's like to be put down in his crib or bassinet already asleep:

He drifts off warm and nestled in your arms, feeding or rocking. A few hours later (or even a few minutes later), he wakes up alone, on a flat surface in the dark. Understandably, he cries out because he's thinking, "Wait a minute, something is wrong. Where am I? Come back and make all that happen again so I can go back to sleep!"

A baby who is put down in his sleeping place—whether it's a bassinet, crib, or otherwise—drowsy but awake at bedtime is more likely to resettle and sleep longer at night. On the other hand, a baby who is placed in bed already asleep will often call out to parents at night because he finds himself in conditions he didn't go into knowingly.

After your baby is about 2 months old, he'll be drowsy after not more than 90 minutes of awake time (see page 73) so watch the clock, swaddle, and place your little one down when his eyes are still open (often the first nap of the day is the easiest). If your baby cries for more than about 1 minute, you can use the Soothing Ladder (see page 62) to calm him and then try to put him down drowsy again. You can do this over and over until he falls asleep. The more you do it, the sooner you begin to see progression. Over the course of a week or so, you may see the number of times your baby needs you to soothe him decrease, until he is used to being put down awake and doesn't need your help at all. This technique is much more effective with young babies, under about 4 to 5 months. It takes a lot of patience initially, but it can really pay off.

PICK UP, PUT DOWN

JoAnne: The first time I put my newborn, Dane, down a little bit awake, he fussed and I had to pick him up and calm him 25 times, until he finally fell asleep! The following nights, the number of times decreased slightly, until after about a week, I could put him down awake and he would soothe himself to sleep.

If your baby doesn't fall asleep on his own yet, it's not a reflection on his future as a bad sleeper—he will get there, we promise. A baby who doesn't fall asleep on his own in the first 4 months will still be a great sleeper later on, if you employ the techniques in Chapter 4. What your baby wasn't able to do today, he may surprise you by doing tomorrow—that's why we ask you to take a curious stance.

2. Loosen the Feeding-Sleep Association

This tip is related to putting your baby down awake. During a feeding, before your baby falls asleep, you'll see her go from drinking milk to merely suckling or pacifying on the breast or bottle. If you pay attention to when *swallowing* (slower, steady, with clear swallows) turns to *pacifying* (faster, more fluttery, little or no swallowing), you can gently take her off the nipple, lay her in her bed, and either allow her to fall asleep without sucking, or help her suck on thumb or pacifier if she prefers that. This may not work right away, but if you repeat this many, many times, your baby slowly but surely becomes able to do that final step of drifting off to sleep, without feeding while she does it. This helps her sleep longer at night, as well as take longer naps, because she doesn't search for a nipple each time she comes into a light sleep or partially wakes up. You may hear advice saying to go ahead and let baby fall asleep while feeding, just wake her up before you put her in bed, but it's much easier on your baby to catch her *before* she falls asleep. We adults all know how hard it can be to try to fall asleep twice!

3. Discern Your Baby's Sounds

Babies are noisy! Why didn't anyone warn you about the grunts, squawks, and gurgles your baby produces at night? One of the keys to promoting your newborn's sleep development is to listen and discern your baby's nighttime sounds.

Talking, whining, fussing, grunting, grumbling, kicking her legs, even pivoting and traveling around the crib—these are all normal noises and movements your baby will make as she figures out how to get comfortable and fall asleep again. These sounds don't necessarily mean, "Come and get me, I need you!" so when you hear them, try to resist jumping to pick your baby up. Give her some space to work things out on her own. Your baby will wake up multiple times a night (as will your older child, and as do you). What matters is whether she can get settled and fall back to sleep again on her own. Wait, listen, and see if she can figure it out.

During REM sleep (also called "active sleep"), babies tend to twitch, move their arms and legs, make sounds, and breathe irregularly, and they can even open their eyes. Roughly

50 percent of infant sleep is active, so that can make for a lot of normal noises at night.

However, if your baby constantly snores, gasps, or snorts while sleeping, tell your pediatrician about this so he or she can make sure it's not a sleep disorder such as sleep apnea.

DOES BABY NEED YOU, OR SHOULD YOU GIVE HIM SPACE?

Jane: I was convinced my 3-month-old was a problem sleeper; he was waking constantly. But in a baby group one day, another mom described how, when she started really listening to her baby's sounds instead of rushing in, her baby's sleep began to stretch out naturally. I came in to group the next week saying, "Never mind, my baby is actually a great sleeper. It was me who was getting in his way, interrupting him during all his grunts, squawks, and squirms!"

It can also help to keep in mind that not all cries are hunger cries. With a newborn, this may take some time to discern. If your baby has fed within the last 2 hours, this is a good opportunity to practice other methods of soothing. Building a repertoire of ways to calm your baby helps her become more flexible. It also loosens the association between food and comfort.

4. Use the Soothing Ladder to Avoid Overhelping

If your baby wakes up at night and needs you, be curious about the least intrusive thing you can do to help her fall back to sleep. Use the Soothing Ladder method to respond to your baby at night.

The Soothing Ladder Method

This method works for the first 4 to 5 months; the earlier you start, the better.

When your baby wakes up in the middle of the night, you use the Soothing Ladder to respond to her with the least intrusive means possible—by doing this, you respond to your baby but avoid over-helping. You start at the bottom of the ladder and spend roughly 30 seconds trying to soothe her, moving up a step if it doesn't work. Maybe one night your baby is calmed by you patting and rubbing her back, but another night all she needs is a soft song or shushing. You won't know unless you start from the bottom and take small steps up. Don't swoop in with the "big guns" (usually a feeding) right away.

During these early months, if your baby wakes up and you think she's due for a feeding, you'll go up the steps of the Soothing Ladder fairly quickly, only spending about 10 to 15 seconds or less on each step before feeding her. By doing this, you are building space for your baby to grow into, when she's eventually ready to drop that feeding. The goal is neither to rush her into dropping a feeding nor to continue assuming she needs to eat beyond the age when she really doesn't need to anymore. Take a curious step back, just far enough for her to show you.

The Soothing Ladder Steps

Create your own ladder, based on what you know about your baby's soothing needs. A typical sleep ladder for a young baby is:

7. Feeding her

6. Picking her up to gently rock until soothed but still awake

5. Jiggling baby in the bed

4. Your touch, patting on the back, rubbing head or tummy, hand over top of the head, and so forth

3. Replacing the pacifier and/or lovey

2. The sound of your voice, talking, singing, shushing

1. Your presence in the room

When your baby makes a sound at night, listen first (remember that babies are noisy but they aren't always telling you they need you). If you decide that your baby isn't just making normal rustling or squawking noises but is truly saying, "Come in here!" go in and use your Soothing Ladder. Start with number 1 on your list and spend around 15 to 30 seconds on each rung of the ladder until you get to the one that works. Do not feel compelled to go all the way up the ladder each time. You can stop when you notice your baby settling.

For example: You hear your baby cry out and you determine that this is a "come here!" cry. You go in and shush her, but she keeps crying, so you find her lovey and pat her on the back. If she starts to calm down, keep patting and shushing rather than picking her up.

It's better for your baby to fall back to sleep in her bed than to fall asleep back in your arms. If she's in her own bed, the next time she wakes she won't be surprised to find herself there.

We've heard so many parents say something like, "I need to go straight to the yoga ball and bounce her!" but when they create and use the Soothing Ladder, they're amazed to see that a step farther down actually works. Each time this happens, it creates a new learning opportunity for the baby. New pathways in her brain are formed, practiced, and strengthened every time she has these experiences.

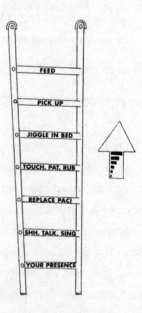

Use the Soothing Ladder to respond to your baby by the least intrusive means, so that you allow her sleep skills to gradually unfold.

Babies change so fast—what they need one week they may not need the next. The Soothing Ladder is the way to track sleep development and to follow *your unique* baby in each moment, rather than using a prescribed cookie-cutter strategy for all babies.

EVAN'S BOUNCING SLEEP ASSOCIATION

Ava: As Evan reached 2½ months, I was beyond exhausted. The amount of time I had to sit on the ball and bounce him back to sleep every night got longer and longer. When I started using the Soothing Ladder with him, I was truly astounded to find that Evan often only needed a few shushes or maybe a little back rub, not the full bouncing routine I thought he did! Over time, I rarely climbed past the first few rungs, and he began to do more soothing on his own.

5. Don't Let Your Baby Cry for More Than a Minute

For the first 4 months, don't let your baby cry for more than roughly a minute (one full minute might feel like more than that because it's so hard to hear our babies cry!). The squawks and grunts are fine, but if your baby is truly crying, attend to her. By meeting your baby's needs early on, you are building trust and a feeling that the world is a good place. In turn, your baby will relax and her stress level will remain low.

It's important to know you can't spoil your baby. Remember, this is how you build trust in the early months. Many parents, using this idea, discover that their baby predictably cries for about 30 to 45 seconds and then falls asleep almost every time. For these babies, crying is a form of stress release.

6. Daytime Independence

Look for moments during the day when your baby is enjoying hanging out by himself. Maybe he's fascinated by a shadow on the wall, marveling over his own fingers, staring at the tree outside the window, making baby pterodactyl sounds, or practicing squirming and rolling. What is the most attuned thing you can do when your baby displays such contentment on her own? Absolutely nothing! Just wait, watch, and wonder. There are two sides to a balanced attachment—proximity and soothing on one side, and your sensitivity to when your baby is just fine on his own or maybe even struggling a little bit on the other. When you attune to these signs of independence during the day, you're cultivating the same skill for nighttime. Remember that your baby's internal attunement (page 26) grows over time in the moments your baby is separate from you. This is when he can practice exploring and building confidence.

7. Transitional Object

More commonly called a lovey or blankie, this is an important aid for falling asleep and self-soothing for most babies. It's helpful to think about it in two stages.

Stage 1 Keep it with you and your baby as much as possible, especially when you're cuddling and feeding, so it has your scent and is associated with comfort (you could even sleep with the lovey for a few nights so it smells like Mom or Dad).

Stage 2 Once your baby shows signs of being attached to the lovey (rubbing it on his face, feeling it with her fingers, or grasping it), typically between 5 and 12 months of age, keep it in the crib for sleeping *only*, so she has a special way to soothe herself that evokes sleepy feelings. Keeping the lovey in the crib and using it only for sleep protects its "potency." Babies are often very happy to get into bed and see their treasured lovey waiting for them.

A lovey is typically a small (size of a cloth diaper) blanket, cloth, or unstuffed animal. You can introduce the lovey any time you want (see "Safe Sleeping Practices" on page 51 for more on safe loveys in the first 4 months), but generally, the sooner the better. For those babies who do attach to their lovey, the benefit to sleep is significant, and it can continue to help with sleep for years to come, both at home and when you travel. It's a good idea to have multiples on hand.

8. Tummy Time

The connection between tummy time and sleep is huge. Regular tummy time will give your baby the strength and coordination she needs to roll, rotate, tuck her legs under her, or anything else she needs to do to get into a comfortable sleep position. When this happens, it's a whole new world for your baby because she gets to choose her favorite body position instead of being stuck in the one you put her in. Lots of babies gravitate to belly sleeping, so once they can roll, they find their way to this preferred pose and sleep for longer stretches. It may feel unnerving to see your baby on her tummy for sleep, but once she can make it to this position on her own, it's okay for her to stay there.

Tummy time gives the neck a workout, strengthens the trunk, and gives your baby more reaching and looking practice. But tummy time may help with more than just motor development—encouraging motor skills is also known to help babies with social development, since the stimulation to motor pathways in the brain seems to encourage growth in other regions as well. Seeing the world tummy-down and head-up also helps your baby to connect the sounds in her surroundings with their exact location (rather than being stuck looking at the ceiling). That's also why carrying your baby is good for the brain—being in a bouncy seat or car seat all the time blocks her ability to turn, look, and see where all the noises in her world are coming from.

BENEFITS OF TUMMY TIME

- Rolling and moving help enormously with sleep. Babies who can move get to choose their favorite sleep position; now they can get comfy like we do at night.

- Babies spend a large portion of the day on their backs for safe sleeping, and in car seats, strollers, and other devices. All that back time needs to be consciously countered with belly time.

- Being on the tummy strengthens the muscles of the neck and back.

- The tummy position reduces the risk of developing a flat head (see page 71).

- Pressure on the tummy increases neurological organization, a fancy way of saying that it helps your baby to regulate and feel comfortable.

- Being on the tummy aids in future fine motor skills, as little hands push and grow strong.

- Tummy time is the first step in the natural progression to rolling, sitting, crawling, standing, and, eventually, walking. On the floor (whether on her back or belly), unaided by devices, should be baby's "default" position.

TIPS FOR TUMMY TIME

- Aim for 10 minutes per waking hour. If your baby can only last for 30 seconds in the beginning, just put her down frequently for those short bursts.

- Instead of plopping your baby down directly on her tummy, start by placing her on the floor on her back. Look at her, smile, say something like, "I'm going to help you roll to your belly," and roll her from the hips gently. (With repetition, she'll learn what's coming.) If her arm gets stuck underneath her, lift the hip on the same side of her body to allow her to pull her arm out. The idea is for your baby to participate in moving to her tummy instead of feeling like she's been stuck there.

- If your newborn is hopelessly face planting, use a small, rolled-up receiving blanket under her chest at armpit level, with her arms reaching forward. Feeding pillows are not a good idea as they give too much support and keep baby from the workout she needs.

- Your baby's favorite thing to look at is your face, so what better way to entertain her and "grow" tummy time than to get right down at eye level with her. Sing, make funny faces, and let her know that you know it's hard.

- Her second favorite thing to look at is her own face, so use a tilted mirror on the floor. See what happens when you put two babies face-to-face to gaze at each other.

- Some tummy time can be right on your chest, as you lie flat. You can press your palms into your baby's and help her push.

- It's okay for your baby to put her head down during tummy time. Think about how big and heavy her head is in proportion to her body; that's a lot of gravity working against her. You can help your baby learn to turn her head to one side and the other; this will help her sleep easily on her tummy once she learns to roll.

- Keep it positive. If you've done all you can to coax your baby into staying a few more seconds but she is clearly distressed, it's time to roll her to her side or back, or pick her up and try again in a little while.

- Don't lose hope. Tummy time progression often feels like a flat line, followed by an epiphany, when the baby bursts into loving it. Eventually, this may become her favorite play position.

FLAT HEAD AND TORTICOLLIS

Many newborns have somewhat lopsided heads. This can occur while passing through the birth canal or after birth as a result of spending too much time in one position. Torticollis, where baby's head is tilted or twisted to one side, usually because the muscles on one side of the neck are tighter, can also be the cause. Although being on their backs (until they can roll to tummy on their own) is absolutely the safest position for sleep, you can help avoid flat spots with some simple tips.

Caution: Don't use rolled-up towels or positioners in the crib to get your baby to keep her head to one side. Never rest your baby's head on a pillow or other type of soft bedding. These increase the risk of SIDS. Always start by checking with your pediatrician if you have concerns about your baby's head shape.

Change Direction Place your baby on his back to sleep, but alternate the direction your baby's head faces—place your baby's head near the foot of the crib one day, the head of the crib the next.

Hold or Wear Your Baby Holding or wearing your baby when he is awake will help relieve pressure on his head from swings, flat surfaces, and car seats.

Frequent Tummy Time With close supervision, place your baby on his tummy on the floor, frequently, during waking hours.

Feeding Time Alternate sides when feeding baby a bottle. You will do this naturally when breast-feeding.

Get Creative Position your baby so that he will have to turn away from the flattened side of his head to look at you or to track movement or sound in the room. Move his crib occasionally to give him a new vantage point.

Varying a baby's head position is typically enough to prevent or treat flat spots. If the flat spot doesn't improve within a few months, your baby's doctor might prescribe a special headband or molded helmet to help shape your baby's head.

Naps and the 90-Minute Awake Window

Your Baby's Naps

In the first 4 months, your baby will sleep in short and long stretches during the day—as short as 5 minutes and as long as 2 to 3 hours.

You can see how newborn awake/asleep patterns progress in the figure on page 303 in Chapter 8's "When the Internal Clock Develops."

Little baby naps typically start out luxuriously long. The tug of sleep is so strong for a very small baby that 2- to 3-hour siestas are common. Enjoy this—shower, eat, read, take a nap yourself. Don't worry too much that your newborn is sleeping heavily during the day because it typically doesn't correlate with restless nights. Just make sure that your baby is exposed to some indirect sunlight and activity during the day, with quiet and dark at night. Soon, her body will adjust.

Your young baby does not need (nor is her body ready for) a nap schedule until she is roughly 5 to 7 months old. Your goal during the first 4 months is to allow her ample opportunities to nap, to understand her sleep needs and how long she can be awake, and to encourage self-soothing. You can look forward to Chapter 4, pages 166–7, for specific schedules for when your baby is a little older.

The 90-Minute Awake Span

Because of your baby's strong sleep drive (see Chapter 8), after about the age of 2 months, she will start to feel drowsy around 90 minutes after waking up (before this age, she'll flicker in and out of sleep much more quickly). There is a magical little window here when falling asleep is easy. When you've missed the window and she's overtired, she may yawn, pull her ears, rub her eyes, cry, or appear a little wired. At this point, falling asleep becomes more difficult because her nervous system is overwhelmed and dysregulated. This 90-minute rule of thumb applies to the start of your baby's day, and also to each window of time she's awake after a nap, throughout the day.

The 90-minute awake span is one of the most successful ways to improve naps and, as a result, all sleep. Sleep begets sleep. One of the most common mistakes parents make is not putting baby down to nap often enough, which results in a chronically overtired baby whose nervous system is overstimulated and who is even less capable of falling asleep. Don't fall into thinking that the longer you keep your baby up, the more easily she'll fall asleep. Many parents assume that their baby is fussy as a result of hunger or boredom, and they try to feed and entertain their baby. Sometimes this is true, but often when your baby is fussy, it's because she's overtired.

THE 90-MINUTE STEPS

- Roughly 75 minutes after your baby wakes up (for the day or from her last nap) or whenever you see the subtle cues listed below, start a simple, soothing, 15-minute naptime routine.

- At the 90-minute mark, put your baby down. Parents are continually shocked and thrilled by how much this helps.

- Even if your baby only naps for 15 minutes, the 90-minute rule usually still applies from the time she blinks awake. Remember this if you're on a stroller walk or in the car and your baby catnaps.

Around 2 to 3 months of age, it is common for babies to sleep in short, brief bursts. If your baby takes frequent catnaps, don't feel as though you must do a full naptime routine before each nap. You might sing her a song while you put her down in her regular sleeping place, take her for a walk, or just put her in the sling or carrier in the house to allow her to doze. When your baby is 3 months and older, the naptime routines become more important.

These are early, subtler cues for sleepiness around naps. If you look closely, you may start to notice these (but we recommend starting with the more mechanical tool of watching the clock).

- staring off into space, dazed look in eyes

- reduced activity

- less interest in surroundings

The 90-minute rule isn't rigid; you have some wiggle room. Often the first nap of the day can come very easily after only 60 minutes of awake time. (Remember that the first nap is also often the easiest one to practice *putting baby down a little awake*). If you see that your 0- to 4-month-old baby seems tired, even though 90 minutes have not passed, it's best to follow these cues and put her down to sleep. Like everything else, this 90-minute span will grow and change as your baby quickly matures. For the first 3 to 5 months, the 90-minute rule will be very helpful. If you feel your baby is growing out of the 90-minute rule, see Chapter 4 for older baby nap routines and schedules.

90-MINUTE AWAKE SPAN HELPS
AVA WITH LONGER NAPS

Allison: We were struggling with naps. I was putting Ava down way too late, after 2 to 3 hours of being awake, which was too long for her. I now put her down 90 minutes after she is awake, and no more than 2 hours. She has been napping anywhere from 1 to 2 hours, which is a huge difference from previously napping 20 to 40 minutes. Especially in the morning: she wakes up around 6:30 a.m. and we have breakfast and play and around 8:00 a.m. I know she's tired. I sing her a song as I put her down and it still takes her 20 minutes of talking/playing in her crib and then she sleeps.

Catnaps

Short naps are really common. Around 2 to 4 months, your baby will be awake for longer stretches. At this point, it's typical for babies to catnap—sleeping for 20 to 30 minutes (just enough time for you to grab a snack, check your e-mail, or take a shower, but not enough time to do all three)—and then pop awake, ready to play again. One reason this happens is that we have to put babies down on their backs to sleep, and they easily startle and wake themselves up in this position. When your baby comes into a light sleep, it can be more difficult for him to go into a deep sleep again in a back-sleeping position. This makes belly sleeping a tempting notion, but remember that research shows putting baby to sleep on his back lowers the risk of SIDS significantly. Soon your baby will be rolling and moving on his own to the most comfy sleep position. Once that happens, the length of his naps will grow to a span of 1 to 3 hours. If you'd like to see where your baby's daytime sleep will be later on, you can look at Chapter 4, pages 166–7, for older baby nap schedule examples.

Remember that even a catnap counts when it comes to the 90-minute awake span. Short naps may still relieve your baby's drowsiness (and release the built-up pressure of his sleep drive, described in Chapter 8) enough so that he won't go back to sleep again—it's like a power nap.

Where Should Baby Nap?

Little babies often sleep better and longer when they're being held or carried. Put a sleeping newborn down on a flat surface and bam, he stirs awake! Nestle him in your arms or put him in the sling and he sleeps for hours. This is common and normal. Your baby doesn't want to be in a motionless, flat environment, but this will change over time. Allow your baby to sleep where you feel it works best, just keep in mind that it's really helpful to have him practice napping in his regular sleeping place, too (his bassinet, co-sleeper, or crib); aim to put your baby down for a nap in his regular sleeping place at least once a day. Often the first nap of the day is the easiest one to practice this.

NAPPING ONLY IN MAMA'S ARMS

Mona: Evan basically refused to sleep for more than 15 to 30 minutes at a time during the day unless I was holding him. If he was in his crib, forget it, I'd go through all the trouble of getting him to sleep, only to have him pop back awake again, whereas if I put him in the carrier or just held him continuously, he'd sleep for hours. I made it my goal to put him in his co-sleeper for his morning nap and that way I knew he had at least some practice there (the rest of the time, I mostly carried him). That morning nap grew into a nice long one, and eventually he started taking all naps in his crib.

QUICK LIST: NAP TIPS

1. **The 90-minute rule.** Your baby will be ready for sleep after roughly 90 minutes of awake time in the morning and after each nap. Watch the clock and start your 15-minute nap-time routine 75 minutes after her last awakening so that you can put her down at the 90-minute mark. Don't miss the optimal window—when your baby is overtired, it's harder for her to fall asleep. The 90 minutes is adjustable because every baby is different and the span grows over time.

2. **Naptime routine.** This will be similar to the bedtime routine (but shorter) and consistent each day. Don't skip the routine. Be sure to put it into place before your baby seems to need it. The nap routine becomes more important as your baby nears 3 months.

3. **Early sleepiness cues.** Babies show signs of sleepiness like becoming still or staring into space before they start to yawn and rub their eyes. It's good to know these early cues so that you can start winding your baby down before she is overtired.

4. **Feedings.** Be creative about getting the recommended number of feedings in. Naps and feedings will naturally be er-

ratic at this age and it's better to follow your baby's lead and feed on demand. If your baby takes a long nap, don't wake her for a feeding, just try to make up for that feeding at another time.

5. **Room environment.** Make the room where baby sleeps dark and quiet for naps. Use blackout shades. White noise, like nature sounds or a low fan, is very calming, especially during the first 3 to 4 months.

6. **Cues from you.** Give baby the genuine feeling that naptime is a rest time for you as well—put on a pajama top, prepare to lie down, even for only 10 minutes. If baby senses your anxiety about all you want to accomplish during the nap, she will have a hard time settling down.

7. **Rest versus nap.** It's okay if your baby sometimes just rests (happy in her bed) during naptime—also, a short nap should be perceived as a successful one.

Fussiness, the Witching Hour, and Colic

Fussiness and the Witching Hour

Most young babies have times during the day when they seem uncomfortable, cry, or fuss more than usual. There are lots of possible reasons for this: immature nervous system, overstimulation, understimulation, hunger, gas . . . the list goes on. A fussy baby is often a *tired* baby, though. Remember that little babies can really only be awake for about 90 minutes before they start to become drowsy, and for babies roughly 2 months and older, the 6:00 to 7:00 p.m. hour is when they're actually ready for bed. Even if your baby follows these guidelines, she may still feel tired and become fussy as a signal that she's ready to sleep.

- Put your baby down after every 90-minute span of awake time throughout the day.

- If your baby is 6 weeks or older and seems to be drowsy and has a longer stretch of sleep in the early evening, consider an early bedtime, around 6:30 to 7:00 p.m.

Many parents notice that their baby becomes extra fussy in the late afternoon and early evening (some parents can literally set their clocks by when the crying and fussing begins). This "witching hour" could be a result of a baby's accumulated stimulation from the day. Her nervous system and her internal clock are still developing, so she's getting conflicting messages from her own body: "I'm tired! No, I'm alert! . . . Sleep! Wake!" This often means that your baby needs more sleep, but, counterintuitively, she may be *harder* to put to sleep. Your baby can't yet balance and integrate all those bodily signals and, as a result, she may have times when she cries no matter what you do.

The witching hour will pass eventually, as your baby matures. In the meantime you can try to:

- Take your baby outside for a walk in a carrier or stroller. The fresh air, distraction, noise, and motion really help.

- Reduce stimulation like bright overhead lighting as the evening progresses.

- Allow your breast-feeding baby to "cluster feed" or feed continuously or frequently during the late afternoon. Some babies even need feeding *and* motion at once during this difficult time. Try breast-feeding while bouncing on a yoga ball or rocking/walking around the house if you can manage these two feats at once.

Colic

All babies cry, but approximately one in five babies (that's really quite a few—20 percent) are described as having colic and will cry piercingly and inconsolably for hours at a time, no matter what you do.

Colic is often defined by the "rule of three": crying at least 3 hours per day, more than three days per week, for three weeks' duration or more (some have debated this strict definition as many babies have colic but won't reach the 3-hour crying mark). Colic is the name given to this extreme crying when it is *unexplained*—there is no identifiable cause (although there are plenty of theories, such as an easily overwhelmed and immature nervous system, or incomplete development of the normal, or "good," bacteria in the gut). A hallmark feature of colic is that not much you try seems to make any lasting difference, and understandably, this can be at turns defeating, depressing, exhausting, and maddening for parents, who often feel alone and out of control.

Definitely call your pediatrician to talk about your baby's symptoms and determine if they fall into the category of colic, or if there's something else going on. If it is colic, the good news is that it does get better—in fact, it almost always seems to disappear magically (and thankfully) by 4 months of age. Babies seem remarkably fine once colic symptoms subside, but parents are often left with an almost "post-trauma" feeling from the experience.

Soothing Ideas for the Witching Hour and Colic

If your baby is very fussy or has colic, it may seem like there's no end in sight, but know that things will improve. The biggest priority for you as an exhausted parent is to get the support and empathy you need to get through this incredibly challenging time.

- Try different approaches, including wearing your baby in a carrier, swinging or bouncing on a yoga ball, using different-sized bottle nipples, adjusting the diet of the breast-feeding mother (with your pediatrician's guidance), giving probiotic drops, applying pressure on baby's belly, giving the baby a warm bath, swaddling, taking baby outside, playing music, turning on white noise machine, taking long car rides—the list is endless. Remember, it's not uncommon that the crying will continue no matter what you do. Feelings of helplessness and extreme frustration are completely normal.

- Get plenty of regular support. Trade off with your partner, hire a babysitter if you can, or enlist a friend or family member to give you regular breaks.

- Find a new baby group to join. You will surely find someone in the same boat as you and you will no longer feel alone.

- Do whatever it takes during this period to try to get your baby to take regular, frequent naps and sleep as well as possible at night. She'll need extra help from you to regulate and get the sleep she needs during the difficult period, and in turn the payoff will be a healthier and stronger brain and body.

There's no reason to worry that a baby who previously had colic or was very fussy will have a harder time self-soothing and sleeping independently in the long run—these skills may just come a little later, once the symptoms subside. When they do, your baby will surprise you by how quickly she is able to catch up and sleep well. Don't despair—even though she'll have strong associations to *you soothing her* (because she truly needs a lot of help), when her symptoms go away you will be able to transfer this role to her.

Sleep Regression

Most parents expect sleep to get progressively better and better in the first 4 months, but if your baby didn't get that memo, you're not alone. Baby sleep is bumpy. It doesn't follow a nice, logical path. Sleep improves and then regresses in fits and spurts: a few blessedly restful nights of long stretches, followed by a few nights of repeated wakings.

Around 3 to 4 months in particular, many babies hit a rough patch with sleep; even those who are champion sleepers as newborns sometimes start to wake up more frequently at this age. It can be frustrating and confusing for parents, who keep hearing that things get easier at 3 months, only to find their infant wide-eyed at 2:00 a.m. You can't imagine how many times we've heard moms and dads exclaim about their 4-month-old, "He thinks he's a newborn again!"

If this sounds familiar, don't worry. The reason for the return of restless nights at this age is probably your baby's rapidly developing brain (in other words, there is a silver lining). The drowsy cloud of the newborn months has worn off and your baby is leaping forward into a new level of consciousness. She's more aware and capable now; there's so much to do and see and explore.

SLEEP REGRESSION AND THE COGNITIVE SURGE

Cara: I was pretty happy since little Alexander was sleeping for longer and longer stretches at night. I was still nursing him to sleep and didn't really think it was a problem because his sleep kept improving. Then, at 3 months and 3 weeks, everything changed. After a 4-to-5-hour stretch, he began waking several times a night, wide awake and clearly ready to party. My husband and I were really surprised by this and quickly exhausted, just like we were at the very beginning. We didn't realize how all that nursing and holding to sleep would become an obstacle to Alexander's sleep as he got older. Eventually we used the Sleep Wave to help him practice falling asleep on his own and his sleep got better again.

Review all of the steps in "Encouraging Self-Soothing" (page 53) so that you can give your baby space to practice and make it through sleep regressions without developing a new sleep association (this is often really hard with a baby who is over 4 to 5 months old, which is why in the next chapter we present a clearer and more structured way to improve sleep for older babies).

A common misperception is that these sleep regressions always signal a *growth spurt*, which results in parents adding more night feedings. Try to avoid doing this automatically because this is the age when your baby is moving steadily toward getting all of the calories she needs during the day (if you do end up adding feedings, in Chapter 4 we can help you wean baby from these extra feedings). Use your Soothing Ladder and see if you can help your baby back to sleep with another method, unless you determine she is definitely hungry. The tricky part is that the same awareness that makes for bumpy nights may also make your baby distracted during daytime feedings (you probably notice her popping off the breast or bottle to check out her surroundings or feeding for just a few minutes before moving on to a new activity). Move to a calm and low-stimulus area like a dark bedroom for daytime feedings whenever possible, to make sure your baby gets enough to eat during the day.

The novelty of this higher level of awareness will eventually wear off. You will make it to 5 to 6 months and we'll be ready to help you solve any nighttime dilemma you still find yourself in. Just hang in there through sleep regressions—they eventually pass.

Although sleep regressions are often developmental, if they persist, talk to your doctor and rule out or address medical problems such as reflux, ear infections, teething, allergies, and colic.

Breast- or Bottle-Feeding and Sleep

The pattern of your baby's feedings will change during the first 4 months, right along with the rest of her development. This is the period of the most rapid consolidation of nighttime sleep, which means that over time the frequency of night feedings will decrease (although not always in a linear progression). At this age, your baby will wake up because she's hungry, but she'll also naturally wake up frequently because her nervous system and internal clock are immature.

We don't recommend that you purposely try to wean your baby from nighttime feedings during the first 4 months. It's incredibly natural (and important for breast-feeding) that your baby eat at night, so it's best to follow your baby's lead. In the next chapter, when your baby is at least 5 months of age, we'll guide you through how to wean her from night feedings if you want to.

> Breast-fed babies are not worse sleepers! Neither formula nor solid foods will help your baby sleep—this is a myth. Breast-fed babies may be more likely to fall asleep while eating, though, so they can quickly create a strong association between nursing and sleeping. If your baby falls asleep while eating, she's more likely to wake up later and call for you to help her fall back to sleep.

Feeding at Night

1 to 6 Weeks

- Doctors recommend feeding your baby 8 to 12 times in a 24-hour period, which usually means every 2 to 3 hours when awake. Your doctor may advise waking your baby to feed if she has slept more than 4 hours at any time, until she has regained her birth weight, after which time you no longer need to wake her. The most reliable indicator that your baby is getting enough to eat is the progression of her growth.

- Look for early cues that your baby is ready to feed, such as increased alertness, physical activity, mouthing, or rooting, rather than waiting for crying, which can be a late sign of hunger.

- It's normal for baby's feeding and sleeping patterns to be erratic during these early weeks as her nervous system is still immature. During this time, if you're breast-feeding, it's best to feed your baby on demand rather than trying to impose a schedule for feedings—this follows your baby's development and is the best practice for ensuring your milk supply.

- It's important to remember that *waking doesn't equal hunger.* If you have fed your baby within the last 1 to 2 hours and she wakes at night, this is a good opportunity to broaden her repertoire of soothing (see the Soothing Ladder, page 62). On the other hand, if your baby wakes after 3 to 4 hours, or at a time when she usually feeds, you can move up the Soothing Ladder quickly, confident that your baby is ready to eat.

6 Weeks to 4 Months

- It's normal to see the frequency of nighttime feeding gradually decrease during this time, as your baby starts to sleep for longer stretches. Your baby's digestive system is becoming more mature along with the organization of his brain and nervous system, two crucial areas of development that directly support sleep. Overall, your baby is taking in the same amount of milk, but gradually shifting those calories to the daytime.

- By 2 to 3 months of age, it is reasonable to assume that two to three feedings during the night are enough for most babies. By 4 months, one to two middle-of-the-night feedings are enough for most babies.

- At this age, if you have fed your baby within the last 1 to 3 hours and he wakes at night, this is a good opportunity to broaden his repertoire of soothing by trying other ways to help him get back to sleep.

- Around 3 to 5 months, it is common for babies to temporarily wake up more frequently—ready to play and excited at the novelty of their new awareness. It's natural to mistake this as a growth spurt and add in night feedings. As you know, babies rarely turn down an offer of milk during the night, so his eagerness to feed is not an accurate indicator of hunger. Review "Sleep Regression" on page 83.

CLUSTER FEEDING

It's common for babies to feed more frequently during the several hours before bedtime. This is called cluster feeding and appears to be a way for babies to soothe and regulate their nervous systems in preparation for their night, rather than being a stocking up of their milk supply. Some parents choose to give a bottle of pumped milk to breast-fed babies for their last feeding of the day as Mom's supply may be low at this time of day. If you do this, just remember to pump during this feeding time, or eventually it will lead to a further decrease in milk at this hour.

Introduce a Bottle

If you're breast-feeding, it's really helpful to introduce a bottle of pumped breast milk between 2 and 4 weeks and give baby a bottle *every single day* thereafter. If we had a nickel for every parent who stops offering a daily bottle to baby—figuring the baby has it mastered—only to see the baby refuse a bottle down the road! It's so much easier to give a bottle every day than it is to turn around a refusal. Having your baby well-versed in bottle-feeding gives you the freedom to know that other people can care for her and handle her bedtime or nap routine. It allows you a break, and gives someone else the experience of feeding. In many families, this becomes a special time for the non-breast-feeding partner to bond with baby.

To prevent overfeeding, keep in mind that most babies don't need more than 5 ounces in one feeding, no matter their age.

GENERAL TIPS FOR INTRODUCING A BOTTLE

- **Select a slow-flow nipple** so that your baby has to work a bit. This mimics natural pacing and lowers the risk that she will come to prefer the bottle if you're breast-feeding.

- **Hold your baby in an almost upright position** while holding the bottle almost horizontal, tipped just enough to fill the nipple with milk. Keep gravity from speeding the flow of milk, again mimicking the pacing of the breast as much as possible.

- **Encourage your baby** to participate by lightly brushing his lips with the tip of the nipple. When he opens wide, place the entire nipple into his mouth so that his lips rest on the base.

- **A bottle-feeding should take about 15 to 20 minutes.** If it's much faster or slower, you may have to adjust the nipple size and/or pace the feed. It's very effective for younger babies and those with colic or reflux to pause and remove the bottle after 12 to 22 swallows for baby to breathe three to five times. Signs that flow is too fast include wide eyes, splayed hands, gulping, gasping, milk leaking from the mouth, and pulling off the bottle.

- **With a newborn baby, bottle-feeding can start small,** at 1 to 3 ounces, building gradually to no more than 5 ounces at a time, as your baby grows.

- **Enjoy this time together.** Hold your baby close, skin to skin when possible. Look for moments to lock eyes and chitchat or sing a soft song.

TIPS FOR HELPING BABY WHO REFUSES THE BOTTLE

- **Not Mom.** Often the smell of breast milk and all the associations of Mom make it much more challenging for baby to go for the bottle. Dad or another caretaker can sometimes, with patience, find success. Sometimes Mom has to leave the room completely.

- **Change the scene.** If you've been re-creating the familiar place and position used in breast-feeding, try the opposite. Walk around the house or outside, sing, dance, and try different positions. Hold baby on your chest facing out, or prop her up facing you on your lap. Don't feed your baby when she's lying flat on her back and never prop the bottle.

- **Bait and switch.** You can try starting on the breast or pacifier and then gently switch to the bottle after your first let-down or once your baby is sleepy or relaxed. It can also help if he is not ravenously hungry. You might notice that your baby will take a bottle when he has just woken up.

- **Persist.** Don't give up. We meet very few babies who truly never take the bottle, as long as the parents keep trying (sometimes it takes a month or more). Try once or twice a day, ideally at the same times, and when everyone is relaxed and calm. Your baby will pick up on any pressure or frustration you're feeling, so breathe; center yourself; and know that with time, persistence, and patience, your baby will eventually take the bottle.

Sleep and Your Milk Supply

If you are breast-feeding and your baby naturally drops a nighttime feeding, it's a good idea to pump at the usual time of that feeding for a few nights and then gradually wean from that pumping. An abrupt decline in demand at a certain time can decrease your overall milk supply and cause discomfort for Mom.

Depending on how much milk your breasts are able to store, you may eventually go for 7 to 8 hours without feeding or pumping. Many moms will pump right before they go to sleep and then either feed or pump again 7 to 8 hours later.

Once your baby is sleeping for longer stretches, it's a good idea to add a daytime pumping session or two if your storage volume is on the low side and you're going back to work, for example. Often, 30 to 60 minutes after the first feeding of the day is the most productive time to pump.

Dream Feeding

Although our first choice is to let baby's sleep unfold naturally, for some babies the "dream feed" technique works very well. Here's how it works: While he's sleeping, gently pick up your baby from his sleeping place (but don't wake him) and feed him before you go to bed. For example, if you put your baby down at 7:30 p.m., you might try dream feeding him at 10:00 or 11:00 p.m. before going to bed yourself. It takes a few days for babies to get the hang of this pattern, but most babies will latch on and eat without fully waking up. If you try this for a few nights to a week, it may help your baby sleep a longer stretch. On the other hand, if you find that your baby wakes up for her next feeding at the same time no matter what you do, drop the dream feed and go back to letting your baby tell you when he's ready to eat.

Parent Sleep: Help in the First 4 Months

We dedicate Chapter 7 to an in-depth look at helping parents (with children of all ages) sleep better. We recommend looking at the tips in Chapter 7 now, but here are additional suggestions for getting the most shut-eye possible during the newborn period.

- **Rotate:** If possible, spread the responsibility for feedings and soothing so each parent gets a turn at a good solid stretch of sleep (even if it's only 3 to 4 hours). Have one parent or helper give a bottle once in a while at night so that the other parent can sleep through a feeding. If you're nursing, pump before bed and leave a bottle in the fridge, so that person can scoot out quickly to grab it.

- **Enlist help:** You cannot do this alone. Nor should you try. Hire a babysitter, ask a trusted friend, hand your baby to Grandma—call on your support system for help. You may feel as though no one but you is capable of taking care of your baby, but other people will find their own ways. It's worth it to relinquish control for a bit and take care of yourself. It's also a good thing for your baby to develop trust in multiple caregivers. If you're a single parent, try to schedule helpers, family members, or friends on a regular basis to help you through these early months.

- **Separate for sleep:** If your home allows, temporarily assign one partner to another sleep space for all or part of the night, or have one parent take the baby into another room in the early morning so the other can sleep. Mom or Dad might sleep in the guest bed or on the sofa one night (or for a portion of the night) for uninterrupted sleep.

- **Block noise:** The parent brain is easily aroused with the tiniest baby peep (especially for a night-feeding mom), so run a fan in the guest room while you or your partner escape there to sleep. Whether you're in the guest room, living room, or right next to your partner in bed, use earplugs if you are the one off duty.

- **Nap:** The traditional wisdom is to "sleep when the baby sleeps." We have mixed feelings about this advice. For some new parents, it's a lifesaver. For others, it makes them feel even more disoriented and groggy to sleep during the day. Experiment and see which category you fall into.

If you feel like you can't wind down and sleep, or even really rest while your baby is napping or sleeping, you're not alone. It's normal to feel some combination of excitement, anxiety, shock, and fatigue like you've never felt before. This is a good time to begin to practice some simple breathing and mindfulness techniques (see the Appendix) to help your nervous system come back to a balanced state, so your body can rest.

Postpartum Emotions

New parenthood is naturally a time of challenging emotional swings from joy at the miracle of your baby, to sadness or anxiety at the abrupt loss of the life you knew and the overwhelming tasks of parenting. It's normal to feel that, at every turn, you don't really know what to do, the Groundhog Day sense of no end in sight, and the mind-numbing heaviness of sleep deprivation. Most parents can identify with the feeling of being moody and blue, at the very least. These feelings are normal for all parents.

Around 20 percent of mothers experience postpartum depression, anxiety, or a combination of the two, making it the number one complication of childbirth. It can appear anytime within the 12 months after birth. Postpartum depression and/or anxiety can feel like it takes over a mother's thoughts and behavior in a strong and unfamiliar way, which can make it scary and hard for her to talk about.

The great news is that postpartum depression and anxiety are very treatable with expert therapy, support groups, and sometimes medication. We're happy to see the stigma and secrecy of postpartum challenges fade away, as society begins to understand it better. More and more moms are reaching out for help and feeling better much sooner.

Sleep deprivation and worry about baby's sleep can contribute to postpartum issues. We find, in our practice, that improving both baby's and Mom's sleep can help moms start to feel more like themselves again. Sleep deprivation is not to be taken lightly and, like other features of postpartum depression and anxiety, it is definitely treatable. We'd love all moms to discuss postpartum emotions with their doctors, families, friends, and therapists to determine what level of support they need.

If you think you might need support during your pregnancy or postpartum, help and information is available through Postpartum Support International (www.postpartum.net; 1-800-944-4773).

☆ TROUBLESHOOTING SLEEP ☆

When Should I Move My Baby to Her Own Room?

For frequent feedings and bonding during the early months and also due to the recommendation by the American Academy of Pediatrics that newborns should co-sleep (in the same room as the parents but on a separate sleep surface) as a SIDS precaution, starting out with baby in your room is a good idea. Since babies' highest risk for SIDS is before 3 to 4 months, a good time to move your baby to her own room is around 4 to 6 months. It's a personal decision that can be influenced by your baby's growing awareness of and activation by your presence in the room, as well as your desire to have your personal space back. However, if you, your partner, and your baby are all sleeping well in your room and you have no desire to move her yet, that's perfectly fine as well.

Should We Have a Schedule?

Not yet! You baby's nervous system, circadian rhythm, digestive system, and more are not mature. This is a time in your baby's development to follow her lead, feed on demand, and follow simple guidelines like helping her nap (after about 2 or 3 months of age), after roughly every 90 minutes of awake time.

My Baby Is Rolling to His Tummy in Bed. What Do I Do?

When your baby first rolls to his tummy in the crib, he will very likely get frustrated and seem unhappy—really he's just unfamiliar with the position and might feel stuck and uncomfortable at first. If this happens, you will initially feel compelled to turn your baby over to his back right away, but this is often a losing battle of flipping and reflipping through the night.

Trust us, this tummy-rolling business is ultimately a very good thing. Help your baby weather this feeling of unfamiliarity by leaving him on his tummy and using the Soothing Ladder. Work your way up the ladder, just as you would at bedtime or with any awakening. This transition is similar to un-swaddling in that you will have a few bumpy nights, but when the novelty wears off, the end result will be a big step toward improved sleep. Most babies sleep better once they've found their way to their tummies, as their limbs are now contained and the pressure on their bellies is calming. The long-term goal is for your baby to find a comfortable sleep position without your help. Lots of tummy time during the day will help your baby feel more familiar with this position. It can also help to show your baby how to turn his head to the side instead of just face planting. For safety reasons, it's best to always put baby down on his back. Remember that if your baby can roll to his tummy, for safety reasons, it's time to get rid of the swaddle.

3-MONTH-OLD FLIPPING TO HIS TUMMY

Rachel: Wesley kept ending up on his belly and it made me nervous, so I kept flipping him to his back, even though I knew he'd roll right back to his tummy. I had the feeling that he liked it better if he got to his belly himself. Sure enough, pretty soon, Wesley was rolling to his tummy midair as I lowered him to the crib!

Is teething waking my baby up?

While the normal age range for teething to start is broad (we once had a mom in class who was born with a tooth, and we've also heard of babies who got their first chomper at 14 months), the majority of babies sprout their first tooth between 4 and 7 months. What typically precedes the appearance of a tooth is a prolonged period of drooling, chewing on everything, and a range of very low to mild discomfort and fussiness.

It's normal to be unsure whether teething is causing your baby to wake up (if only she could just tell you!). If you're noticing extra fussiness during the day and decreased interest in feeding, and you can see little clear or whitish bumps (the bottom middle and top middle teeth, in that order, are typically the first to come in), there's a pretty good chance that your baby is about to cut a tooth. Don't assume that teething is going to bother your baby a lot. Quite a few babies will sail through teething without any significant sleep disruption, while others are noticeably bothered during the night.

If your baby is *actively* cutting a tooth (meaning it's currently coming through the gums), and sleep has clearly been derailed, consider addressing the pain so that he can get good sleep during the two to three days it usually takes. Talk to your pediatrician about giving a pain medication thirty minutes before bedtime, and make sure you use the correct dose. You can also use homeopathic remedies or whatever you have found to be helpful—just be sure to clear this with your doctor. By addressing the pain during the two to three nights of active cutting, you are helping your baby to get the sleep he needs so that he can better tolerate the pain during the day, without adding sleep deprivation to his plate. It will also prevent you from overhelping him during the night, which can quickly create new unhelpful sleep associations. Acute teething pain usually lasts no more than two to three days, so try to be aware of not assuming that your baby needs more help at night for weeks because of teething.

Babies may have a tendency to take in less milk during the day, when actively teething. You can avoid adding nighttime feedings by assuring that they feed well during the day.

TEETHING TIP

Give your baby a cold, wet washcloth or gel-filled teether to chew on before daytime feedings. The coolness (avoid the freezer as it can be too cold) can help to numb her gums a bit and up the chances that she'll have a full feeding.

My baby will sleep only in a swing, vibrating chair, hammock, or other device. Is this okay? Will he ever sleep in his crib?

You've probably heard the term "fourth trimester," which refers to your baby's first 3 months out in the world. This term came about as a way of describing how we humans come into the world less mature than many other species, due to the size of our brains. This means that simulating the environment in the womb can be extremely helpful for soothing and sleep, and this is why many 0-to-3-month-old babies respond so well to rocking, bouncing, and swinging.

If these devices work in the first 3 months, use them to soothe your baby and try not to worry too much about the future. Remember that during these early months, responding to your baby's cues when she needs your help is key to her feeling that the world is a safe place where her needs are met. At the same time, stay curious about her abilities so that you can discover when your baby is able to fall asleep without the help of these devices. With this mind-set, your baby will show you when she doesn't need as much help anymore.

This early need for movement is finite—it won't last. As their brains quickly mature, babies are ready for the next step and will sleep better without the movement, just like we do. Review the steps in "Encouraging Self-Soothing" (page 53). One of the most common responses to our sleep approach is, "Wow, I didn't know my baby was so capable!" If your baby is still reliant on movement to fall asleep when she reaches 5 months, we will help you change this pattern in the next chapter.

My baby is sick. What to do during the night?

Sniffles, tummy upset, ear infections—babies can pick up all kinds of bugs and viruses. As much as we wish we could protect them from illness, we know that exposure to these colds and flus is a big part of what stimulates their immune system to become strong and resilient.

When you know your baby is sick and he wakes during the night, attend to him promptly and do whatever he needs to feel soothed and comfortable. This part isn't difficult for most parents; the hard part is giving baby space again once he's feeling better. You may notice that your baby's sleep patterns are bumpy for a few nights, even after the illness passes. Go back to your methods for encouraging self-soothing and give your baby a little space to show you what he can do now that he's feeling better.

It's a good idea to always check with your pediatrician before you give your baby any medications, even those sold over the counter, and make sure that you understand the dosage and directions. Even when your baby is sick, all of the safe sleeping rules still apply, including no pillows or blankets or anything other than their lovey in the crib.

Why does my baby take super-short naps?

Babies evolve from the super-sleepy newborn state—when naps go on and on—to a more aware and conscious state. After this happens, they are more likely to fully awaken when they transition into a light sleep. More babies than not will move to these alarmingly short catnaps of about 30 minutes, anytime between about 2 and 6 months of age. Once your baby's brain and body mature even more and she can roll to her favorite sleep position, her naps will lengthen again. The tips most likely to support your baby's progress toward longer naps are:

- Put your baby down awake.

- Discern your baby's sounds (at the end of a short nap, don't rush in!).

- Give your baby plenty of tummy time between naps.

Some parents have success using the Soothing Ladder at the end of a very short nap to get baby back to sleep quickly to "finish" their nap. This is always a good thing to try from time to time, as the day will come when your baby is ready to stretch out that nap. In the meantime, during the catnap phase, don't worry, and know that it's perfectly normal. Just watch the clock and put your baby down 90 minutes after her last awakening. This is a very challenging time, as your day feels endlessly consumed with naps and feeding and little else. It's fine to have some of these naps take place in the car, carrier, or stroller, so that you can get out and walk, do errands, meet a friend for coffee, or go to a class.

Can my baby just nap on the go?

As your baby approaches the 3-to-4-month mark, you may notice her having a harder time sleeping when out of the house. Again, this is because her brain is developing and her awareness and interest in the world are growing steadily. She is much more curious and stimulated by her environment, and this makes those peaceful restaurant meals, with baby sleeping soundly by your side, more difficult. The world is just too exciting now and she needs her familiar cues and nonstimulating environment to fall asleep, just like you probably do. Of course, we all know someone who can fall asleep anywhere, at the drop of a hat; there's always a chance that you have a baby like that, but it's not the norm.

My baby woke up after just 45 minutes of going to bed!

Babies and young children often have a brief arousal roughly 1 hour after falling asleep (most likely because they move from quiet to active sleep during this time). If you hear from your baby 30 to 60 minutes after she goes to bed, it's likely because she hasn't yet practiced self-soothing back to sleep. Try putting her down awake at the beginning of the night, or for her first nap, and using other steps explained in "Encouraging Self-Soothing" (page 53). If she really cries out, use the Soothing Ladder to help her.

My baby has reflux. What do I do for sleep?

The range of reflux symptoms is broad, from the "happy spitter" all the way to GERD (gastroesophageal reflux disease), the most severe form of acid reflux. Always start by working with your pediatrician or specialist (pediatric gastroenterologist) to determine the best treatment protocol for your baby. Some doctors may recommend a particular sleeping position for your baby, so talk to yours and review the safest way to help your baby get comfortable for sleep.

Depending on the severity and progression of your baby's reflux (with treatment and over time, symptoms will subside), you may see sleep development unfold more slowly. The Soothing Ladder, on page 62, allows you to follow your unique baby, but it may take more time if she has reflux. You might practice putting her down a little awake only once a day or at bedtime, until her reflux starts to improve. Your baby may need a lot of help from you during these early months. As long as you stay curious, you will be ready to take those small steps back when her reflux improves and she is ready to do more self-soothing. Your baby will eventually sleep well, even if her sleep is initially more challenging.

4.

Baby + Toddler
(5 Months to 2 Years)

TROUBLESHOOTING ☆

Troubleshooting the Sleep Wave, pacifiers, new motor milestones, climbing out of the crib, separation anxiety, throwing loveys out.

☀ HEALTHY SLEEP HABITS ☀
Your Baby's Sleep

You have a different baby in the house now. She's no longer a tiny, bundled newborn but rather a laughing, babbling—maybe even talking little human being. You can see it in her eyes, can't you? The lights are on; she's engaged and aware of the world around her (thanks to new, more sophisticated activity in her brain's frontal cortex).

All of these changes are good news for sleep, because it means her self-soothing capabilities are growing fast. Have you noticed her sucking on her hand, or rocking back and forth to calm down? Maybe she's grabbing her chubby feet and popping them in her mouth, turning her head and nuzzling a blanket, singing to herself, or rolling to her belly in her crib. These behaviors are all part of her budding ability to self-regulate. On top of this, her circadian system is now more mature (see Chapter 8) and craves a good, regular sleeping schedule.

At this point, bedtime and nighttime sleep should no longer feel like a lot of work to you. If you're still hushing everyone within a one-mile radius, feeding or rocking until your child is in a deep sleep, or tiptoeing out of the room like a ninja-parent, praying that she doesn't peep . . . you don't have to do this anymore. It could be you're bouncing or feeding your baby back to sleep multiple times a night, endlessly inserting and reinserting a pacifier, or pushing your toddler in a stroller to help her nap. Whatever it is, at this point you're working so hard, but the truth is that your baby has become dependent on *you* to soothe her to sleep, when *her own body and brain are capable of this job.*

We know how frustrating this can get: you try and try to help your baby sleep, but you still end up exhausted and you feel as though you're doing something wrong. Don't worry, you're in good company—sleep issues are very common at this age. A lot of babies and toddlers struggle with sleep troubles like:

- Being unable to self-soothe and fall asleep independently

- Waking up in the night out of habit rather than from hunger

- Needing a parent's presence or a stroller, car, or another device to nap

- Going to bed too late, and therefore not sleeping eleven to twelve hours

- Waking up too early, and therefore not sleeping 11 to 12 hours

If your baby falls into one of these categories, remember that she's probably tired and wants to sleep, just like you do! Fortunately, even though sleep issues can feel like a major struggle, improving sleep is very doable if you consistently follow the right plan.

In this chapter we will guide you through improving sleep for babies ages 5 to 24 months. You'll establish an early and consistent bedtime, a regular nap schedule, and a pattern of self-soothing that helps your baby fall asleep independently and sleep through the night. In this chapter, we'll teach you the Sleep Wave, a technique for falling asleep independently that you can use with babies 5 months and older, as well as toddlers and even preschoolers. We'll also walk you through how to approach feeding and weaning at night, and all of the other common questions and issues you may have.

As you read, keep in mind that the healthy sleep habits outlined in this chapter will improve your baby's sleep right now, and also stay with your child for many years to come. An early and consistent bedtime and the ability to self-soothe and sleep through the night: these practices will become the norm and your child will expect and even *want* them in place down the road.

SLEEP NEEDS FOR BABIES AND TODDLERS

Babies 5 to 11 months
14 to 15 hours total
Three naps until
about 9 months, then
two naps

Toddlers 1 to 3 years
12 to 14 hours total
One nap

Why Does Your Baby Wake Up?

Here's a fact: all babies wake up at night. The "good sleepers," the "bad sleepers"—all pass through light sleep and into a twinkle of consciousness during the night as they transition through stages of sleep. You do this, too. When you wake up slightly you might roll over, adjust your blankets, plump your pillow . . . and drift back. Usually you're not even fully awake—at least not for long enough to remember it the next day. Your sleep feels seamless to you, but in fact it reaches the border between sleep and wakefulness multiple times every night.

When it comes to babies, the difference between the so-called good sleepers and bad sleepers is *what they do when they partially wake up.* Some roll over, grab their blankies or loveys, tuck their knees under them, and fall asleep again. Others call out for help to be soothed back to sleep. Our main goal in this chapter is for your baby

If babies don't know how to self-soothe, they wake up fully instead of going back into a deep sleep.

to become a little expert in her own ways of getting comfy, self-soothing, falling asleep, and drifting back to sleep throughout the night without your assistance.

One of the main reasons babies signal for help at night is because they're looking for the soothing trick that put them to sleep in the first place. If your baby nods off feeding or rocking in your warm arms and then, inexplicably, finds herself awake and alone in her crib, you can see why she summons you. Imagine if you fell asleep in your cozy bed, your favorite soft blanket tucked under your chin, and then woke up a few hours later, blanketless, on the living room floor. You'd reach around a bit for your blanket, wonder where you were, and you'd be disoriented enough to fully wake up and try to solve the mystery (and get your original sleep things back). That's what it feels like for your baby when she slips into a dreamworld surrounded by certain stimuli—your arms, your motion, breast, or bottle—and then blinks awake under totally different circumstances later in the night.

What looks to parents like their child's sleep problem is often just the result of *unhelpful sleep associations*. Sleep associations are the conditions under which your child falls asleep that, over time, she links to the act of soothing and sleeping. Certain sleep associations are good and helpful, but others delay sleep at bedtime or disrupt sleep in the middle of the night because they require the input of Mom or Dad. If your baby can't re-create the exact soothing method that put her to sleep initially, you're likely to hear from her in the wee hours. If you're still putting your baby to bed already asleep (or virtually asleep), this will be the first thing to change in order to improve both her daytime and nighttime sleep. The goal is to put your baby to bed with her as a conscious, knowing participant—without any sneaking out or surprises.

BEDTIME: THE CORNERSTONE OF GOOD SLEEP

Bedtime sets the tone for the whole night. The way your child goes to bed will often determine the quality of her sleep overall. If she goes to sleep with you holding or feeding her, she's more likely to look around for you when she stirs at night. If she drifts off with her own soothing methods (rolling, wiggling into her favorite position, nuzzling her blankie or lovey, listening to the rain sounds in her room), she can re-create this any time she wakes up at night.

This is why we focus on bedtime first. Newborns often need to be soothed to sleep, but by 5 to 6 months, babies become capable of taking over this job (with some room to practice). After this age, it's important to look at the associations and circumstances around bedtime. You will always help your child with comforting routines, stories, songs, cuddles, and so forth, but once she's in her crib or bed, if there is anything you do that she can't do herself later, you will want to replace this with a soothing method *she can be in charge of* all night long. Follow safe sleeping guidelines (see "Safe Sleeping Practices," page 51) when deciding what to put in your child's crib. Read about loveys and other transitional objects on page 66.

UNHELPFUL SLEEP ASSOCIATIONS	HELPFUL SLEEP ASSOCIATIONS
Rocking, bouncing to sleep	Loveys, blankies (stuffed animals for toddlers)
Breast- or bottle-feeding to sleep	Baby rocking back and forth
Swings, vibrating chairs, and other devices	Nature sounds or white noise all night
Pacifiers that baby can't reinsert	Sucking fingers or thumb
Music that turns off during the night	Moving into favorite sleep position
Stroller rides or car trips	Singing or talking to self in the crib

Babies also wake up in the night for feedings. Later in this chapter (page 146) we'll help you decide how to approach breast- or bottle-feeding at night. You do not have to wean your baby in order to improve her sleep—you can work on her self-soothing skills while keeping feedings in place. If you are ready to wean, we will walk you through the steps for this, too.

As you work on sleep with your baby, remember that all children go through periods of difficult sleep. Think about it: their brains and bodies are in a constant state of change and growth. Teething, new motor skills, language acquisition, cognitive development, separation anxiety, travel, illness, nightmares, transitioning to the big bed (the list goes on!)—all of these normal parts of development will disrupt sleep patterns at some point. Working on sleep is not something that you do one time to "fix" the problem and voilà! If you think this way, you're bound to be frustrated and confused by temporary setbacks. Instead, we're going to teach you concepts and practices that lead to a good, healthy sleep foundation. When you have this, you can weather these bumps and sleep disruptions in the best way possible, and then quickly get sleep back on track for the whole family.

AWAKE VERSUS ASLEEP

Multiple research studies have found that babies and toddlers who are put into bed already asleep are more likely to wake up during the night and less likely to be self-soothers. A National Sleep Foundation poll on children's sleep found that infants and toddlers who were put to bed asleep tended to sleep about an hour less at night than those who were put to bed awake. Those who were put to bed asleep were nearly three times as likely to wake two or more times compared to those who are put to bed awake.

Your Child's Bedroom

The sights, sounds, and feel of your child's bedroom environment play a big role in promoting sleep. The following are important for babies, toddlers, preschoolers, and school-age children, and they apply no matter where your child sleeps.

Light Your child is exquisitely attuned to light, which is the primary signal to her internal clock (see Chapter 8). Install blinds or hang curtains that block early morning rays and make the room very dark for naptime (we often ask parents if their baby's room is dark and they say it definitely is; when we look for ourselves, we see that it's not even close to being dark enough). Bright home lights can suppress the release of melatonin (which naturally rises as we near bedtime) and interfere with your child's ability to fall asleep. In the evening, lower the lights in the house an hour before bedtime and use a dim lamp during bedtime routine to help your child's body wind down. If she wakes in the night, use a nightlight (see "Light, Electronics, and Bedtime" on page 120) instead of bright overhead lights. Darkening shades or curtains that can be pulled back in the morning are best, so the room can have natural light. In the morning, pull back the shades—this is like pressing "start" on your child's internal clock.

Sound Use a low fan or nature sounds to block ambient noise, from siblings, barking dogs, and so forth.

Smell Keep the air fresh in your child's room, so that the smell and air quality are pleasant. Open the windows during the day to let air circulate. Use a low fan or air purifier to keep a gentle flow of moving air.

Feel Give your child a comfortable, firm sleep surface and soft sheets (make sure to follow safe sleeping guidelines, page 51). If your older child is using a pillow, it should be the right size for his body, supporting his neck in alignment with his spine, not craned upward. Most children don't need pillows until they are at least 2 years old, and many don't use them until they move to a big bed.

Temperature Keep the room cool, around 65 to 68 degrees Fahrenheit. It may sound chilly, but cooler temperatures are generally better for sleep. If it's hot and you do not have air-conditioning, use a fan to bring in cooler outside air at night. Don't overbundle your baby for sleeping.

No Television Children who have a television in their bedroom tend to sleep less at night and are also less likely to take a nap than those with no TV in their room.

Design Your child's room should be a peaceful space that makes you both feel relaxed and comfortable.

Early, Consistent Bedtime

One of the best ways to help your baby sleep is to set an early and consistent bedtime—between 7:00 and 7:30 p.m. works well for most. When babies and young children stay up later than this, they often become overtired and overstimulated, as levels of stress hormones like cortisol begin to rise in their bodies. This can make them activated, moody, and even less likely to be able to wind down and fall asleep.

The sweet spot for putting your baby to bed is before this happens. Try not to wait until she shows classically "tired" signs like yawning and rubbing her eyes—the optimal bedtime is when your baby is quietly talking, playing, and in a good mood.

Staying up too late can also cause your baby to wake up earlier in the morning (counterintuitive, right?), whereas an early bedtime often begets longer and longer stretches of sleep over time.

Setting an early bedtime can feel like a major adjustment, especially if you're an evening person. But an early bedtime truly optimizes sleep for babies and young children, whose bodies are naturally programmed for early rising. You might notice that your baby wakes up at the same time in the morning no matter what time she goes to bed (put her to bed at 9:00 p.m. and she wakes at 6:00 a.m.; put her to bed at 7:00 p.m. and she wakes up at 6:00 a.m.—that's a powerful internal alarm!). Putting your child to sleep early allows her the best chance of sleeping a full 11 to 12 hours. Your baby's circadian system is quite mature now, so regularity is important.

This kind of schedule creates a dilemma for a lot of parents: with such an early bedtime, Mom or Dad gets home too late to see the kids. We know this is a tough spot (and we've had to juggle this fact with our own families, too). But a full night's sleep is so important to your child's development; it's better for her to be well-rested than to routinely keep her up for the purpose of seeing you. You might also see that when Mom or Dad comes home from work, the energy and excitement disrupts bedtime routines and delays sleep even more. It doesn't mean you can never be flexible, but the majority of nights, keep to your child's bedtime. Carve out another time, like the morning routine or a weekend swim class, to give the parent who misses out in the evenings the much-needed bonding time. For parents who work late and aren't able to get baby down at 7:00 p.m., 7:30

or even 8:00 p.m. is okay, as long as baby still gets at least 11 hours of sleep. Some babies adjust better to a later bedtime than others.

WORK SCHEDULES AND BEDTIME

Erin: My husband John rarely got home in time to see Riley before her bedtime. When I tried keeping her up so they could see each other, her sleep really fell apart and it truly wasn't worth it. We came up with the solution of having Daddy get up with her at 6:30 in the morning and spend an hour playing and having a bottle. They came to treasure this time together and I got a luxurious extra hour of sleep! This eventually gave John the confidence to begin spending more one-on-one time with Riley on the weekends.

Just as some adults are natural night owls and others are "larks," or morning people, kids can also have these innate biological tendencies. However, often what looks like genuine night owl behavior is the result of an inconsistent bedtime, bedtime routine, or difficulty self-soothing. If you truly have a night owl child, you may notice that she's able to stay awake until 8:00 p.m. and sleep until 7:00 a.m. consistently and is happy with this schedule. If so, that's great, and it may work well with your own sleep schedule, too. On the other hand, if your night owl baby still wakes up at 6:30 a.m., you'll want to make sure her bedtime is no later than 7:30 p.m. Even children with night owl tendencies can usually do well with early bedtimes if they are consistent. In fact, a baby with this tendency might need you to be extra consistent and clear with bedtime practices to help her wind down and get a full night's sleep.

Bedtime Routines

Babies are highly sensitive to routine. A calming, consistent set of steps leading up to bedtime signals to your child's brain and body that sleep is just around the corner. Your baby is a little scientist and she's always looking for patterns in her environment. She *wants* you to do things the same way each day—repetition is soothing to her. In the newborn months, you had a lot of wiggle room to do whatever worked—sometimes you put your baby to sleep at 9:00 p.m. and other nights 6:30 p.m., sometimes you sang a song and rocked her to sleep and other nights she fell asleep while feeding. But if you haven't already, now is the time to start doing the exact same thing, in the same order, every night before bed.

Sample Bedtime Routines

Your baby's routine can last for 30 to 60 minutes or more, depending on how many steps it contains and whether you have multiple children. These are just examples. You will find your own special steps; just be sure you choose soothing rather than activating ones, and keep the same order, with a calm tone:

6-MONTH-OLD	12-MONTH-OLD	20-MONTH-OLD
Bath	Bath	Bath
Pajamas	Pajamas	Pajamas
Feeding	Feeding	Books
Books	Baby-led play (see page 121)	Lights out

6-MONTH-OLD	12-MONTH-OLD	20-MONTH-OLD
Say good night to objects in the room	Books	Tell a story about the day
Lights out	Say good night to objects in the room	Song
Songs, cuddle/sway	Lights out	Good night kiss
Bed	Songs, cuddle/sway	Bed
	Good night kiss	
	Bed	

The Soothing, Repetitive Routine

Make your baby's bedtime routine an enjoyable, calming set of steps that are the same from night to night. The "what" of the routine doesn't matter as much as the "how." Even turning on a certain type of music, lowering the lights in the house, and doing very small behaviors such as drawing the curtains, turning on the fan, saying good night to objects in the room with a quiet voice, or arranging blankets *just so* become a cue for sleep if you repeat these steps every night. Drowsiness develops into a Pavlovian-like response for your baby if your actions are calm and consistent. Watch the way your simple behaviors, if they're slow, almost methodical and consistent, can trigger a calming reflex in your baby.

It's best to do the last steps of your routine in your baby's bedroom, and the *very* last step (for example, singing a song) with the lights out, so that your baby has a moment with you in the dark before you leave the room.

Dim Lights and Disconnect

Dim the lights in your home an hour before bedtime to help your child's brain and body wind down. Avoid having your baby watch TV before bed, as this can delay her ability to fall asleep. It's also better not to make TV a strong sleep association that your baby, and eventually your child, grows into needing.

LIGHTS, ELECTRONICS, AND BEDTIME

The lights in your home—including overhead lights and light from electronic screens on devices like tablets and computers—can interfere with your child's ability to fall asleep. This is because light suppresses the release of melatonin—a chemical that naturally rises as we begin to feel drowsy before bed. This is especially true of blue light, which is emitted by a lot of electronics. Use dim lights for nightlights (red light has the least powerful effect on melatonin secretion, so you could replace your baby's nightlight with a red bulb, which will be the least alerting light source).

Wind down the House

Shift the energy in the house (including your own) roughly 30 to 60 minutes before your baby's bedtime. The older they get, the more children believe that by going to sleep they're missing out on a party in the living room. If your child gets the sense that the whole house is settling down, it becomes much easier for her to let go and shift into bedtime mode.

Routines Grow with Babies

Yes, consistency is key with routines, but remember that your baby's routine will grow with her. Sometimes we meet families who say their toddler's routine is still bath, massage, rocking, and milk—a great routine for a very young baby, but not a great fit for an alert, curious older one. The trick is to make your bedtime routine age appropriate and engaging (like telling a story about the day with your toddler), while still being calm.

> Some babies like to have their bedtime books read to them as they move around and explore the area, rather than in the quintessential side-by-side pose. This can also help them tap into their internal regulation and be in charge of calming down their nervous systems in preparation for sleep.

Baby-Led Play

Baby-led play warms up your child's self-soothing skills before bedtime. To do this, you simply get down on the ground and follow your baby's interests and play behaviors for 10 to 20 minutes. This is an option—try it out and see if it helps you and your baby shift modes. If it fits in your bedtime routine (it's often easier to accommodate if you have only one child), you can decide when in the routine it will come.

At 5 to 6 months, baby-led play can be simply watching your baby practice rolling, picking up a similar toy, and occasionally narrating what she is doing or mirroring her movements and sounds. As her play grows more complex and creative, you may be called upon to join your child in imaginary play. The key is that it's calm and that you *follow* rather than lead.

We often hear about babies starting to cry the minute the parent enters their bedroom to start the routine. Including baby-led play in their room, as a predictable step in their bedtime routine, can really turn this around. Now, your little one will look forward to this special time, when she gets to be in charge and show you a thing or two.

☽ SLEEP SOLUTIONS ☽

Falling Asleep Independently and Sleeping Through the Night: The Sleep Wave

If you put your baby to sleep at the beginning of the night using feeding, motion, or something similar, this is the place to start to improve her sleep. Remember that babies are smart little pattern detectors, and typically by 4 to 5 months, they become very aware and very attached to their sleep associations. If you are still soothing your baby all the way to sleep (or virtually to sleep) at bedtime or in the middle of the night, this association is probably very strong. At this age and older, it's difficult to change this pattern gradually (for example, by using the Soothing Ladder in Chapter 3). To transfer the role of soothing to your baby after 4 to 5 months of age, you'll need a sleep approach that is very clear.

In fact, you may notice that with your older baby, helping actually makes things *worse*. We often find that the same feeding, swinging, or rocking that supports newborn sleep seems to hinder an older baby's sleep. Over time, as parents continue to help their child, sleep plateaus or even regresses. These are some signs that your baby's cognitive development is clicking along, her awareness is growing, and she is ready to shift to doing the soothing herself:

- Your "helping ways," like feeding, rocking, or strolling, begin taking longer and longer to get your child to sleep.

- Your baby wakes more during the night, skips naps, or takes very short naps.

- Your baby wakes up the minute you lower her into the crib or very soon after.

- Your baby arches her back or struggles slightly as you hold and try to soothe her to sleep.

- Rather than becoming sleepier, your baby seems activated by your presence.

These are signs that you, with the best of intentions, are actually getting in the way of your baby's sleep. Your baby is telling you, "I need to do this soothing-to-sleep part on my own!"

It may not seem like it right now, but your baby *is* able to fall asleep independently and sleep for long stretches at night (if not a full 11 to 12 hours). The problem is that if your baby has become reliant on external soothing, this is now masking her innate ability to sleep well. Even though older babies are *able* to take over the role of self-soothing, they get confused by the blurred lines around who is actually doing the soothing.

Setting up new sleep patterns will actually grow your baby's brain. We know that as babies practice new behaviors, like accessing their self-soothing abilities, they create and begin to strengthen neural pathways in the brain. It's kind of like creating a new path in a forest: at first, you can barely see it, but as you travel it over and over, it becomes clear and obvious. For babies (and for all of us), those well-traveled pathways become easy and natural to follow the more they are traveled.

The Sleep Wave will help you "pass the baton" of soothing to your capable baby. In this section, we'll walk you through this technique, a simple and effective method that will allow your baby to practice putting herself to sleep and will help her sleep for a full night, too (as you'll read, you can decide to keep feedings in place if you wish). Read through this entire section before starting to use the Sleep Wave (you can use the Sleep Wave Planner in the Appendix, page 316).

Remember that babies don't need to be trained to sleep—they naturally have this capacity. Using the Sleep Wave will help you back away from habits that are not needed and create a clear pattern to your behavior and response; once your baby detects, tests, and trusts that pattern, she can relax, turn inward, and access her natural ability to fall asleep.

Before You Start the Sleep Wave

1. **Review Healthy Sleep Habits.** Make sure you have put the Healthy Sleep Habits, which are outlined earlier in this chapter, in place. Please read through this section before moving forward.

2. **Make Adjustments to the Room Environment.** Make sure that you have the right bedroom elements (page 113) in place and that your child is comfortable and familiar with her room. If your baby is sleeping in your room, but your goal is for her to transition to her own room, this is a good time to do it. Allow her a little awake playtime to get comfortable in her room before starting your sleep plan. You can "dress" the crib in her new room for play, adding a bright sheet, toys, and maybe a mobile, during the day. Have her spend some playtime in there for a few days, both with you nearby and on her own. Redress the crib for sleep and practice putting her down there for naps or the first segment of nighttime sleep. Your child should be familiar with her sleeping place before starting the Sleep Wave.

3. When you start the Sleep Wave, you'll be **removing your "unhelpful" sleep associations while making sure all "helpful" ones are in place.** For example, it's a good idea to give your child a lovey if you haven't already.

4. **Set Your Baby's Schedule.** In the Healthy Sleep Habits section, we asked you to set an early bedtime. Now that you're starting the Sleep Wave, you'll also set your child's

wake-up time to be at least eleven hours after bedtime. So, for example, if bedtime is 7:00 p.m., then wake-up time will be no earlier than 6:00 a.m. You can see examples of nighttime and daytime sleep schedules for babies on pages 166–7.

5. **Choose the Right Time**

Is your family ready for a structured sleep plan? Make sure:

- Your baby is at least 5 months old (if you're considering the Sleep Wave with a younger baby, see page 142).

- There is no minimum weight requirement for using the Sleep Wave. However, if you are thinking about weaning from night feedings and you have any concerns about your baby's weight gain, growth, or health in general, consult your doctor.

- You and your baby are healthy and have no vaccines scheduled in the next 2 weeks.

- The house is stable for the next two weeks, meaning that you will not travel, go back to work, or undergo any other major changes.

6. **Parents Must Be on the Same Page.** We can't emphasize enough how important consistency is when you're working on sleep, and one of the most common places for a break in consistency is between the behaviors of each parent. This happens for many reasons: one parent badly wants a

change, while the other feels fine with the status quo; one parent feels uncomfortable with the plan; one parent is an expert on the plan but the other isn't fully versed in the details; one parent adheres to the plan consistently, but then goes out of town . . . you see what we mean!

This is why we strongly recommend that, if there are two parents in the house, both of you read this chapter and then sit down together and write out the plan for yourselves (you can use the "Sleep Wave Planner" tool in the Appendix on page 316). Your baby will pick up on your calm consistency and feel secure when all parties are on the same page. This can make or break your success in changing a sleep pattern.

Sleep can be a big source of tension for many couples, especially if each person has a different idea of what's best—and the middle of the night is the worst time to debate and decide how to respond to your child. If you've each got your own tactics, it leads to too many tricks in the bag and the sense that nothing is working. One of the benefits of following a structured sleep plan is that you no longer have to doubt yourself or each other as you troubleshoot sleep issues. This is why when we do sleep consults, we ask both partners to be present so that they can hear and understand the plan together.

The Sleep Wave Method

When your child is practicing a new way to fall asleep, there's often protesting and crying involved—you are changing a pattern she is so used to! It's at this point that parents get confused about how to respond—do I go in the room, do I comfort her, do I leave her alone? If you don't respond to your child at all, she'll likely start to wonder where you are and, after a while, she might begin to feel worried or fearful. But if you swoop in and help soothe, you'll confuse her as to who is in charge of soothing to sleep. The Sleep Wave is the way to do both—respond and let your child know you're close, while making it crystal clear to her that soothing to sleep is her job. *Your goal here is to "pass the baton" of soothing to your child.*

When you do this, you'll be surprised to see that your baby has her unique way of getting comfy and falling asleep. It's actually a very sweet and amazing process to watch (once your baby has shifted from protesting to accessing her own abilities). We've seen babies do this in so many ways—some roll to their bellies and tuck their knees underneath them, some put their legs up the side of the crib, others rock back and forth, nuzzle their blankets . . . each individual baby has a special way of making herself comfortable and drifting off to sleep. You won't know your baby's personal technique for falling asleep (and your baby won't know, either) until you give her enough space to develop it.

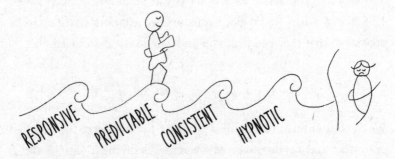

RESPONSIVE PREDICTABLE CONSISTENT HYPNOTIC

You are like a wave as you respond to your baby.

The reason we call this method the Sleep "Wave" is that we want you, the parent, to imagine yourself as a wave in the ocean. Your repetitive, rhythmic visits, as you roll in and out, are a constant, predictable response for your child. You come and go in a reliable way, and this is key to a healthy attachment. Your baby—who is a natural little scientist, constantly looking for patterns—will learn how you move through this method, always responding to let her know you're there, but not reverting to doing the soothing for her. Once she detects, tests, and finally trusts your wave pattern, she will relax, turn inward, and access her own self-soothing abilities.

For the fastest learning, we recommend using the Sleep Wave starting at bedtime and continuing to use it in exactly the same way with any nighttime wakings, after any nighttime feedings, and with naps the next day—this gives your baby the most consistent pattern of your response. If your baby is feeding at night, read the section on feeding and decide either to wean or keep these feedings in place. As you'll read on page 142, you can use the Sleep Wave at bedtime and after feedings as well (with or without weaning those feedings).

The Exact Steps of the Sleep Wave

1. **Put your baby down awake.** After bedtime routine, put your baby down drowsy but awake. Give her a pat and say a few words, like "It's time for sleeping. Mommy's right outside. I love you," and leave the room. The statement you say before leaving the room is your "script," which you will use during your visits if your child is crying. Create your own script and write it down so you and anyone else who

puts your baby to sleep is saying and doing *exactly* the same thing. It's crucial that it is repeated word for word and not changed or expanded.

Good to know: Your baby's brain has an abundance of "mirror neurons" that absorb emotions from people around her. Approach this process with confidence so that your baby feels good about sleep. Be positive and envision a good outcome—your baby is very sensitive to your physical and emotional state. Your tone should be calm and matter-of-fact. What you're conveying to your baby is that you believe in her abilities and will respond reliably until she trusts the new pattern.

2. **The 5-minute check.** If your baby starts to cry (really cry—not just fuss, squawk, or whine), wait for 5 minutes. Go into the room, stand either at the door or at the side of the crib (somewhere where your baby can see and hear you), and say your script in a matter-of-fact, confident tone. Your visit should only last as long as it takes to walk in, say your script, and walk out (about 7 to 10 seconds). The check is *only* to let baby know you're there. The check is not at all meant to calm her down or help her fall asleep. Don't soothe, touch, or pick your baby up. Let your baby sense that you give her credit for what you know she's capable of, and you will continue to do your checks until she trusts the pattern and falls asleep. This is key. Initially, the parent who feels more confident is the best one to do the checks, but you can alternate parents, too. If one parent needs to step outside the house to regroup while the other

one takes over and does the checks, that's okay! It's not uncommon for babies to protest and cry for 20 to 60 minutes at bedtime, and occasionally this period is longer on the second or third night.

Good to know: When the Sleep Wave isn't working as well as we expect, it's often because the parent is staying in the room too long, trying to calm, soothe, and help. The paradox is that the well-meaning helping actually makes it much harder for the baby to turn inward. When you deviate from your plan and change your behavior even slightly (by rubbing her back when you go in for one of your checks, for example), your baby then has to spend energy guessing what you're going to do next, or decoding your behavior and wondering if her protest has resulted in this help from you.

3. **The Wave.** If she's still crying, wait another 5 minutes and repeat step 2 *exactly*. If the crying stops, reset the time to zero and go back in if cries start again and last for 5 minutes. Returning *every* 5 minutes, if she's crying, helps your baby detect your pattern. Resist the urge to lengthen the time. Your baby needs your visits to be 100 percent predictable.

If your baby is whining or crying intermittently, it can be hard to tell exactly when to go in. Use your best judgment and try to give your baby space if she's simply talking, grumbling, or mildly protesting, but do your check when she has been truly crying for 5 minutes.

Good to know: Sometimes parents tell us, "This doesn't

work. Every time I go in, my baby gets louder and madder."
What we say is that's *exactly* what we expect to happen
initially. You've got to be prepared to "ride the hump." This
is the period, usually the first, second, or third night, when
your baby is testing the new pattern and may protest for a
long time. The reason we want you to keep the intervals at
exactly 5 minutes is that this amount of time is short
enough and the frequency always predictable so that there
is no risk that your baby moves beyond the *protest* stage
into even the *wondering where you are* stage. Yes, she'll get
louder and madder, but with the frequency and predictability of your visits, she will still feel safe and secure. You
are responding to her, you're just not responding the way
you used to. Once she trusts your new pattern, she will
stop protesting, relax, and turn inward to her own very
capable sleep abilities. This can take time. Babies are very
good little scientists. They like lots of data before they feel
certain. We know the Sleep Wave works, because, over the
years, we've seen it happen for thousands of parents and
babies.

4. **Good morning.** Set a wake-up time that is 11 hours after
   bedtime. Before this time, you will implement the Sleep
   Wave for any awakenings your baby has. If your baby is
   still feeding at night and you wish to wean from one or
   more feedings, you will need to do so gradually (see page
   149). Anytime after the set wake-up time, greet your baby
   and make it clear that this is morning. Gently open the
   blinds, give her a big smile, and sing a little song. Soon her

internal clock will register when it's time to wake up. We don't recommend waking your baby up in the morning even if 11 hours have passed. Ideally, you'll let her sleep end naturally.

If you're consistent, most babies figure out the pattern in two to four days and nighttime sleep will improve. Learning often happens more quickly if you apply the Sleep Wave at nighttime and daytime sleep simultaneously. Read more on naps and the Sleep Wave at naptime later in this chapter.

Crying

It's really difficult to hear your child cry. If you're like most loving parents, you might worry that you're harming your child by allowing her to cry without helping—especially because you probably know just what to do to fix the problem (feeding, rocking, lying down with your child), but instead you're sitting on your hands! Some parents worry that their child will be mad at them in the morning, or that it will hurt their relationship with their baby or their baby's sense of attachment.

Your baby is crying because she's protesting change. You're doing things differently now—you're altering a well-entrenched pattern. You (or a swing, stroller, or another sleep association) used to be in charge of soothing, and now your child is the one in charge. It's a difficult shift to make and we can't blame our babies for having strong feelings about it! When she cries, your baby is initially saying, "Hey, hey, hey, what's going on here? This isn't the way we do things!" If you are consistent she will move to, "Huh, I'm starting to detect a pattern here," to finally, "I trust this pattern, feel safe, and now can get down to the business of soothing myself to sleep." You *are* responding to your baby, you're just not taking back the role of soothing to sleep.

Remember that it's okay for your baby to feel frustrated and to struggle. You can't expect her to be content at every moment. Imagine that your baby wanted to climb a bookcase, or your older child wanted to eat chocolate bars for dinner but you said no—there are lots of moments in which you know you could do something to make your child temporarily happier, but that wouldn't lead to longer-term happiness. Remember that sometimes the moments of frustration are your baby's best learning opportunities. We've been there, too, so we know this can be hard!

We also know thousands of precious and happy babies, toddlers, and kids who have gone through this period of shifting to using their self-soothing capacities. The feedback we consistently get from our families is that when they stay consistent with the plan, they are proud and amazed at their child's abilities, and the whole family is happier, less stressed, and more balanced overall.

LOVING MAMA NERVOUS ABOUT LETTING BABY CRY

Lindsay: I was one of those expectant moms who thought her baby would magically sleep on her own. She would nap during the day and sleep peacefully at night in the bassinet next to our bed. I thought I would never allow Blake to cry. After all I am her mama and she just needs Mama's love. Flash forward 4 months and baby has worked her way into our bed and is nursing at all times through the night. My husband was on board with the Sleep Wave, but I was reluctant—I did not want to disappoint my sweet girl, I did not want to hurt the bond and trust that I had been working so hard to attain. Close to her turning 5 months, the sleep deprivation started to get the best of me as well as my lack of any personal space, so I decided that we would give the Sleep Wave a try. On the first night, I cried more than she did, which was 5 minutes. On the second night she took 12 minutes to settle in, and on the third night, no tears at all! We are now three weeks plus into the Sleep Wave and she is sleeping through the night! Five months really is the magic age. We are a much happier, healthier, and well-rested family.

There is no reason to think that periods of crying (against the backdrop of loving and attentive parenting) have a negative impact on children. Quite the opposite, in fact: research on this topic says that structured sleep plans work, and that they increase well-being for the whole family. What we have discovered, happily, is that the checks can be this frequent and still work extremely well, if the plan is followed carefully.

We recommend checking on your child every 5 minutes so that her tears are ones of protest, not worry, fear, or abandonment.

This is neither a "cry-it-out" nor an "attachment-style parenting" approach. Remember that in psychological terms, attachment means being there to support your little one, *while also encouraging her to learn, develop, and move toward independence.* This is fundamental to raising a happy, healthy child. Passing the job of soothing (which

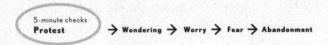

Five-minute checks keep baby in the protest state, so she doesn't move into a state of wondering, worrying, fear, or abandonment.

will involve some tears of protest) to your capable baby is very much in line with attachment theory.

MANTRAS FOR PARENTS

These are short, helpful, and supportive thoughts to tell yourself or to envision while you and your child are working on sleep. Create your own or use ours:

- It's okay for my baby to struggle or feel frustrated.

- My baby is protesting because we're changing a strong pattern. She has feelings about it, and that's okay!

- I'm helping my baby get enough sleep, so that she is healthy and feels rested during the day. She needs to sleep well.

- I want her brain and body to get the "nutrition" they need from adequate sleep.

- We, as parents, need to get back to sleeping normally so we can be attentive and available to our children during the day.

- I want my baby to go to bed feeling confident in her ability to get comfortable and fall asleep on her own.

- Picture your child sleeping peacefully and how much the family will enjoy one another when you've all slept well.

- I want my baby to acquire healthy sleep habits for a lifetime.

- I want my baby's sleep development to be on track rather than delayed.

- We, as parents, are ready to feel better rested so we can have some time for each other.

- Our mantra for you: Every time you complete a 5-minute check consistently, a big chunk of money goes into your "bank account." You are accruing sleep wealth. If you break the pattern, you lose all of your money!

The Sleep Wave with a Verbal Child

Babies and kids vary a lot in their behaviors and the sounds they make while you're using the Sleep Wave. When you're working on sleep with a toddler, he might stand at the side of the crib, talk, and summon you in a much more sophisticated way than would a 9-month-old baby. It might feel hard to hear your toddler call to you with such clear words, but the fundamental idea of the Sleep Wave is the same no matter what your child's age.

If those clear cries of "Momma" or "Dada" pull extra hard at your heartstrings, we understand. You can, however, find solace in the fact that, by this age, your little talker knows in an even more concrete way that, between checks, you are not far away. He also has the brainpower to detect, test, and quickly trust the repetitive, predictable pattern of your behavior during your checks. It may feel more difficult to stay consistent, but there is no concern that he will feel abandoned or worried.

If your child is at the age (typically 18 months or older), when his verbal abilities are advanced enough, you might want to try the following:

- Do some rehearsals during the day with puppets or stuffed animals to show your toddler what bedtime will now look like.

- Make sure that your child's bedtime routine is growing with him, adding in quiet, child-led play, books, and songs that are interesting and calming.

- If your child is more than 2 years old, we recommend reading the information in the next chapter, which deals with bedtime resistance and the Sleep Wave with older children.

Consistency Is Key

Remember, you are a rhythmic and steady wave. You let your baby know that you are there, so he doesn't feel abandoned or fearful. He may get pretty loud, but he won't be worried or fearful because of your responsive, predictable presence. But also remember, if you blur the lines by soothing him even a little on your visit, it will confuse him and prolong the process. Give him space to practice his skills. Exude confidence in him; he will absorb that feeling.

One of the reasons we underscore consistency in this approach is that we've noticed it actually leads to parents being more responsive overall. When parents try "gentle" methods that involve a greater amount of soothing on the parents' part, it tends to make the baby cry even more (because he's confused) or, if it doesn't work, it results in parents taking a harsher approach or not responding to the baby at all—which we would never advise.

Your baby is geared to test the world. Your job is to give him plenty of reliable data. The more you stay calm and consistent, the sooner he will grow to trust the pattern of your response.

TWO PARENTS, ONE CONSISTENT PLAN

Katya: We were nervous about trying the Sleep Wave with Nadia but it really was a complete game changer. We were the dorks who wrote our script on a dry-erase board to make sure we were being consistent! The advice for me and my husband to create our plan together and be on the same page made all the difference. It also helped my anxiety to be encouraged to wait until 5 months, when Nadia was cognitively more mature and aware that we still existed when we weren't right there. She progressed very quickly and, within two to three nights, was falling asleep on her own with ease.

THE SLEEP WAVE WITH 6-MONTH-OLD ELLA

Tara: Initially, the Sleep Wave worked great for Ella, after only a few nights. A few weeks later, she began to protest at bedtime again. We realized that my husband, Colin, was staying too long for the checks and trying to help, by shushing and rubbing Ella's back, which blurred the lines for her. Once he followed the "no soothing" instructions to a T, it made all the difference in the world, and Ella went back to falling asleep on her own very easily.

TOP ELEVEN REASONS THE SLEEP WAVE ISN'T WORKING:

1. The parent doing the 5-minute checks is doing *even a little bit* of soothing (beyond responding with presence in the room and the few words of the script), for example, rubbing baby's back while in the room. This is very confusing and motivates the baby to continue reaching out externally instead of turning inward. When this happens, the baby isn't working on his innate soothing capacity because he's distracted by trying to get the parent in the room to soothe him.

2. The parent is anxious, unsure, resentful, exasperated—you name it! The parent who checks needs to be confident, calm, and matter-of-fact.

3. Daytime sleep patterns. It's important that baby has enough naps during the day, as this improves regulation

and the ability to fall asleep easily. Naps should end by 3:30 or 4:30 p.m.

4. Weaning too quickly. Read more on weaning in the next section.

5. The room is too warm or baby is overdressed.

6. Baby needs more tummy-time exercise during the day so he's free to move around the crib and choose his own sleep position. See "Tips for Tummy Time" on page 69.

7. The crib is in the parents' room. This is much more difficult, because older babies tend to be very activated by the presence of the parents. If baby is in the room with you, see Chapter 6.

8. Feeding is the very last component of the bedtime routine. Move the feeding earlier in your bedtime routine and read a story, sing songs, or walk around and tell everything in the room "good night," as the last steps before going in the crib. This also allows baby's tummy to settle before being put down.

9. Bedtime and naptime routines are nonexistent or are not age appropriate. We often see parents who drop the naptime routine altogether or are doing a bedtime routine that is suitable for a much younger baby.

10. The baby is going through a developmental surge such as sitting, crawling or, most disruptive, pulling to a stand in the crib. During any of these periods, your baby is very

excited and single-mindedly intent on practicing his new ability. It's very common for him to wake much more frequently and resist falling back to sleep. When a baby first sits or pulls to a stand, he often needs your help lying back down during each 5-minute check. Once you know that he can get back down by himself, you can let him be.

11. Parents give up too soon and break the consistent pattern. It's often just at this moment you're ready to cave and pick up your baby that he finally falls asleep on his own for the first time. This is such a critical turning point. If you give up, you've lost hard-earned ground and given your baby the message that if he protests long enough, you'll pick him up. If you hang in there, new pathways for self-soothing will emerge in your little one's brain—this is the route to his feeling happy and comfortable falling asleep on his own, now and in the long run.

Using the Sleep Wave While Continuing to Feed at Night (Also for Babies 4 to 5 Months Old)

You can work on self-soothing and falling asleep independently while continuing to feed your baby at night. This is the preferred method for many moms who wish to continue breast-feeding at night (regardless of baby's age), *and* for babies who are ready for the Sleep Wave before the age of 5 months.

To do this, use the Sleep Wave at bedtime to help your baby fall asleep independently. Then, when your baby wakes up for a regular feeding, you can feed her and put her back in bed, awake. Your baby may protest that you've put her down awake, but you can again use your 5-minute checks to respond to her until she falls asleep independently again. If she begins to fall asleep during the feeding, don't let her—pop her right back into her bed, even if the feeding was shorter than usual. (We don't recommend waking your baby again if she's already fallen asleep—just try to catch her before she drifts off.) When you use this method, your baby is getting all the consistent practice at self-soothing without you having to change your nighttime feeding patterns. If you do this consistently for a week or two, your baby may naturally begin to wake up less frequently, as she becomes an expert little self-soother.

This method also works very well for babies younger than 5 months. The reason that we *usually* recommend waiting to use the Sleep Wave until your baby is 5 months old is that this is an age at which most babies have the skills to soothe themselves to sleep, by rolling, moving, rubbing their eyes or face, rocking back and forth, and so forth. However, sometimes we meet babies who are ready for the Sleep Wave at an earlier age (4 to 5 months), when it's too early to think about weaning from night feedings. This is usually because they are neurologically more mature—for example, they have good motor skills, are already un-swaddled, are showing signs of being able to self-soothe, their sleep has recently regressed, or it's taking longer and longer for parents to put the baby to sleep.

Here's the story of a quite young baby who was clearly ready to self-soothe to sleep. This baby naturally dropped her night feedings, but she needed the space to figure out how to fall asleep at the beginning of the night. She's a great example of how different every baby can be.

THE SLEEP WAVE WITH A 3½-MONTH-OLD BABY

Sarah: When Clarissa was 3½ months, it was taking longer and longer to get her to fall asleep at bedtime. Nothing I tried seemed to soothe her and I literally spent 2 to 3 hours on the bouncy ball before she would finally give up the fight and drop off to sleep. The amazing part was that she would then proceed to sleep for 11 hours straight, every night! It only made sense to me that she was clearly ready to fall asleep on her own. Julie said Clarissa was a real outlier and we could give it a try because she was developmentally on track and growing well. Sure enough, she responded very quickly to the Sleep Wave and soon was easily falling asleep on her own. The best part was that she seemed so much happier at bedtime. Needless to say, so was I!

Waking Up Too Early

Waking up too early is one of the most common and most stubborn sleep issues. Babies and little kids are very prone to waking up early because they are easily cued by morning light and their internal clocks tell them to rise roughly with the sun. The end of your baby's sleep (toward morning) contains more light sleep than the beginning of the night. In addition, your baby's sleep drive (see Chapter 8) is not as strong as it was in the first half of the night. All of these factors mean that in the early morning, your baby is more likely to come into a light stage of sleep, become restless, and call for you instead of going back into a deep sleep. The problem is that even though babies and toddlers often wake up at 5:00 or 5:30 a.m., they typically aren't *ready* to wake up at this hour, in that their bodies actually need another hour of sleep.

If you're using the Sleep Wave to help your baby sleep a full 11 hours at night, the 5:00 a.m. hour may be your most difficult waking to work on. Your baby is *so close* to being ready to wake up for the day, and her body is beginning to send her chemical signals to this effect. You'll need to be extra consistent, and often for a few weeks, before this pattern shifts. Here's how you can work with this problem and stretch your baby's wake-up time.

- Don't put your baby to bed later, hoping she'll sleep later. Your baby will likely wake up at the same time, or even earlier if you do this—the difference is that she'll have had even less sleep.

- Surprisingly, putting your baby to bed 30 minutes earlier often helps her sleep later the next morning. This is because well-rested babies are less likely to wake up during the early morning hours.

- If your baby wakes up before 6:00 a.m. and she is grumbling, fussing, or talking, you can let her be. You don't have to go in.

- If your baby starts to cry, wait 5 minutes and use your Sleep Wave checks until her scheduled wake-up time.

- When the clock strikes 6:00 a.m., and if your baby is awake, go to her and let her know it's morning, say hello, open the blinds, feed her, and signal to her that it's time to start the day.

Why does this strategy work? Because when you pick your baby up, feed her, talk to her, and, most important, expose her to sunlight or the lights in your home, all these behaviors send signals to her circadian system. If you do this at 5:30 a.m. when your baby wakes, it regulates her internal clock to expect feeding and social interaction at that time. When you hold the boundary of 6:00 a.m. (or 11 hours after bedtime), her internal clock will begin to adjust accordingly. It's okay if your baby doesn't fall asleep again—keeping her in her sleeping space and holding off on feeding, social interaction, and light until the wake-up time will still work—it's just going to take some time.

It can take two to three weeks or more for your baby to shift into waking up at the right time. This is a tiring and frustrating process for some parents, we know. If you are reliable with your baby's wake-up time in the morning, it will change eventually, but you have to be incredibly consistent. If you go in at 5:40 a.m. one morning, you can expect your baby to wake up at that time the next day, or even earlier (what starts out as a *little* earlier than the right wake-up time very easily slides to being *even earlier* the next morning). Make sure your baby's room is very dark and you've blocked early morning sunrays, keep to your Sleep Wave plan until 6:00 a.m., and your baby will adjust eventually. In the meantime, make sure you go to bed extra early during this time to get the best possible night's sleep yourself.

Breast- or Bottle-Feeding, Weaning, and Sleep

When it comes to eating at night, babies vary widely, with some naturally dropping feedings as the first year progresses, while others continue to wake up for a feeding every 3 hours. Parents also vary a lot in whether and how they choose to wean at night. Some wish to stop night feeding, for example, if both parents are going back to work, while others decide to continue feeding and let the baby naturally wean over time.

There isn't one right approach to feeding at night because every family's needs are different. You certainly don't have to wean your baby from night feedings. It's very normal and natural for babies to feed during the night, and your baby does not have to follow a timeline. If you're not ready to wean your baby in a structured way (using the steps we have outlined in this section), it can still help to give him some space to move toward sleeping longer stretches and dropping feedings on his own. The best way to do this is to *put your baby down awake at the beginning of the night.* The more practice your baby has with self-soothing, the more likely he is to naturally drop feedings during the night because he now has the ability to put himself back to sleep. See page 142 for using the Sleep Wave while keeping night feedings in place.

BENEFITS OF BREAST-FEEDING FOR BABY AND MOM

BENEFITS TO BABY

- Breast milk contains antibodies that change with baby's environment. Breast-fed babies have fewer colds and other infections, including respiratory and ear infections.

- Breast-feeding is good for baby's digestive system.

- Breast-feeding lowers baby's risk of diabetes. Evidence suggests that breast-fed babies are less likely to develop medical conditions later in life such as obesity, high cholesterol, and high blood pressure. Breast-feeding also lowers baby's risk of developing certain cancers.

- Exclusive breast-feeding lowers the risk of allergies and asthma.

- Breast-feeding lowers the risk of SIDS.

BENEFITS TO MOM

- Breast-feeding lowers stress through the release of oxytocin.

- Breast-feeding reduces the risk of breast and ovarian cancer, and the longer Mom breast-feeds, the lower the risk.

- Breast-feeding reduces the risk of osteoporosis.

- Breast-feeding promotes weight loss.

- Breast-feeding lowers the risk of developing metabolic syndrome: diabetes, high blood pressure, high cholesterol, and cardiovascular disease.

If you choose to wean night feedings, this is an option after your baby reaches 5 to 6 months of age. By this age, most babies no longer need to eat during their 11 to 12 hours of nighttime sleep. (This is just a guideline, as there are often babies who fall outside of these numbers on either side.)

So why do older babies still wake up and happily chug away in the middle of the night? This is a tricky principle about night feeding—over time, it can become more of a habit than a necessity. Just because your baby *wants* to eat doesn't mean he *needs* to eat; we like to say that if you fed us a sandwich at midnight, for three nights in a row, we'd probably wake up at that time on the fourth night with a rumbling tummy, looking for our sandwich! Even if your baby does eat at night, after 5 to 6 months, he is likely capable of getting all the calories he needs in the daytime instead.

Weaning Baby from Night Feedings

If your baby has been eating regularly at a certain time of night, his body is programmed to anticipate the feeding and feel hungry at that time. Weaning very gradually ensures that your baby does not feel hungry; this gives your baby the best chance to work on his self-soothing skills without feeling disrupted or uncomfortable because of hunger. We don't recommend going "cold turkey" on existing night feedings.

Contrary to much of what you might read, we have found, over many years of practice, that a *very* gradual weaning is the most effective, because your baby is less likely to notice and miss the slight decrease in milk each night. This is also the most sensitive approach, as we can be confident that your baby doesn't feel hungry as he's trying to fall back to sleep. Weaning incrementally is also the friendliest approach for your breasts (if you're breast-feeding)—by avoiding the abrupt drop-off in demand that can cause milk supply to decline or clogged ducts to form.

Gradual Weaning Formula

These are guidelines for how to gradually wean your baby at night. You will use these guidelines while you implement one of the "weaning methods" below.

If you're breast-feeding, decrease 30 seconds, *every other night*.

If you're bottle-feeding, decrease ½ ounce, *every other night*.

It may seem painstakingly slow to wean this way, but once your baby becomes an expert in falling asleep on his own (as you use the Sleep Wave), he may naturally drop feedings on his own, which speeds up the weaning process. This often happens when babies are accustomed to feeding as a way to pacify to sleep (rather than strictly out of hunger). When their skills at self-soothing take off, they naturally sleep for longer periods and don't wake up to eat.

WEANING A 5-MONTH-OLD FROM FREQUENT, PACIFYING FEEDINGS

Evelyn: I had always nursed our daughter, Mia, to sleep. For the first 4 months, this worked well for everyone, and Mia's sleep stretched out longer and longer, until she was sleeping 8-to-10-hour spans at night. Then, it all fell apart at about 4 months, when she started waking more and more often during the night. Especially in the hours after midnight, she was waking every hour. I resorted to nursing her back to sleep each time, and most of the feeds were very short, under 1½ minutes. Needless to say, I was beyond exhausted and worried that Mia wasn't getting good sleep. The Sleep Wave worked really well because Mia was fully capable of falling asleep on her own; she just needed her sleep association to change from nursing to self-soothing. I only had to gradually wean her from one long feed, as the others were super-short and I knew she wasn't really hungry.

Weaning Guidelines

Weaning very gradually from nighttime feedings as you implement the Sleep Wave works very well. As you follow the weaning guidelines, you'll put your baby back down awake after each feeding and use the Sleep Wave 5-minute checks if he cries.

Before you start, take some notes about your baby's current feeding patterns at night (if you're breast-feeding, you might use the timer on your phone during each feeding). He may be feeding anywhere from once to multiple times a night. Draw a timeline for the night and mark where the feedings generally are, including the amounts or durations (ounces of bottled milk or minutes of breast-feeding) at each feeding. You can use the Sleep Wave Planner in the Appendix to take notes.

Start with no more than 5 minutes or 5 ounces. In other words, if your baby nurses for 8 minutes during one feeding, you can start weaning by nursing him for 5 minutes on the first night. This is because babies 5 months and older usually get plenty of milk to assuage their hunger in 5 minutes or with 5 ounces (starting with less than 5 ounces is fine if that's how much your baby is used to). If you're nursing way more than 5 minutes, you can choose a faster wean and decrease 1 minute each night until you're down to 5 minutes, after which you would move to the gradual wean. If breast-feeding, you can stop the weaning at about 1 to 1½ minutes, as at that amount, considering letdown time, hunger is no longer an issue. If bottle-feeding, you can stop at 1 ounce. As you'll read in both weaning methods below, don't feed your baby at all unless it's been at least 3 hours since the last feeding (this comes in handy if your baby wakes at unpredictable times), and you will put your baby down *awake* after each feeding. The more you do this, the more your baby practices self-soothing, and his sleep will continue to improve.

It's also fine to choose to wean from one feeding at a time. If you do, we recommend weaning the earliest feeding first. This may seem counterintuitive, as your instinct will be to keep the feeding in the middle of the night, but babies typically stretch out their sleep longer and longer from bedtime on, so it makes sense to follow this natural pattern as you wean. Some parents choose to keep one feeding in place for various reasons: concern about Mom's milk supply, weight considerations, or a working mom's desire to connect with baby at night. Use the gradual weaning formula for the feedings you do want to eliminate and keep the one full feeding in place. If you do keep one feeding in place, consider making this a "dream feed" (see page 156), in which you feed your baby without him waking up—this allows you to stay consistent with how you respond to your baby every night. You can always use the same gradual approach to wean this final feeding when you and your baby are ready.

Weaning Examples

In both of these examples, it would take about 15 nights to wean completely (unless baby naturally stops waking up for one of these feedings). It sounds like a long time but, in the grand scheme, it's quite quick, and remember, babies often drop a feeding on their own along the way. If your baby does drop a feeding for at least three nights in a row, you can consider that feeding weaned. If it's only one or two nights, stick to the gradual wean.

BREAST-FEEDING WEANING EXAMPLE

TIME OF NIGHT/ DURATION	NIGHT 1	NIGHT 3	NIGHT 5	NIGHT 7 . . .
12:00 a.m., 5 minutes	4½ minutes	4 minutes	3½ minutes	3 minutes
3:00 a.m., 7 minutes	5 minutes	4½ minutes	4 minutes	3½ minutes
4:00 a.m., 3 minutes	no feeding, 3 hours have not passed.			

BOTTLE-FEEDING WEANING EXAMPLE

TIME OF NIGHT/ AMOUNT	NIGHT 1	NIGHT 3	NIGHT 5	NIGHT 7 . . .
11:00 p.m., 1 oz.	no feeding, amount is only 1 oz.			
1:00 a.m., 6 oz.	5 oz.	4½ oz.	4 oz.	3½ oz.
4:00 a.m., 3 oz.	2½ oz.	2 oz.	1½ oz.	1 oz.

Now we will walk you through two choices for how to wean. In the first, you follow your baby's lead in terms of when to feed (although you will determine the amount), and in the second, you wean your baby on a schedule. Our favorite approach is the first, because it allows you to follow your baby's natural progression. She may surprise you and start waking up less frequently—you'd never know this if you fed her before she actually calls out to you. At times, weaning will feel quite mechanical and slow, but the good news is that once you're done, you've made a huge stride toward that full night's sleep for your entire family.

Weaning Method 1—Following Your Baby's Lead

The benefit of using this method is that if your baby naturally sleeps longer one night, you won't have to wake up. You can follow the progression of her sleep this way.

- Take notes on when and how long/how much your baby is feeding at night.

- Note all feedings that are over 1 to 1½ minutes or 1 ounce and that have at least 3 hours of space in between them. Looking at the examples above, make your own timeline for weaning.

- When your baby wakes and it has been at least 3 hours since she last fed, go in, pick her up, and feed her according to your weaning schedule.

- When your baby has fed for the slightly decreased amount of time for that night, gently take her off the breast.

- Put your baby right back down *awake*. Say your script and leave. If she cries, respond to her with the 5-minute checks of the Sleep Wave.

- If your baby wakes up and it hasn't been 3 hours, you can use your 5-minute Sleep Wave checks to respond to her until she falls asleep independently. If it's close to 3 hours, say 2½ hours, it's a good idea to go ahead and feed her. Remember, you're weaning from these feedings anyway and it's better to err on the side of not trying to get a hungry baby to fall back to sleep. As long as you stick with the weaning guidelines, these feedings will all soon be a thing of the past.

Weaning Method 2—Following a Schedule

With this method—which uses the dream feed concept—you will wake up *before* your baby's feeding and feed her according to your weaning schedule. This method works best for babies whose feedings come at very predictable times. The benefit of this method is that it breaks the cycle of baby's hunger signaling her to wake up, and you responding with a feeding.

- Take notes on when and how long/how much your baby is feeding at night.

- Note all feedings that are over 1 to 1½ minutes or 1 ounce and that have at least 3 hours of space in between them. Looking at the examples above, make your own timeline for weaning.

- Once you have your feedings mapped out according to these guidelines, set an alarm for yourself that is 1 hour before your baby's usual feeding time.

- Gently pick up your baby and feed her according to the gradual weaning formula.

- If your baby wakes before you're scheduled to feed her and it *hasn't* been at least 2½ hours, use your 5-minute checks from the Sleep Wave to respond to her. You can be confident that she is not hungry at this point. However, if she cries for 30 minutes, go ahead and feed her, as she may now be hungry.

- If your baby wakes before you're scheduled to feed her and it has been 3 hours, go ahead and feed her. It's better to err on the side of feeding, to avoid trying to get a hungry baby to put herself back to sleep. The deck is stacked against her at that point and that's the opposite of our approach. It's not necessary to be rigid. Once your baby is falling asleep independently, the weaning becomes relatively easy.

- Put your baby back in her crib awake and use your 5-minute checks if you need to.

Dream Feeding

If you wish to keep a feeding in place at night (for milk supply reasons, or if you think your baby isn't ready to sleep a full 11 hours without eating), you can feed your baby before *you* go to bed, while weaning the rest of the feedings. To do this, simply go quietly into your baby's room while he is sleeping, pick him up gently in the dark, feed him, and return him to the crib. This takes a few nights for some babies to get used to, but most will latch and drink while asleep.

Some moms like this method as they'd rather feed than pump before they go to bed, and it's a nice way for a working mom to spend a little extra precious cuddle time with her baby.

Regressions, Illness, Travel

What if your baby gets sick or you're traveling and you feed him at night again after you've started to wean? Generally, if you've only fed your baby for one or two nights in a row at a certain time, you don't need to re-wean—you can simply use the 5-minute checks once he's healthy again or you've returned home. If you've fed him for three nights in a row or more, it's now a good idea to return to your gradual weaning schedule, since your baby's body has gotten used to the feeding.

Maintaining Your Milk Supply

If you decide to wean at night, it's important to consider your milk supply. Dropping feedings for a long stretch at night can lead to a decrease in supply overall, so many breast-feeding moms pump right before they go to bed as they're weaning gradually. That way, once the night feedings are weaned, most moms can still sleep for 7 to 8 hours without having to get up to feed or pump. If you know you're a low-volume milk producer, you may want to pump twice, once at your bedtime and once in the middle of the night, to keep your supply up. It's important to have plenty of support from a lactation consultant if this is the case for you.

THE MYTH OF THE FOOD-SLEEP CONNECTION

It's a bigger challenge for parents to let go of this idea that filling the tank at bedtime and during the night will equal better sleep! It makes perfect sense that this is difficult, as parents are used to the world in which their little newborn absolutely needs to feed during the night. The problem is that long after this is no longer true, parents are feeding their babies at night and hoping it will translate to more sleep. But the correlation between calories taken in right before sleep and duration of sleep is not strong for older babies. (This is why research shows that introducing solids or giving baby rice cereal before bed does not improve sleep.) By the age of 5 months and older, the opposite is true: too much milk right before bed or during the night becomes activating to babies, waking up their digestive systems and creating lots of peeing and big wet diapers. Think of your baby as you would yourself from this age on. If you drank a ton of liquid at bedtime and throughout the night, your body would have a hard time sleeping as well!

Starting Solids and Sleep

There are quite a few approaches to introducing babies to solid foods—you'll find the one that best suits your family. Research supports the long-term health benefits of favoring vegetables and non-sweet foods, while limiting fruit and avoiding juice altogether. Another effective strategy is to avoid praising or urging your child around food; once he picks up on how much you want him to eat something, he will be a lot more likely to refuse. All you have to do is offer him healthy food— how much he eats is up to him. The first several months of eating solids are a time for your baby to explore and get to know all the different tastes, smells, and textures of food. The quantity is not nearly as important as the richness and enjoyment of the experience. If you feel curious and relaxed around food, your baby will, too.

Here are some things to keep in mind about solids and sleep:

- Introduce a brand-new food in the morning so that you have time to observe your baby for any type of reaction, and so that his body has time to digest the food before bedtime.

- As you go from one meal a day to three, usually by around 8 months, at times you'll feel that all you do is feed and nap your baby. Favor keeping his naptimes and bedtimes consistent and fit the meals in when he's awake. Sometimes that will mean giving a little snack or a mini lunch between naps, in order to fit everything in.

- Now it's especially good to remember to move milk feedings earlier in your naptime and bedtime routines (or remove them completely when baby is ready) so as to disassociate feeding with falling asleep.

Naps

Naptime can and should be a beautiful, restful break for you and your baby. For your baby, it means letting her brain and body rejuvenate (she has an optimal span of awake time before her "sleep drive" builds to the point at which she needs sleep). Babies and toddlers still need a lot of sleep during the day, and if they move past their optimal window for falling asleep, they can become overtired, fussy, and unable to learn and interact well. If you're home with your child, naptime also gives *you* a break to take a shower, eat, work, or even sleep yourself.

Here is a rough outline of how your child's naps will develop:

5 months	three naps (if baby catnaps, she may even take four naps a day)
9 months	two naps
15 to 20 months	one nap
3½ to 5 years	Most children stop napping in this age range.

Nap Environment and Sleep Associations

Remember when your baby slumbered in the middle of a bustling coffee shop? After the first several months, babies usually don't sleep deeply or for long periods when on the go. Your baby will probably get the healthiest sleep in her quiet, dark, comfortable room and familiar bed.

Just as with nighttime sleep, the best naps happen when your baby self-soothes and falls asleep independently in her own crib. If your baby is not yet self-soothing, she may take fewer or shorter naps because when she transitions between stages of sleep or enters a light sleep, she will stir, wake up fully, and be unable to return to a deeper sleep. A baby or toddler who is not self-soothing to sleep is also more likely to resist taking a nap altogether because she is reliant on you and may be very particular about her sleep associations: you may have to hold, rock, stroll, or carry her to sleep *every time* if this habit is entrenched. Sometimes this is okay in the beginning (you may enjoy lying down to nap with your baby, or plan to take a walk every day at naptime), but usually, over time, parents start to feel trapped by these habits, and baby's naps become harder.

Evaluate your baby's nap environment for any unhelpful sleep associations (page 112). The most common unhelpful ones at naptime are stroller or car rides, parent's presence, feeding, or rocking to sleep. For the best sleep, your baby should go into her crib or regular sleeping place calm but awake, so that she can grab her blankie, roll around, talk to herself, get comfy, and doze off.

NAP CHECKLIST

Review the Healthy Sleep Habits as many of these apply to daytime sleep as well. For example:

- **Nap routine.** Use a routine with naps just as you do with nighttime. Your nap routine can be a shortened version of your nighttime routine. For example, turn down the lights and close the shades, nurse or feed your baby, read a short book, switch on her white noise, walk around the room saying "good night" to her toys, sing a song, put her in her crib, say "It's time for sleeping, Mommy's right outside. I love you," and walk out.

- **Transitional object.** Since your baby is now in charge of her own soothing to sleep, a lovey will help her find comfort and it can be a powerful tool for sleep both at night and for naps (see pages 66–7 for more on loveys).

- **Slow down.** Your mood has a major influence on your baby's ability to wind down for sleep. If you're anxious and impatient to get her down, this will be activating to her little brain. Switch yourself into rest mode. Lower your voice and move slowly and carefully in her room while you do her routine. It's amazing how small, peaceful gestures signal to your baby that sleep is near and elicit a calming response.

Using the Sleep Wave at Naptime

You can use the Sleep Wave method for naps. Here are a few additional notes:

- The fastest way for your baby to practice falling asleep on her own is to use the Sleep Wave for both bedtime *and* naps, so that she detects a consistent pattern of how she is put down for sleep.

- After you put your baby down for a nap, if you've been doing consistent 5-minute checks and she continues to cry for 30 to 45 minutes with no sign of progress, go in and simply say, "Okay, naptime is over" and pick her up. Try again in another 45 minutes or so.

- If your baby sleeps for a short time (20 to 45 minutes) and starts to cry when she wakes, only wait about a minute and go pick her up. It rarely works for a baby to put herself back to sleep after a short nap, because the pressure of her sleep drive has been relieved just enough so she's not sufficiently drowsy anymore.

- If baby is awake but content after a "too short" nap, let her hang out on her own until she signals to you that she's no longer happy. This helps build the window into which her naps can grow. Even when the nap has been fabulously long, if your baby wakes happy and babbling, resist the urge to swoop in right away. Remember, cultivating a sense of comfort in alone time is key to your baby's *internal attunement* (page 26). Coming to get her when her babbles clearly change to calls for you is a great opportunity for an attuned, rather than automatic, response.

- As you're implementing the Sleep Wave for naps, you may have days when you feel like your baby has barely napped at all. If baby is overtired and irritable and you're desperate to get her to nap, put her in the carrier, stroller, or car for a nap. If you rock or feed her to sleep in her bedroom as you used to do, you are reinforcing a strong sleep association, which can be confusing and might prolong the process for your baby.

If you're using the Sleep Wave, working on naps almost always takes longer—many babies fall asleep easily at bedtime after just days of using the Sleep Wave but continue to have trouble falling asleep at naptime or taking short naps for several weeks. It's okay— her nighttime sleep is the most important. Your baby will eventually nap well. Just when you're ready to give up, you will likely start to see improvement.

Scheduling Naps

For younger babies (ages 5 to 6 months) who are just getting into the rhythm of regular naps, we recommend using the *span of awake time* (this is the length of time babies of this age can be awake before the pressure to sleep builds sufficiently for a nap) to gauge when naps should occur during the day, just as you did with your younger baby, putting her down after about every 90 minutes of awake time. Then, when your baby is 6 to 7 months old and over, you can establish a set nap schedule based on the *time of day* (see nap schedules, pages 166–7). Age is just a guide. When your baby starts to fall asleep independently and sleeps for at least an hour at a time, it's a good sign that she's ready to move to a time-of-day schedule.

Here is how the typical *span of awake time*, in between sleeps, develops for babies and toddlers. Usually the first span of the day (after your baby wakes up) is the shortest, with the longest span coming at the end of the day, before bedtime.

OPTIMAL SPAN OF AWAKE TIME

5 to 6 months	1½ to 2½ hours (sometimes with one 3-hour span in the last half of the day)
9 months	3 to 3½ hours
15 to 20 months	4 to 5 hours (depending on the length of nap)

5-to-6-Month-Old Babies—Using the Span of Awake Time

At this age, you can use the span of awake time to know when your baby should nap. To do this, note when your baby wakes up (for the day, as well as after each nap), and use this to figure out when she's ready to sleep next. The first awake span of the day is often the shortest one (usually no more than 90 minutes). For this first span of awake time, start your naptime routine after your baby has been awake for about 75 minutes so you can lower her into her bed at the 90-minute point. As she gets older, you may notice that your baby might be able to stay awake for longer and longer periods—sometimes even a 2½- to 3-hour awake span in the middle or end of the day. This is a normal progression but also differs somewhat from baby to baby.

For example, your baby might wake up at 6:00 a.m. and be ready to nap again at 7:30 a.m., sleep for 2 hours, and be ready to nap again 2½ hours after that, and so on, possibly being awake for 2½ to 3 hours before bed. Continue to nap your baby throughout the day, having the last nap end no later than about 4:00 or 5:00 p.m., for a 7:00 p.m. bedtime.

6 to 7 Months to Toddlerhood—Using the Time of Day

As your baby grows, she is able to be awake for longer periods, and her daytime sleep consolidates from three or four naps, to two and eventually one. Look at the sample sleep schedules on pages 166–7 to see where your baby falls in this progression. Your particular baby's schedule will depend on what time she wakes up in the morning and the length of her naps. Often, at this age, you can observe your baby moving naturally into a regular, "time of day" nap schedule.

When you first establish a nap schedule, your baby may, at times, be awake for longer than her optimal awake time until she grows accustomed to the schedule. For example, if you put your 6-to-7-month-old down at 8:00 a.m. and she only sleeps for 30 minutes, she may have to stay awake for 3 hours to make it to her next scheduled nap. That's okay—your baby's internal clock will adjust and she will most likely start sleeping longer if you keep her naptimes consistent. It's also okay to flex the times a bit during this adjustment period. One nap may always be shorter than the other (for example, for a 9-month-old, a 2-hour morning nap followed by a 45-minute afternoon nap). As your baby reaches 7 to 9 months, she will likely need to have her last nap end no later than 3:30 or 4:00 p.m. for a 7:00 p.m. bedtime.

Arranging your life around a child's nap schedule can be an adjustment. We know how this goes: Your baby wakes up and, if you have a diaper bag packed and ready to go, you have a 2-to-3-hour window before needing to be back for another nap! We understand this can feel limiting, but having a well-rested child is worth it. As your baby grows and as naps go from three to eventually one, the stretches of time in between will lengthen and you'll have more freedom. It may also work for your baby to have one nap per day on the go: on a stroller ride, in the car, or on a walk in a sling or carrier in the afternoon, for example.

Nap Schedule Examples

0 TO 5–6 MONTHS OLD
(USE SPAN OF AWAKE TIME)

6 TO 9 MONTHS OLD (THREE NAPS)

	EXAMPLE 1	EXAMPLE 2
Bedtime	7:00 p.m.	7:30 p.m.
Wake time	6:00 a.m.	6:30 a.m.
First Nap	7:30 a.m.	8:30 a.m.

	EXAMPLE 1	EXAMPLE 2
Second Nap	12:00 p.m.	12:30 p.m.
Third Nap	3:00 p.m.	3:30 p.m.

9 TO 15–20 MONTHS OLD (TWO NAPS)

	EXAMPLE 1	EXAMPLE 2
Bedtime	7:00 p.m.	7:30 p.m.
Wake time	6:00 a.m.	6:30 a.m.
First Nap	9:00 a.m.	9:30 a.m.
Second Nap	2:00 p.m.	2:30 p.m.

15–20 MONTHS TO 2–3 YEARS (ONE NAP)

	EXAMPLE 1	EXAMPLE 2
Bedtime	7:00 p.m.	7:30 p.m.
Wake time	6:00 a.m.	6:30 a.m.
Nap	11:30 a.m.	12:30 p.m.

3 TO 5 YEARS (ONE NAP)

	EXAMPLE 1	EXAMPLE 2
Bedtime	7:00 p.m.	7:30 p.m.
Wake time	6:00 a.m.	7:00 a.m.
Nap	12:30 p.m.	1:00 p.m.

Transitioning Nap Schedules (Three→Two→One Nap)

When your baby is in the midst of transitioning from three to two to one nap, there will typically be a period of time when she may not *need* the last nap every day, but she'll also be extra tired and not quite rested without it. In other words, she's in between and won't consistently take the last nap, but she is fussy and tired because fewer naps are not quite enough. Don't underestimate how tough this transition period can be for kids (and parents)—it's normal for your child to be extra clingy, easily frustrated, or groggy during this time while her body is adjusting to a new schedule. You might want to put your baby down earlier, at 6:45 p.m., for a week or two while she makes the adjustment.

How to know when your baby is ready to go from three to two naps:

- Baby is about 9 months old.

- Naps have gotten "chunkier," at least an hour or more.

- Baby is no longer falling asleep for the third nap for one to two weeks straight.

- The third nap of the day begins to interfere with bedtime.

- The first nap of the day begins to drift later.

- Note: When they switch to two naps, most babies sleep at roughly 9:00 a.m. and 2:00 p.m.

How to know when baby is ready to go from two to one nap:

- Baby is 15 to 20 months old.

- The first nap of the day is drifting later or skipped.

- The first nap is long but the second nap is skipped, or your baby resists falling asleep for her second nap for one to two weeks straight.

When your baby is ready to switch to one nap, one way to think about this is that naptime has "consolidated" and that her one nap will most likely be longer than each of her two naps were, but not as long as both combined. This is a gradual process that can take weeks. During this transition time, your baby may take two naps on some days and one nap on other days while her body adjusts. When she does take one nap, you can move your baby's bedtime 30 minutes earlier or more if she seems very tired.

When first switching to one nap, most babies begin their nap at around 11:30 a.m. or 12:00 p.m. This tends to move later, to 12:30 p.m. or 1:00 p.m., as they grow.

When you move to one nap, make sure that your toddler gets some fresh air and activity in the morning. Give her a snack or mini lunch, and take time for a 15- to 20-minute wind-down routine. Keep things as routine and predictable as possible as your child adjusts. She may seem a little fussy or tired that last hour or so before her nap and also before bedtime. After a few weeks, her body will adapt to her new schedule.

Wait, Don't Drop That Nap Too Early!

One of the most common mistakes parents make is rushing into fewer naps. Often your baby will appear to be dropping a nap at an earlier age than mentioned above. We call this a temporary "nap strike," and it's usually due to excitement over a developmental advance or circumstance in the house (such as a visitor). Many parents have thanked us for advising them to hold off on dropping a nap too early. Even if your baby doesn't fall asleep for her second nap, it's okay; consider this a rest time (rest time is really important for your baby's growing body), and keep it in place until she's clearly showing signs that she's ready for one nap only. Sometimes she might nap a little later in the morning and then rest or take a shorter nap in the afternoon. Or she may do the reverse. Pay attention to not letting her second nap go beyond about 3:30 p.m. for a 7:00 p.m. bedtime. This is one of the few times that we would recommend gently waking your child. If this becomes a pattern, adjust her nap earlier so you don't have to wake her.

KEEPING THE SECOND NAP

Emily: At 11 months, Devin almost had me convinced he was ready to go from two naps to one because, for over a week, he pretty much didn't take his second nap. He had just started cruising and was excited to practice in his crib instead of napping. I was really happy to get the advice to hang in there and continue putting him down at his usual time, because on day 8 or 9, like nothing had changed, his nap came back! He so clearly still needs it and was just taking a little nap holiday.

This also applies to dropping naps completely, which most children are not ready to do until they are at least 3 years old. If your toddler spends naptime sitting in his crib, rolling around, and talking to himself, don't panic and don't assume he's ready to stop napping altogether. Keep your toddler's nap schedule and routine in place and he will eventually fall back into the rhythm of sleeping. Even if your toddler doesn't nap for a week straight, keep putting him down at the same time (use the Sleep Wave if necessary), and move his bedtime slightly earlier temporarily, until he starts napping again.

☆ TROUBLESHOOTING ☆

I'm trying the Sleep Wave but my baby is still crying. What should I do?

Review the top 11 reasons the Sleep Wave isn't working (see page 140). The most common reasons are:

1. Parent doing the checks is doing more soothing than just coming in for the 5-minute checks.

2. Parent is not exuding confidence and calm (rather anxiety, uncertainty, or frustration).

We almost always identify one of these two top culprits as the issue, and once they're tweaked, the Sleep Wave progresses.

My baby gets more upset when I go in after 5 minutes. Can I stop going in?

We know it's hard but don't stop going in every 5 minutes if your baby is crying. When your baby cries, she is protesting the change and has not yet come to trust the new pattern. Stick with her reliably through this phase of "riding the hump." This consistency can be hard for you to keep up, but it's exactly what makes the process of turning the soothing part over to baby easier on her.

By doing your checks every 5 minutes, your baby will never wonder or worry about where you are or why you're not responding to her. The rhythmic, repetitive, wavelike quality of your visits will create trust and reassurance, which will make it possible for her to relax and do what she is capable of doing: self-soothe to sleep.

So I can never go and soothe my baby at night?

Absolutely you can! The consistency we stress in the Sleep Wave is for establishing a new pattern. As a general rule, *if your child has been sleeping well through the night* and all of a sudden wakes up at an unusual time, listen first. Determine whether she's simply whining and trying to get comfortable again, or if it seems she's truly calling for you and sounds upset. If it's the latter, go to her. Use the Soothing Ladder (Chapter 3) to soothe her. In other words, don't immediately pick her up, change her diaper, and so forth, but also don't feel as though you have to use your 5-minute checks.

We recommend that you respond this way when a night waking is *out of the ordinary*—it's not a pattern—because we don't want you to feel rigid or nervous about your baby waking up. Once you have established good sleep habits and your child is sleeping through the night, there will inevitably be nights where you randomly hear from her. Don't be afraid of these hiccups! Again, if it's very unordinary for your baby to wake up, listen and work your way up the Soothing Ladder.

The next night, if she wakes again at the same time, you can be confident that it is a *pattern* and she is waking and looking for you out of habit. At this point, go to using your Sleep Wave 5-minute checks consistently.

I picked my baby up during the Sleep Wave. Did I ruin our progress?

It's so hard to hear your baby cry. We truly understand where you're coming from if you broke the pattern of the Sleep Wave and picked your baby up. You'll probably notice that your baby cries for a longer period the next time you put her down. Remember that she is a scientist, and she needs reliable data, so now she'll need to conduct another experiment! Of course, as always, if you think your baby has a fever, has had a nightmare, or something along those lines, we'd recommend going to her.

Can I use the Sleep Wave if baby is in my room?

Yes, you can, it's just more difficult to implement if baby is in your room, as he is activated by your presence. See Chapter 6, "Special Circumstances."

The Sleep Wave has worked beautifully but my baby still cries for 5 to 10 minutes almost every time he goes to bed. What should I do?

Crying has a function in addition to communicating discomfort or unease, which is that of stress release. Some babies just need to cry for a short time as a way of letting go of accumulated stress. It might be a good idea to try moving naptime or bedtime a little earlier in case overtiredness is contributing. You can also check to make sure baby's bedroom is set up for peaceful sleep: cool, very dark, and no abrupt or loud noises. If all of this, plus the other foundational pieces in the Healthy Sleep Habits section, are in place, your baby may just need to let off a little steam before going to sleep. Be sure to still do your 5-minute checks so that your baby knows you're close by.

What about pacifiers at night?

If your baby can reinsert her pacifier on her own during the night, it shouldn't disrupt her sleep. You might increase her odds of finding her own pacifier at night by placing multiples in the crib. However, if your child cannot reinsert her own pacifier, it's a good idea to remove it before starting the Sleep Wave.

What do I do if I think my baby pooped and we're using the Sleep Wave?

If you suspect your baby has pooped and is crying, you can go in by dim light and change her (if you can change her in her crib, that's great, but if you need to get her up, that's okay, too) and then put her back in the crib. She will likely be upset that you are breaking the pattern, but once you know she is dry and clean, you can resume your 5-minute checks.

My baby was falling asleep faster and faster using the Sleep Wave for the first three nights and then on the fourth night she was right back at the start, waking frequently and taking a long time to go back to sleep. Help!

This truly can be disheartening, but you'll be happy to know that it's perfectly normal and will pass. It's a phenomenon called an "extinction burst," when old behaviors (those we're trying to make extinct) come back for one last curtain call. Don't be thrown by this; what your baby needs is for you to stay centered and super-consistent, and you should see your baby go back to the progress she was making initially.

My baby's sleep has regressed. What should I do?

One of the most common issues with using the Sleep Wave is that parents think it's a onetime fix. We can't tell you how many sleep consults we've done where the parents say some version of, "I hired someone else to help with this a few months ago and it worked great, but now he's waking again."

Babies and children (in fact, all people) will always have times when they sleep less well. Sometimes we'll know why (they're sick, going through a developmental surge, having a nightmare, obviously teething, or have been traveling) and sometimes we just won't know why. Babies keep changing, and we can't expect them to be robotic in their sleep patterns.

We find many times that parents interpret sleep regressions as being caused by "growth spurts," so they respond by adding feedings in the middle of the night. Adding feedings back in is almost never necessary. Remember, after about 5 months, most babies can get all of their nutritional needs met during the day. It's natural to think the wakings are hunger related, but they are much more likely to be due to developmental surges, which excite and activate a baby.

Keep the Sleep Wave "in your pocket" at all times, so that you can pull it out and use it every time you need it, again with great commitment and consistency. The good news is that the second, third, and fourth time, your child will recognize it much more quickly and soon relax, knowing that you are nearby and that the soothing part is up to her.

We're all sleeping better, but we're not feeling better.
Once sleep begins to improve for the entire family, it's very normal to feel a little worse before you feel better. You may even feel groggy and out of sorts for a while. Healing from sleep deprivation is a process. Imagine that it's like peeling layers off of an onion, which exposes deeper layers of your fatigue. This sounds ominous, but time will resolve this feeling and you will eventually be truly rested. See tips for healthy adult sleep in Chapter 7.

My baby is rolling, sitting, or standing in the crib. What do I do?
When your baby gets a new motor milestone under her belt, it's generally good news for sleep because she's able to find a comfortable sleep position and self-soothe.

Still, each new physical talent can temporarily throw sleep off course. Now your baby is excited to practice her skills at all times of the day and night, but she also may be getting into positions that she doesn't know how to (or doesn't want to) get out of.

If your baby is sitting, crawling, or standing, gently guide her back down into her favorite sleep position during each of your 5-minute checks. The idea is to guide or "mold" her body to show your baby how to eventually do it herself. Even if she immediately pops back up to a sit or stand, only "mold" once per visit. If she is sitting or in a crawling position, you can swiftly and smoothly guide her into her favorite lying-down position, usually on her side or tummy.

If she has figured out how to pull to a stand at the crib rail but can't get back down again, gently lift her hands from the rail, bend her knees, and guide her into her favorite lying-down position. The idea is to show her how to do it herself (the opposite of her being picked up and "magically" plopped into a lying-down position). Whether it's sitting, on hands and knees, or standing, once you know that your baby can lie back down by herself and begins to do so, you no longer need to guide her down.

What do I do if my baby climbs out of the crib?

If your baby is starting to climb out of the crib but is under 2 years old, make sure the mattress is at the lowest level and try putting cushions (couch cushions work well) around her crib at night, just in case. Some little mini gymnasts can launch themselves from the crib at an early age and take us by surprise. Other toddlers stay happily in their cribs until age 3 or even older. If, no matter what you do, your baby is still able to climb out of the crib, for safety reasons, you will have to move her to a toddler bed (see Chapter 5, page 231).

> *Julie: We don't normally like sleep sacks much as they restrict baby's freedom to move around the crib. However, we met parents who put their 2-year-old in a sleep sack as it prevented her from getting a leg up high enough to climb out of the crib. Pretty brilliant!*

Does my baby have separation anxiety?

You may worry that your baby doesn't like falling asleep on her own because she's separated from you, and it's true that babies and toddlers go through periods of separation anxiety—this is developmental and also depends on your child's temperament. Know that it's okay for your baby to protest separating. Over time, with your consistent patterns, she internalizes the idea that her most important people are right nearby, that she's okay in her comfortable crib, and that you always greet her in the morning.

My baby is throwing loveys and stuffed animals out of the crib. What should I do?

That trusted, soothing lovey—at some point your baby might figure out that if she launches it out of the crib, you'll come back in to retrieve it. You give it back to her, turn to leave, and she's already flung it back overboard.

First, try going in a handful of times and simply give the lovey back. The first time you do, say, "It's time for sleeping," and walk out. The subsequent times, don't say anything. Be as boring and quick as possible so that the visit won't feel fun for your baby. If you're doing the Sleep Wave, retrieve the blanket only once during each 5-minute check. Do this in a very quick and unobtrusive manner, so that baby doesn't really notice that it's back near her hands.

5.

Child Sleep (2 to 6 Years)

TROUBLESHOOTING

☀ HEALTHY SLEEP HABITS ☀
Your Child's Sleep

Toddlers and preschoolers are amazing little beings. They have advancing language, impressive cognitive powers, and budding personalities. They explore and test the world with growing independence.

It's easy to see how these very same skills can lead to new, and sometimes tricky, challenges when it comes to sleep. Little kids are master negotiators—quick to try out crafty schemes for delaying bedtime and resisting naps—and their awareness and imagination can lead to separation anxiety, fears of the dark, and nightmares.

Even if your child used to be an easy sleeper, he may now be refusing naps, digging in his heels at bedtime, calling for you, or even padding down the hallway to greet you in the middle of the night. In this chapter we'll help you address all of these very common sleep issues.

TYPICAL SLEEP CHALLENGES FOR TODDLERS AND YOUNG CHILDREN ARE:

· Bedtime resistance

· Requiring a parent's presence to fall asleep at night or fall back to sleep in the middle of the night

· Getting out of bed after bedtime

· Waking up too early

· Resisting naps or requiring a special setting such as a stroller ride for naps

· Giving up naps too early

· Nightmares and night terrors

Your 2- to 3-year-old needs 12 to 14 hours of sleep in total and most likely still takes one nap.

Three- to 5-year-olds need 11 to 13 total hours of sleep. Some continue one nap until about 4 years old.

Five- to 10-year-olds need 10 to 11 hours total.

Remember how much sleep your young child needs—it's still a lot!

This total sleep time includes naps, which most children need until they're roughly 3 to 5 years old. Little children are often early risers, so it's very helpful to keep your child's bedtime early. Especially if your child needs to start the morning early for day care, preschool, or elementary school, getting to bed around 7:30 p.m. is the way to carve out enough time for a full night's sleep. If your child resists bedtime and getting to bed early is difficult, we'll help you address this issue later in the chapter.

Bedtime and Sleep Associations

If you've read Chapters 3 and 4, you're familiar with the idea of *sleep associations* (the behaviors, soothing methods, or elements of the environment that your child associates with sleep) and the importance of how your child falls asleep. We will review this information here because it looks a little different for older children.

The way your child falls asleep determines a lot about how he sleeps through the night. This is because *all children wake up during the night as they pass through stages of sleep.* Many times during the night, your child (just like you) transitions between sleep stages and shifts into a light sleep. He stirs and wakes partially. When this happens, he either rolls over, pulls up his covers, tucks a stuffed animal under his arm, and drifts back to sleep, or he calls out to you to help him.

- If your little one falls asleep on his own at bedtime and goes back to sleep on his own during the night without help, he has practiced his own special ability to self-soothe and feels confident to do this at bedtime as well as when he wakes partially at night.

- If your child relies on your presence to fall asleep at bedtime or calls out to you for help falling back to sleep during the night, he isn't a "bad sleeper"; he just hasn't yet practiced and become comfortable with his own self-soothing to sleep.

There are lots of reasons that children have trouble sleeping through the night without help, but one of the main reasons is that they wake up in the night with different sleep associations (even slightly different ones) than they had when they went to bed.

Here's an example of a 3-year-old who wakes up one to two times a night.

AT BEDTIME:

- Mom or Dad lies down in his bed until he's asleep or almost fully asleep.

- The light in the hallway is on.

- Sips of water are given to him by request.

- The blankets are tucked in by Mom or Dad repeatedly before he falls asleep.

BUT IN THE MIDDLE OF THE NIGHT:

- He wakes up alone in bed.

- The lights are off.

- He has no accessible water.

- He can't retuck his own blankets.

> A National Sleep Foundation poll found that infants and toddlers who are put to bed asleep were nearly three times as likely to wake up and need help at least twice per night than those who went into bed awake.

One of the first steps when you're working on sleep is to look at the exact environment in which your child goes to bed. If there are any behaviors or elements of his bedroom that he cannot re-create for himself in the middle of the night, you will need to address each of these. This might mean changing the behaviors you do at bedtime, or arranging and practicing things so your child knows just what to do in the middle of the night. For example, make sure that there is an accessible sippy cup in case he needs water, and do "rehearsals" during the day in which you help your child practice pulling up and retucking his own blankets. The goal is not to do anything to help your child fall asleep at bedtime that he can't do on his own in the middle of the night. If your child is used to you lying down until he falls asleep, or has any other strong sleep associations that you need to change at bedtime, this usually requires a consistent, structured plan—we'll help you accomplish this later in the chapter with the Sleep Wave or the Reverse Sleep Wave.

Here are the most common unhelpful sleep associations for toddlers and preschoolers, and examples of how you might change them.

UNHELPFUL SLEEP ASSOCIATION	HELPFUL SLEEP ASSOCIATION
*Mom or Dad's presence	Song, kiss good night, leave room
Calling parent for water	Placing a sippy cup near bed
Calling parent to tuck in blankets	Being able to manage blankets on own (rehearse this during the day)
Hallway lights on at bedtime	Dim nightlight on all night
*Sleeping in parents' bed (when independent sleep is desired)	Feeling comfortable in his own bed to fall asleep and sleep continuously through the night
Strollers, rocking, or other motion delivered by parent	Rolling and moving body around in bed to get comfortable
Falling asleep in another room, for example, in the living room	The feeling, sounds, and sights of your child's own crib or bed

*These are common unhelpful sleep associations that are very strong and require parents to be especially consistent to change. They are fully changeable, though, so don't worry if you're in this pattern and want to switch to your child sleeping independently.

What if your child goes to bed independently, but then after a nightmare, Mom lies down in bed until he falls back to sleep? This counts as an unhelpful sleep association, too, because if the child drifts off with Mom stroking his head, the next time he comes back to a light sleep, *where's Mom*?! (You'll always soothe and help your child if he has a nightmare, but we will help you do this without creating an unhelpful sleep association.)

Your Child's Bedroom

The sights, sounds, and feel of your child's bedroom can have a big impact on his sleep. In the last chapter, we went through all the basic elements of a child's bedroom for any age, so if you haven't done so already, read pages 113–15 in the previous chapter for creating the right bedroom environment (light, sound, feel, temperature, design). In addition to these important bedroom elements, here are a few that you'll want to consider with a toddler or young child:

- **A wind-down space.** Have a dim lamp by the bed that you can use for reading and a few comfortable pillows so you can sit on or beside your child's bed. It's really helpful to dim the lights an hour or so before to help your child's body wind down for sleep. Turn off bright overhead lights in the house before you start your bedtime routine (see Lights, Electronics, and Bedtime, page 120).

- **Nightlight.** Many young children like having a nightlight for falling asleep and waking up at night, especially if they need to pee. Use a very soft nightlight. Even the dimmest light can seem like too much after your child's eyes adjust to the dark.

- **Design.** Does your child's room evoke a sense of calm? Think about using colors and patterns that are soothing.

Organize your child's room so he feels peaceful during naps and at bedtime. Ask your little one if it feels cozy to him.

- **Have your child make his bed.** When he's old enough to pull up the covers (even if you secretly redo it later), it's a nice ritual to help him be involved and take care of his sleeping place.

- **No television.** Children who have a television in their bedroom tend to sleep less at night and are also less likely to take a nap than those with no television in their room.

Regular Bedtime

An optimal bedtime for children ages 2 to 6 is between 7:00 and 8:00 p.m. Where your child falls in this range will depend on age, morning wake-up time, and naps. For example, a 3-year-old who is napping from 1:00 to 3:00 p.m. may do well with an 8:00 p.m. bedtime. A 4-year-old who has stopped napping and wakes at 6:30 a.m. will do well with a 7:00 p.m. bedtime. Remember that your child should go to bed when he's in a good mood, not when he's yawning and bleary-eyed.

If your child is a night owl and falls asleep at 9:00 p.m., he's probably not getting the best quality and length of sleep that he needs (unless he's sleeping until 8:00 a.m. every morning, which is hard to do with most families' schedules). To shift his bedtime earlier, you can gradually move bedtime. To do this, put your child to bed 15 minutes earlier every two to three nights, until you've achieved the right time. While you're in the process of shifting to an earlier bedtime, gently wake your child up in the morning if he is sleeping too long, because if your child sleeps in until 9:00 a.m., he legitimately won't feel drowsy enough to fall asleep until 9:00 p.m. (remember that your child's wake-up time is like pressing "go" on his internal clock). Of course, it's okay for your child to sleep in to catch up on sleep sometimes, but especially when you're trying to shift a sleep pattern, it's best to keep your schedule as regular as possible, on both weekdays and weekends. This gives consistent cues to his internal clock.

In fact, a regular bedtime is as important as an early one. When your child's bedtime moves around, he's not getting the maximum benefit of regulated circadian rhythms. Ideally, your child should go to bed at the same time every night, on weeknights and weekends (within reason, of course). Morning wake-up time and naps will adjust this slightly, but it shouldn't be by more than 30 minutes on a regular basis.

A large study of more than 11,000 little kids (ages 3 to 7) showed that having a regular bedtime, independent of the time of that bedtime, was linked with better reading, math, and spatial capabilities. Children with irregular bedtimes also had more behavioral issues, such as moodiness and hyperactivity, and kids with late and irregular bedtimes were the most affected. Moving bedtime around is like giving your child a mini case of jet lag on a regular basis, whereas a regular bedtime keeps her internal clock in sync—this affects many aspects of her thinking, mood, and behavior.

You most likely already have a bedtime routine for your child. Even so, read this section to make sure it's the most sleep-conducive routine possible.

Bedtime Routines

Routines make kids (and grown-ups, too, for that matter) happy. Clear, consistent rituals and patterns allow kids to know what's coming, and the order and structure make them feel secure. When children don't have regular routines, there can be endless confusion and protesting, but when the whole house knows what to expect, the evening tends to flow more smoothly.

Sample Bedtime Routines

Here are some examples of bedtime routines. Create your own in a way that works for the family. Remember that it doesn't matter exactly what you do. What matters is that it's clear, consistent, and calm.

2-YEAR-OLD	3-YEAR-OLD	5-YEAR-OLD
This routine starts at 6:15 p.m. and bedtime is 7:15 p.m.	This routine starts at 6:30 p.m. and bedtime is 7:30 p.m.	This routine starts at 6:30 p.m. and bedtime is 7:30 p.m.
Dim lights in home	Dim lights in home	Dim lights in home
Bath	Bath	Bath
Pajamas	Pajamas	Pajamas

2-YEAR-OLD	3-YEAR-OLD	5-YEAR-OLD
Brush teeth	Child-led play	Brush teeth
Read two stories	Brush teeth	Read two chapters of a book
Turn off the lights	Read two stories	Go to potty
Say good night to objects in the room	Share a story of your day with each other	Turn off the lights
Sing one song	Go to potty	Talk about your "highs" and "lows" for the day
Kiss good night, put in crib, tell your child you'll check on him in 5 minutes (see Reverse Sleep Wave on page 205), walk out of the room	Turn off the lights	Kiss good night, say you'll check on him in 5 minutes (see Reverse Sleep Wave), walk out of the room
	Sing two songs	
	Kiss good night, say you'll check on him in 5 minutes (see Reverse Sleep Wave), walk out of the room	

Consistent and Calm

You can craft your child's routine however you wish. All that matters is that the steps are consistent every night and that the behaviors and tone are progressively more calming toward the end. Do the last few steps of your routine in your child's room.

Try not to make television part of the bedtime routine—screen time before bed is linked to later bedtimes. Your child should definitely not engage with close-range electronics, such as computers or handheld screens for at least an hour before bed. The artificial light from these gadgets can have an alerting effect on the brain and make it harder for your child to fall asleep.

LIGHTS, ELECTRONICS, AND BEDTIME

Light is a powerful signal to the body's circadian system. Lights in your home—including overhead lights and those from electronics—are known to suppress the secretion of melatonin, a chemical that naturally rises as we become drowsy before bed. This is especially true of blue light, which comes from many computer screens, tablets, and other close-range devices. Bright home lights and the use of electronics in the hours before bed can delay your child's ability to fall asleep.

Allow Enough Time for Winding Down

Your child's routine may take up to an hour to complete, if you think of it as starting with a bath after dinner and ending with you giving him a kiss and walking out of the room. Don't underestimate the amount of time it can take to move through all of the aspects of your child's routine (especially if you have multiple children). Not allowing enough time can make you feel rushed and stressed, which makes it harder for your child to wind down and fall asleep.

If your child's bedtime is 7:30 p.m., then by 6:30 p.m. the house should shift into wind-down mode (you can even call it this, or come up with another phrase to help the family understand that it's time to shift their energy). It doesn't mean that your child is getting into bed now; it just means the house has shifted into a calm, gradual march toward bedtime. This can be a pleasant time—put on jazz music, turn down the overhead lighting—the idea is to signal to your child that sleep is coming down the road.

Bedtime Chart

The idea of a bedtime chart is to have a visual representation of each part of the bedtime routine so that the whole family is on the same page in terms of the order and the expectations before bed. A chart can be as simple or as fancy as you want to make it. It's just a way for your child to see her bedtime routine clearly and help her move through the steps. In the next section, you'll see an example of how to create a bedtime chart and use it as motivation for your child.

Child-Led Play

This is a way to help your child shift into a self-regulating mode—it's the opposite of *you* doing things *to* him, like bathing and dressing, and it sets the stage for your child falling asleep independently. Child-led play varies depending on age, temperament, and interests. The key is to avoid teaching, initiating, or changing the play. All you really have to do is follow. For example:

> *You've dimmed the lights in your child's bedroom and put a few simple toys or books on the floor. You sit or lie down on the floor with him and wait and watch to see what he does next. Just watch! Often it's enough for your little one to simply feel your presence and interest as she explores the room. You can pick up a similar toy or a complementary toy and join in, even if it's really simple. It's not necessary to always expand, but at times you can add*

something, like "Can my guy help build that barn?" or "I'm gonna roll my ball next to your ball." Child-led play is good to do at any time, but for bedtime, keep it quiet and calm.

If you're adding child-led play into your routine, try it before bath, or after pajamas, before reading a book.

Be Specific and Clear

It can help little kids to have very specific expectations and limits when it comes to bedtime routines. Clarify that your routine always has two stories and two songs. If your child spends a lot of time haggling over which book to read, choose a handful of books and allow him to pick two from that stack.

Help with the Transition

Your goal with bedtime routines is to be supportive and warm, but also very clear in handing off the responsibility for falling asleep to your child. We promise you, he is very capable of falling asleep on his own. It's just a matter of helping to make the transition clear and comfortable. Make sure that the last step of your routine happens in the dark, while you're still in the room. Turn off the lights and sing songs, tell a story, or talk about the day *before* walking out. If your child is very used to your presence while he falls asleep, you might want to give him some experience being alone in his room at the end of bedtime routine, before you officially leave. After your child is in bed and the lights are out, pop out quickly to fill his water glass or say, "I have to check something, I'll be right back," and leave the room for 1 minute.

Heather: I worked with a family whose son was crying when Dad left the room after the bedtime routine. We realized it was because the child went from a bright room with Dad, to being alone in the dark abruptly. The parents made a very specific routine, with a visual chart. After stories, Dad turned off the light and sat on the bed to talk about the day briefly. The son then had a moment with Dad in the dark, his eyes could adjust, and it eased the transition to bed. After 2 to 5 minutes in the dark, and with the child still awake, Dad kissed him good night and walked out. With this small adjustment, the son was comfortable falling asleep on his own.

Talk Through Bedtime Changes

We'll repeat this idea many times in this chapter because it's so important: *anytime you're working on sleep with a verbal child, talking with them and explaining the new plan is key.* In this case, it might mean saying during the day, and with a reminder before bed: "We're going to try something different today to help you get ready for bed and say good night." Explain how your bedtime chart works and review the exact steps and the number of books and songs you'll have before saying good night. If you're going to use the Reverse Sleep Wave (page 205), this is the time to explain or remind how it works.

Gentle Good Morning

If you need to wake your child up in the morning, do so gently. Partially pull back a curtain and sit next to him on the bed. Allow him a few minutes to adjust and wake up quietly with your presence, rather than starting the day with an abrupt wake-up.

Your Child's Relationship to Sleep

Think about your little one's overall relationship to sleep. Does he (and do you) feel like it's something we *have* to do—a dreaded activity to check off the list? Or is it something that we *get* to do—a pleasurable time to value and look forward to? Sleeping well is just like eating well and exercising; it's part of taking care of ourselves and allowing our minds and bodies to be at their best, so that we can enjoy life to its fullest. Be a model for your child and let him see how you value and take care of your own sleep. Think of it as a family priority, not a chore; this is something your child will carry with him throughout his life.

We tend to spend a lot of time coaxing our kids to sleep, discussing expectations, talking about bedtime routines, and so forth, so balance this out with talk about sleep that doesn't involve *you trying to get your child to do something.* That should be easy, because sleep is a pretty amazing topic and there's plenty to get you started. Talk about what sleep is, why it's neat, and why people need to sleep. For example:

Everybody in the whole wide world sleeps every night just like we do.

Did you know that while you sleep, your body becomes stronger and your brain makes connections and remembers information?

When I don't sleep enough, sometimes my head feels a little cloudy. What does your body feel like when you don't sleep enough?

Sleeping is like breathing. It's what our bodies just know how to do!

Your body and mind need about 11 hours of sleep at night because you're growing and changing so fast—sleep is really important for all of us though. Grown-ups need about 8 hours of sleep.

Did you have any dreams that you remember from last night? Dreams are like stories told by our brains while we sleep. Your brain can be pretty creative at night, can't it?

After I say good night to you, I can't wait to lie down in my soft, cozy bed, read my book for a little while, and then close my eyes and go to sleep!

Positive Bedtime

Since you're aiming to create positive, warm associations with sleep, don't use bed or bedtime as a negative consequence—for example, by telling your child he'll go directly to bed without stories, or using the bed or crib as a space for time-out. In general, we don't recommend using time-out as a punishment because this is not a helpful learning experience for your child. But if you use the concept of time-out to mean that your child has a moment to calm down and regulate himself, we still suggest using another space in the house to do this. Also avoid sending your child to time-out during bedtime routines, or using an early bedtime as a form of discipline—use the positive techniques presented earlier in the chapter instead.

Balanced Days, Peaceful Nights

The world's best-crafted bedtime routine won't cut it if your child is feeling stressed. When we humans are in a state of stress, the "downstairs brain" takes charge and we go into flight, fight, freeze (or faint) mode—think of running away when the pjs come out, fighting and stalling at every step of the routine.

Overscheduled or chaotic days lead to bedtime struggles and restless nights, and a lot of factors can tip our lives out of balance, like:

- Nonstop after-school classes and enrichment activities like sports, music, and dance

- Way too much homework at a time when families need to connect and wind down

- Overwhelmed parents who feel they need screens (TV, computer, tablets) as babysitters

- Parents' busy lives and the feelings of stress they carry

- Everyone getting home late and healthy bedtimes rarely being met

On the other hand, if you pay attention to how your day unfolds and make sure that your child has downtime, he can shift out of stress mode and access his more sophisticated "upstairs brain." When this happens, he's regulated, emotionally calm, and is able to follow directions and enjoy books, songs, and snuggles. He's ready to welcome sleep.

How to Achieve Balance with Your Children

Pare Down

Eliminate some activities and schedule free, unstructured time. Put your pjs on early and discover what boredom feels like. One wise parent we know tells her children, "When you're bored, your brain is growing!" Lean into the open spaces in your day. Take a walk. Tumble and wrestle on the bed. Have everyone help out with dinner prep. Take early baths with extra bubbles. Create a visual schedule or chart that everyone uses to help you feel organized and keep the week balanced.

Check In

Sit and snuggle, talk about your "highs and lows," rub your child's feet if he'll let you—find moments when you're really together and not distracted. With some kids it doesn't work to ask them direct questions, so get down on the floor and join your child in what *he's* doing (instead of expecting an adultlike "how was your day" conversation). When you're drawing, doing a puzzle, or playing a card game, conversations start to flow. It's good for working parents to know that quality means more than quantity when it comes to spending time with our kids.

Think About You

Your mood rubs off on your child. Fighting with your partner, working too much, not taking care of your own sleep and exercise, not calling on family, friends, or other helpers to relieve you sometimes— all these things increase stress in the house, and your child picks up on it. This is where the "secure your own oxygen mask first" analogy applies.

Put a Limit on Homework Time

It's helpful to talk to your child's teacher and find out how much homework time is reasonable. Set the timer and when that amount of time is up, put the homework away. Most teachers want to know if it's taking longer than they expected for the homework because this gives them information about how everyone is understanding the material. Current research shows little value from long hours of homework; it's better to reconnect and have some fun after a long day.

Turn off the Screens

Just try it. We promise you'll do just fine. As with any habit, you may go through a little withdrawal, but the reward will be big: calmer nervous systems, brains primed for relaxation, and time to really be with each other.

Make Bedtime Routine Sweet and Relaxing

Read the previous section on bedtime routines and craft one that you all enjoy. Hold tight to bedtime—it may seem rigid, but keeping bedtime consistent helps everyone feel less stressed the next day.

☽ SLEEP SOLUTIONS ☽
Bedtime Resistance: Helping Your Child Get into Bed

Preschoolers are brilliant designers of stall tactics, which means that sometimes just getting through the bedtime routine and actually *getting your child physically into bed* can feel like pushing a boulder up a mountain. "No, I need to put my other pjs on! I need the water in the *fishie* cup. Now I need to get a different blankie for my bears!"

The negotiating and stalling can try your patience as a parent and take the enjoyment out of bedtime. If this rings true, take a deep breath and read through this section for tips on helping your little one get through the bedtime routine and get into bed. (Following this section, we'll help you figure out how to help him stay there all night.)

Schedule

Little kids still need roughly 10½ to 11 hours of sleep at night, so if your child is waking up around 6:30 a.m., a good bedtime is 7:30 p.m. This depends on your child's individual sleep needs, but also is determined by what time he wakes up, whether he naps, and the timing of his naps. Around age 3, kids who are napping may not be tired until a little later than their usual bedtime, whereas when they stop napping they'll be tired an hour or so earlier. This is because as your child grows, his "sleep drive" (Chapter 8) does not build as quickly. Napping for too long (more than 2 hours) or too late (past 3:00 or 3:30 p.m.) will mean that your child's sleep drive hasn't built up enough to make him fall asleep at bedtime. This is also true of kids who have stopped napping but sleep late into the morning or take even a little ten-minute "power nap" in the car. Both napping and sleeping in reduce your child's sleep drive and can make bedtime difficult.

Motivate

Your child may need a little motivation to drive him through the steps of getting ready for bed, so you don't feel as though you're dragging him along. You might start by putting the best, most alluring step at the end of the routine. For example, if your toddler likes to sing a certain song with you or use a flashlight to make shadows on the wall, make that the final step in the bedtime routine. Tell your older child an ongoing story that has a "cliffhanger" every night, so he's motivated to put on pajamas, crawl into bed, and hear the next installment. Remember that the best incentive for getting into bed is your undivided attention. Set aside books you love to read and create a repertoire of songs you love to sing. Your child will know if you're truly enjoying this time together or merely going through the motions, so take good care of yourself and your mood will be contagious.

A visual chart can be very helpful. You can ask your child to check in with the chart and complete his routine. After doing so, he (or you) can put a star or choose a sticker to show that the routine was completed for that night (you can also do this for your morning routine). Resist praising or showing big excitement; this can backfire and increase resistance. Focus on the effort and process, not the end product. Remark on his accomplishments by saying, "Look at all these stickers. You're following your chart!"

Here's a simple chart you can make in 10 minutes.

- Take a large piece of poster paper.

- Draw an illustration of each step of your child's routine (bath, pajamas, brushing teeth).

- Pin up an envelope of stickers next to the paper (buy some surprise stickers on your own so they are exciting to your child).

- After your child completes the routine, but before getting into bed, have him choose a sticker and put it on the paper in a designated spot.

BEDTIME ROUTINE CHART

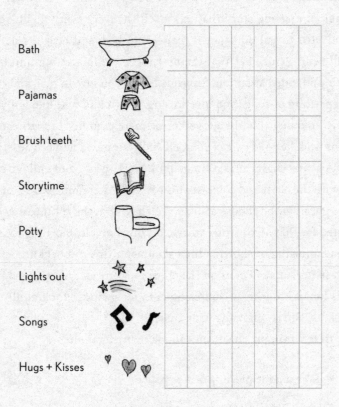

Bath

Pajamas

Brush teeth

Storytime

Potty

Lights out

Songs

Hugs + Kisses

Make a Bedtime Storybook

Take photos or draw pictures of each step in your bedtime routine and write the story of how it goes every night. Your child can draw the pictures and help you make the book, or you can do it yourself and read it with her during the day or as part of your routine. Telling the story of your routine and how the evening goes will help her make sense of this new plan—kids often love to see themselves and their routine in a book. You can also have these books made by an online photo book service.

Last Call for Stuff!

If you find yourself answering random questions that your child has concocted to lure you back into the room, or you're repeatedly rearranging blankets and loveys after bedtime, it's time to institute a "last call" policy. While your child is climbing into bed and you're winding down the routine, tell him that this is the "last call for stuff," in which he can ask for water, request his favorite stuffed animals, ask you to check his boo-boo, help him put on or take off socks, make a trip to the potty, or ask any of the questions he might have. The last call is a way to meet your child's needs but to contain the interaction so that it doesn't dribble over after the clear handoff of you saying good night and walking out of the room. Remind your little one during the last call that if he asks for something *after* last call, he is now in charge of his stuff (his blankets, water, and stuffed animals).

THE CREATIVE BEDTIME STALLER

Andrea: My son Jonah was a super-creative staller. "My socks fell off; I pushed my crib away from the wall; All my animals jumped out of my bed," etc., etc. Thankfully, he loved the idea of "last call for stuff," and as I made sure to include this check-in during his routine, he felt heard and contained. It became much easier for him to accept and understand when it was time for him to stop calling out and begin to soothe himself to sleep.

Falling Asleep Independently:
The Reverse Sleep Wave, the Sleep Wave, and the Gradual Parent Wean

Here we will explain three techniques for helping your child sleep: the Reverse Sleep Wave, the regular Sleep Wave, and the gradual parent wean.

Which Should You Use? All Are Effective, but Consider That:

1. The Reverse Sleep Wave, if successful, is a gentle and easy system, and it's one you can keep in place as a sweet, ongoing nightly ritual that helps your child transition to bed. We recommend trying it first. It's very successful for many families. If it does not work, you can use the regular Sleep Wave or the gradual parent wean, and then go back and put the reverse one in place once your child is falling asleep on his own. Most children who are at least 2 can understand the concept of the Reverse Sleep Wave and stay in their beds in between the checks.

2. If you have been lying down or sitting with your child until he falls asleep, or having him sleep in your bed for a long time, you may feel most comfortable with the gradual parent wean. However, we still recommend trying the Reverse Sleep Wave first—you might be surprised by the result!

3. The Reverse Sleep Wave is primarily for helping your child fall asleep at the *beginning* of the night. If your child wakes up in the middle of the night, the regular Sleep Wave is the better option. In this case, you would use the Reverse Sleep Wave at bedtime and the regular Sleep Wave in the middle of the night.

4. If your child has been sleeping in *your* bed, use the Reverse Sleep Wave or the regular Sleep Wave, not the parent wean.

No matter which technique you choose, don't skip over this very important step: *Talk to your child about the plan during the day—this is an essential step in working on sleep with children over the age of 2.* The more you can explain in clear, simple language and even include your child in your plans, the more success you'll have. For example, once you've read through this chapter and decided on your new sleep plan, you can say something like: "It's my job to help you sleep better, so we're going to have a new plan at bedtime." Then explain the plan. Have these talks during the day (not while the plan is in motion at night).

The Reverse Sleep Wave

Remember that having the confidence to fall asleep alone at the beginning of the night is a major benefit to children, and it determines a lot about how your child sleeps through the night as well as how he sleeps over the long term.

So once you're through the bedtime routine and your child is in bed, how do you support him falling asleep independently?

The underlying pattern in bedtime problems is usually the same:

Your child protests or calls for you, and you respond. The Reverse Sleep Wave is a way to shift this dynamic completely, by setting up what we call "5-minute check-ons" that you do for your child *automatically*, without him calling out to you. When you put your child to bed, you'll tell him that you're going to check on him in 5 minutes— this gives him the peace of mind to know you're coming back and he doesn't have to craft any tricky requests or negotiate to get you back in the room. Kids love this idea; if they just wait quietly, *you* will come to *them*! It's an elegant little twist on the concept of the Sleep Wave (see Chapter 4) because it gives your child a repetitive, consistent reminder of your presence, but it keeps your child in charge of soothing and falling asleep independently. Your child can stop spending energy trying to get you to respond, and instead feel calm and relaxed knowing you're already planning to come back.

REVERSE SLEEP WAVE STEPS

- Explain to your child, in a calm moment during the day, what the new plan will be and how the Reverse Sleep Wave works. Say, "We're going to do something different tonight to help your body relax. We're going to do our bedtime routine of brushing teeth, reading two stories, turning out the light, singing one song, and putting a cup of water by your bed. If you stay quiet, in your bed, Mommy (or Daddy) will check on *you*! I'll keep checking on you until you fall asleep."

- Show your child how you will stick your head just inside the door and softly say, "I'm checking on you. I'll be back in 5 minutes. Night night," and then you will leave right away.

Make sure she understands that the Reverse Sleep Wave is quick and isn't a conversation starter. Her role is to stay quietly in her bed and wait for your next check-on. During the day, you can use puppets or stuffed animals to demonstrate and rehearse with her to see how this will look. Depending on your child's age, she can either watch or take a role; children often love to take the parent's role.

- The first time you do a check-on, wait only about 30 to 45 seconds before going in. The idea is to make sure you do your check *before* your child calls out, gets out of bed, or starts to cry. At first, she may not have the patience to wait 5 minutes because she doesn't "get" the new pattern yet.

- Stick your head just inside the door and say very softly, just loud enough for your child to hear, "I'm checking on you. I'll be back in 5 minutes. Night night." Then leave. You're not waiting for a response or having any expectation of whether she's asleep yet. You're simply letting your child know that you are checking on her. Make this check very quiet. If you have a creaky door, put some oil on the hinges to make it possible for you to open it quietly without disturbing your child.

- Gradually lengthen the time between your check-ons until you've reached 4 to 5 minutes. By this time, your child will have detected the pattern and will come to trust that you will indeed come, without her having to reach out for your attention in any way.

- Continue 5-minute checks until your child is asleep.

Over the next week or two, you should see the number of checks drop dramatically. Most children are asleep by the third one. If this doesn't happen and you feel that the checks are still going on and on, you can now choose to set a limit and let your child know that you will only do two or three checks.

At first, your little sleeper will be very excited and expectant, waiting for you to come, but after a while, she will relax as the predictable pattern of your Reverse Sleep Wave becomes clear. This builds a very sweet bridge from awake time with you, to separating to fall asleep, and you can keep this ritual in place for a long time.

The Reverse Sleep Wave doesn't always work right away—your child might pop up and get out of bed before you can do your check-

The Reserve Sleep Wave is short, sweet, and automatic—it changes the dynamic at bedtime.

on (even a 15-second one). If this is the case, don't worry, you can still use the Reverse Sleep Wave once your child begins to stay in his bed and fall asleep on his own. Read the following section on the regular Sleep Wave and you'll see how you can apply it until your child is ready for the Reverse Sleep Wave.

The Sleep Wave

In Chapter 4, we taught you the Sleep Wave—a method for helping your baby fall asleep independently and for sleeping through the night. You can use the Sleep Wave to help an older child fall asleep independently, too—whether he's sleeping in a crib or a bed.

The Sleep Wave is the best option if you've tried the Reverse Sleep Wave but your child is still getting out of bed and/or crying, or if you simply think that your child is not capable of understanding and staying in bed in between checks. Many parents use the Sleep Wave when moving their child from the crib to the big bed, from *their* bed to their child's own bed, or if their child's sleep has regressed.

The basic principles and method of the Sleep Wave are the same with older kids as they are for babies. The goal of the Sleep Wave is to give you a repetitive (wavelike) way to respond to and reassure your child, while keeping a clear distinction in terms of who is soothing to sleep. Through the Sleep Wave, you stay very consistent and reliable for your child, coming and going in a predictable pattern. Your child, over time, will pick up on this pattern, relax, and eventually turn inward and access his ability to fall sleep. Remember that your child is capable of falling asleep on his own, but habits and associations become so powerful and entrenched that they've overshadowed his natural abilities. It can look like it's impossible for your child to fall asleep on his own. It's not. You just have to shift the dynamic and institute a new, consistent pattern.

THE SLEEP WAVE

Remember this method from Chapter 4? We'll explain how you can use the same steps with your older child.

Put your child down awake.

The check.

The wave.

Good morning.

Kids often protest change; it's normal for your child to have feelings about doing bedtime in a different way! The Sleep Wave is the way to respond predictably and consistently, without helping with the soothing-to-sleep part. When you're very repetitive and consistent, it's almost hypnotic for your child. He'll be able to detect the pattern, know what to expect, relax, and access his own soothing mechanisms.

When using the Sleep Wave with a walking, talking child who is in a real bed, you have extra challenges as well as extra tools to help. The main challenge is that now your little one isn't confined by the crib, so this newfound freedom can bring on multiple attempts to come looking for you. The good news is that an older child has the ability to understand and participate in a new plan, as well as the sophisticated brainpower to know in a very concrete way that you are nearby.

The Key to Success = Consistency

The number one key to success with the Sleep Wave is consistency— sticking to your plan with complete steadiness, with the goal of not breaking your pattern at all. Especially as children grow—with stronger bodies, louder voices, and big personalities—their protests can be very powerful. As a parent, it's hard to hear or watch your child protest; we know how tough this can be. Keep in mind that the end goal is a good, healthy sleep for your child; the more consistent you are, the faster and easier the process will be for everyone.

When we say "consistent," we mean even your small behaviors, such as what you say and how you move, must stay the same. For example, below you will read about options for returning your child to bed. When you choose a script to say, repeat it *exactly* each time, without adding a single other phrase, an exasperated sigh, a sharp tone, or any yelling. The precise consistency of your voice and your body movements are key. When you deviate from your exact plan, it confuses and activates your child. He will begin to reach out and test even more to see what your next response will be. If he knows it's never changing, he will eventually relax and self-soothe to sleep.

Before you start the Sleep Wave, you will create a plan and a "script" to say to your child once he's in bed. Do not deviate from this. When you change your response, even slightly (by saying a different phrase, responding to his request for a new stuffed animal just one time, and so forth), it will make him more likely to keep getting up or crying and the whole process will be prolonged.

Please read about crying on page 133 if you have doubts or worry at all about your child's emotional response to the Sleep Wave. Sleep struggles can get ugly sometimes because parents want to be accommodating but eventually reach a limit and start feeling frustrated, resentful, and out of control. That's when putting a new sleep plan in place and sticking to it consistently is really important. Make a fresh start with your child by creating/writing down your sleep plan, talking it through with your partner and your child, and implementing it in a very clear way.

Sleep Wave Choices

How you implement the Sleep Wave with your child depends on whether he's in the crib or a big bed, and what exactly he does when you put him into bed. Here are the possible scenarios:

If Your Child Is in a Crib

To implement the Sleep Wave if your child is still in the crib, you can follow the exact steps of the Sleep Wave as outlined for babies in Chapter 4, starting on page 127.

If Your Child Is in a Bed

To implement the Sleep Wave with a child sleeping in a bed, you will complete your bedtime routine (make sure to read all the above information on routines), kiss your child good night, and walk out of the room. Your child may protest this change in many different ways, so read the following options depending on your child's behavior:

If Your Child Cries, but Stays in Bed

You don't need to check on your child if he's talking, singing, or mumbling, but if your child is crying or protesting strongly, use the Sleep Wave 5-minute checks as outlined in Chapter 4 starting on page 127.

If Your Child Gets out of Bed

Here comes the tough one! Many toddlers get out of bed after parents say good night and walk out (you may even feel someone tugging at your leg *before* you get out of the room). If your child gets out of bed, there are a few ways to respond using the Sleep Wave, all of which involve the idea of "expanding the crib."

Expand the Crib

Many parents are not prepared for the persistence with which their little one will get up out of bed over and over. One mom told us that the first night she moved her son to a toddler bed, he got out of bed 110 times!

It helps tremendously to now imagine your child's bedroom as an expanded crib. Instead of being contained by the crib, you can now choose a gentle but clear way to contain your child in the bedroom, rather than allowing her to join you repeatedly in the living room. This is very effective in reducing her excitement at being able to get to where the action is. Keeping her in her room also keeps her in the darkness, where her brain is better able to fall asleep, and the sense of a fun game is also diminished if she can't come pitter-pattering down the hallway time after time.

Depending on factors such as whether your child's bedroom door is usually open or closed, which direction the door opens, what kind of a climber he is, and so forth, there are several choices for how to accomplish the idea of the expanded crib. Before you start, check the room carefully for any safety issues, for example, blind cords, electrical outlets, and anything your child could pull over or climb on.

- Use a baby-proofing gate at the bedroom door. This is probably the most common approach. The gate needs to be strong and high enough to be effective.

- If your child is used to having the door closed, you can simply close it. The tricky part about this choice is that most doors open into the room, which makes it difficult to open it to do your checks if your child is standing right at the door.

- There are gadgets you can buy that hold the door firmly in an ajar position, which some families have used for this purpose.

- If you don't use any of these choices, you can sit on the floor or in a chair just out of sight, in the dark, outside your child's room.

Sleep Wave Steps

Once you've decided on your method for keeping your little one secure in her comfy room, you're ready to use the Sleep Wave steps to help her learn the new pattern of falling asleep independently. You'll want a one-line "script" to say to your child when you're doing your 5-minute checks—for example, "It's time for bed." Repeat this script in a very calm, confident way. For some children these strategies may work better without any words from the parent at all. This is your choice and depends on your child's temperament and age. The trick is to not engage or stimulate her during these visits. The goal is to be so repetitive and non-engaging that she eventually figures out that it's not really worth getting up after all. Whichever way you choose to respond, remember, the most important thing is to *stick to it!*

Look over the following four examples and choose how you will respond, depending on your child's behavior after you say good night and walk out of the room.

1. **If your child is at her gate or door, crying,** wait 5 minutes, and then go and walk or carry her back to her bed, say your script, and leave right away. Even if she doesn't get out of bed, be sure to do the 5-minute checks if she's crying. If you haven't yet read about the Sleep Wave and the concept of the 5-minute checks, please go to Chapter 4, page 127.

USING THE SLEEP WAVE WITH THE TODDLER BED

Marianne: When we first moved Bella to her toddler bed, she popped up repeatedly. She would stand at the gate and just scream at the top of her lungs. The first night, my husband walked her back to her bed and said his script, 45 times! We were sure it wasn't going to work. But the second night, he had to do it only 28 times, and the third night, it was down to 10. She's a strong little one, but by week's end, she was going down easily and not getting out of bed at all.

2. **If your child is at his gate or door, but not crying,** you don't have to go at all. Some parents still choose to go every 5 minutes and walk or carry their child back to his bed, say their script, and leave right away. When you get your little one back into bed, be sure not to do any additional soothing or bedtime rituals for him: "Last call for stuff" is over, so no elaborate tucking in or pulling covers up. Teach him to do those things for himself, otherwise they turn into reasons for calling you back in.

3. **If you've chosen not to use a gate or close the door,** sit just out of sight outside your child's door, in the dark, and walk or carry him back to bed every time he gets up. In this case, it's best to use very few words, or not to talk at all, as he will already be quite activated by your presence. Remember that you're not disciplining your child, sending him the message that he's done something wrong, or that you're upset. You're simply establishing a new pattern. Make sure that your body movements and emotional tone convey this by being patient and neutral.

4. If you choose one of the check-in methods above and find that little or no progress is being made, you'll want to shift

to a less engaging approach, which usually means no talking. Either way, if you stick to it, your child will eventually become convinced that you're not going to change your tune and that getting up isn't so much fun after all. It's only then that she will turn to her inner soothing abilities and find her own way to fall asleep.

Remember: Important Notes About the Sleep Wave with Children

Be Calm and Concise

When you're walking your child back to bed, don't engage in conversation or negotiations. Don't use threats or consequences, plead, or express frustration with your child. We can't overstate this! You don't want bedtime to be associated with tension, and sometimes *negative* attention from you confuses or reinforces your child's behavior. Be calm and confident, unwavering, repetitive, and boring. Say the *exact* same thing each time you go in, such as, "It's time for sleeping," or say nothing at all. If you feel exasperated or upset, try switching off with your partner in doing the checks.

Kids Are Tenacious

Expect your child to get out of bed 50 times at first. Hopefully this won't happen, but you should prepare for your child to truly test the limits of this new bedtime arrangement. If he detects the pattern, and gets comfortable after one to two checks (in which you walk him back to bed), that's great—you've got an easygoing sleeper on your hands! Just know that it's completely normal for children to pop out of bed many times, cry, and express their feelings in all sorts of different ways in response to a big change like this. Be ready to ride this out and let your child know that this is truly the new way of doing things in your home.

You may feel as though 5 minutes is too short and that you're interrupting his progress toward self-soothing to sleep. If this is the case, at this age it's fine to extend the time to 6, 7, or 8 minutes. The key is to choose a time and stick to it. You want your child to feel the predictability, the rhythmic wave, of your visits.

What to Say the Next Day

Children have a basic need to feel capable and significant. The next day, let your child know that you noticed he was able to fall asleep on his own, and maybe ask how his body feels after a good night's sleep. If getting there was a big struggle, you might say, "You kept trying and finally did it!" Research points to the fact that big praise and lots of "good jobs" actually backfire, as kids tend to give up or tune out very quickly. Kids are more likely to try harder and stick with something difficult if we acknowledge the effort and the progress they're making, while also helping them connect with how *they* feel about their accomplishments. It also helps to stay calm about their progress and normalize sleep for them, because if they catch wind of how invested you are in this whole business, they will be inspired to resist.

> *Julie: When my son used to say, "Mommy, I can't fall asleep," I would tell him, "Don't worry, honey, all you have to do is close your eyes and take deep breaths and your body will do the rest!"*

Don't punish your child or take away anything if he doesn't meet your expectations with the new bedtime plan. Simply acknowledge the struggle and notice his accomplishments when they happen. For example:

> *Wow, I noticed it was really tough for you to follow your new sleep plan last night, wasn't it? I had to help you back into bed lots of times. Is there anything you think would help you tonight? (This isn't an opportunity for your child to change the plan, only to make a small modification like a new sippy cup or a different book, so she feels like she's part of the plan, too.)*

Or,

> *Wow, I was noticing how you fell asleep with your lovey last night, just like we talked about. Your body knows just what to do, doesn't it?*

If you stick with your plan and your response is consistent, you'll probably notice that your 5-minute checks eventually decrease (although don't be surprised if they increase the second or third night). After a week or two of a *consistent* response, most kids fall asleep independently.

4-YEAR-OLD ELI AND THE MAGIC MONKEY

Ben: When Eli was 4, he refused to go to bed on his own. I made the mistake of "resting" next to him until he fell asleep. Then, I would sneak out—or I'd fall asleep, too, only to wake a few hours later, confused and frustrated. This went on for a few weeks. Every time I tried to leave before Eli was asleep, it would result in tears. I was exhausted and weak and would give in. Repeatedly. When we decided to stay consistent and truly change the pattern, we realized that an extra bit of encouragement made a big difference. At the time, Eli was very interested in a character he invented and called "The Magic Monkey." The Magic Monkey started writing Eli supportive letters that would "appear" under Eli's pillow: "I know you can do it." "It's hard, but you're almost there." "Don't worry, Eli. This can take a little time." Eventually, he was falling asleep without me in the room.

The Gradual Parent Wean

If you have been helping your child fall asleep in her own bed for quite a while (by lying down with her in her bed, on the floor, in a chair, on a futon . . . we've heard it all!), one approach is to very gradually shift yourself out of the room, moving about six to twelve inches each night. This strategy can be very useful if lying down with your child is a well-entrenched pattern and you just can't fathom the idea of extricating yourself—we've met lots of parents who fall into this category. The process takes some time, but it's often a relieving option for parents who don't think they can use the Reverse Sleep Wave or the regular Sleep Wave.

When you fade yourself out of your child's room, your child knows what's happening, but it's so gradual that he becomes comfortable with the change as it unfolds. He also has a clear sense that you are still there, even if he can't see you, as he's watched your path as you slowly exit. Since the parent's movement is very gradual, children usually don't protest. If your child does, let him know, during a preview or rehearsal during the day, that once Mom or Dad says good night, you won't be talking at all. If he gets out of bed, simply take him back to bed, without any words (very much like you would when sitting in the dark hallway if using the Sleep Wave). By the time you're out of the room, your child is falling asleep on his own. During this process, keep your child's bedtime and routine very consistent and predictable.

GRADUAL PARENT WEAN STEPS:

- As with any changes planned for kids this age, start by explaining them during calm, daytime moments: *Daddy's going to move a teeny, tiny bit each night, until he is sleeping in his own bed.* You can do a little playacting with animals or dolls, showing your child what it's going to look like.

- Decide what you are going to sit or lie on. Ideally, it's the same or similar to what you've been using. If you've been lying in your child's bed, you'll need a sleeping bag or pad of some kind. Make sure that, whatever you choose, it will fit through the doorway and into the hallway.

- The first night, only move a few inches away. Each night continue to move six to twelve inches. Stay in your spot until your child is asleep.

- Depending on the distance you have to travel, you should be completely out of the room and down the hallway in about 10 to 14 days. It's a painstaking process, but don't try to speed it up too much. It's the gradual nature that makes it reassuring to your little one.

- Once you are completely out of the room, you can begin to use the Reverse Sleep Wave, which is a great way to maintain a connected feeling as your child falls asleep.

- If your child's sleep regresses after this process is over and the Reverse Wave doesn't work, be ready to use the regular Sleep Wave, so that you don't create the lying down pattern again.

Sleeping Through the Night

Kids wake up and call out in the middle of the night for different reasons. Read through this section and decide which approach is best to help your little one sleep all the way until morning.

Make sure that you have read all of the information in the Healthy Sleep Habits section of this chapter. Your child's environment and sleep associations are key to sleeping through the night. Review the sleep associations on page 182 to make sure your child isn't waking up at night because she can't pull up her own covers, she can't reach her sippy cup, or her room looks different in the middle of the night than it does at bedtime. For example, if your child wakes up in the night calling for you and asking for you to retuck her covers or find her stuffed animal, practice having her tuck her own covers and locate her animals on her own during the day. Talk this through with her to review *exactly what she will do in the night* now, instead of calling to you for help. Encourage her, stay positive, and acknowledge any accomplishments (however small) the next day.

Julie: The moms in my toddler groups over the years have come up with creative solutions to the "tucking" dilemma and other sleep associations. Some have described teaching their child to sit up, find the edge of their blanket, and then pull it over them as they lie down. Others will hang a blanket over the crib or bed rail so that their child can easily pull it over them during the night. Many will tuck a sippy cup into the corner of the crib or on a nightstand so that it can be easily reached. Once mom described how, during the day, her child loved to pretend to be a little kitty, getting ready for bed and making sure that all of his "stuff" was handy!

If your child is waking up too early in the morning, read "Waking Up Too Early" on page 224.

If your child wakes up afraid after a nightmare, you always want to go to her right away. See page 234 for how to help your child with nightmares.

If you've adopted all of the Healthy Sleep Habits, addressed any unhelpful sleep associations, and your child is not having a nightmare, you can now use the Sleep Wave (page 209) for night wakings. The key to using the Sleep Wave for night wakings is to go immediately back to the predictable pattern of the 5-minute checks and resist changing it up. The steps will be exactly the same. Staying consistent can be extra challenging in the middle of the night, when you're groggy. But resist the easy way out (lying down with your child or bringing her into your bed), as this will make it harder, in the long run, for your child to sleep continuously in her own bed.

If your approach at bedtime was sitting just outside the door in the dark hallway (if you're not using a gate or a closed door), you'll have to do this again during night wakings.

Remember that the Sleep Wave works when you keep the pattern of your response *exactly* the same, and that applies to bedtime, middle of the night, and naptime. If you keep it 100 percent consistent, your child will detect the pattern and shift more easily to self-soothing to sleep.

Waking Up Too Early

Do you hear "Mama!" or feel someone tugging on your blankets before the sun comes up in the morning? Early waking is a really common sleep pattern for young kids. In contrast to the first half of the night, in which your child has more deep sleep, in the last part of the night he experiences more light sleep. At this point, he's more easily awakened and also isn't as tired as he was earlier in the night— making it harder to fall back to sleep.

We've met families in which the child wakes up at 5:00 a.m., climbs into bed with parents, and everyone falls back to sleep until their regular wake-up time. If this is the case in your house and the whole family is sleeping well, then there's no problem! But often an early riser makes for shortened sleep for at least one person because he or she cannot fall back to sleep, or sleeps restlessly after the early riser wakes up. If this is the case for you, you can work with this pattern and shift your child's wake-up time.

To do this, it helps to keep his environment completely dark and quiet until it's time to get up. The body's internal clock uses light cues (both sunlight and home lights) and, to a lesser degree, things like social interaction and eating, to help it know when it's time to wake up. Your goal is to save all of these sources of stimulation until after your designated wake-up time, and to have a very clear boundary that keeps your child from eating, playing, social interaction, or, most important, being exposed to light until that designated time. If you are very consistent with this, your child's body will eventually adjust.

This can take weeks, so do not give up! Shifting wake-up time is one of the hardest parts of working on sleep. Expect this process to take some time. We know it can be frustrating, but it's worth it for the eventual payoff of waking up at the proper hour.

HERE'S HOW TO HELP THE EARLY RISER:

- Don't shift your child's bedtime later, because this can backfire and cause him to wake up even earlier. A good bedtime for a 2-to-6-year-old is still 7:00 or 7:30 p.m. (depending on his nap schedule). It often helps a child to sleep later in the morning if he is put to bed a little *earlier* (try about 30 minutes earlier). Make sure your child is napping well, too. It seems counterintuitive, but a well-rested child is less likely to be restless in the early hours.

- Make sure that your child's room has blackout shades or curtains so that no morning light creeps in to signal him to wake up—not even a sliver!

- If your child can read numbers, have a clock in his room

that he can see from his bed. Let him know that when the clock says "6:30 a.m." he can get out of bed. If he cannot read time, you can buy a nightlight that works on a timer and changes colors or symbols at the designated time.

- *Talk to your child* about how before the designated wake-up time, he will be in charge of his own "stuff," which means he can take his own sips of water from a sippy cup by the bed, pull up his covers, hug his stuffed animals—you will not be coming in to do these things for him until it's wake-up time.

- Practice anything your child cannot do (such as pulling up covers or drinking water) during the day or before bed so he has a rehearsal.

- When your child does stay in bed until wake-up time, acknowledge his progress. "Hey, you stayed in bed this morning like your plan says!"

- If your child cries for more than 5 minutes or pops out of bed, go right into your Sleep Wave method until wake-up time, walking him back to bed or doing your checks if he's still in a crib.

- Be precise about the wake-up time. If you decide that wake-up is 6:00 a.m., don't go into your child's room (except for 5-minute checks if he's crying) until the stroke of six.

- Once the wake-up time has arrived, if your child is still awake, walk into his room and greet him, say good morning, and open the blinds to let his internal clock know that it's now daytime. It's okay if your child hasn't fallen back to sleep at this point—you are still helping to shift his internal clock. If he's still asleep at the wake-up time, let him be. It's best to let him wake up naturally.

Naps

Most children need to nap until they are at least 3 or 4 years old; until this age, naps are still a critical way for your child's mind and body to refresh. Before this age, if your child goes the whole day without sleeping, stress chemicals continue to rise in his body. He's no longer optimally alert, so he doesn't learn as well and he can become irritable, inflexible, and less creative. Most 2-year-olds do well with a nap around 12:00 or 12:30 p.m. (assuming they wake up in the morning around 6:30 a.m.), and this time can gradually move back to 1:00 p.m. by the time the child is around 3 or 4 years old. See nap schedule examples on pages 313–4.

Dropping the Nap

Here's how you'll know your child might be ready to stop napping:

- **He's between 3 and 5 years old.**

- **He lies awake at naptime for one to two weeks in a row.**
  Note: This doesn't mean that your child simply resists lying down to take a nap. It means that he is lying down and rest-

ing, but he does not fall asleep. Naptime resistance (protesting getting into bed for a nap in the first place) is common and doesn't necessarily signal that your child doesn't need a nap.

- **On the days that he does nap, bedtime has started to be a big issue.** Your child either resists bedtime or gets into bed but doesn't fall asleep until 8:30 or 9:00 p.m. In this case, if your child stops napping, he might be able to fall asleep at 7:00 p.m. and get the same amount of sleep overall as he did when he napped.

- **If your child is in day care or preschool, he doesn't nap there either.** If your child does nap at child care but not at home, that's a sign that he probably should nap at home, too.

Nap Resistance

Around age 2, many little ones start protesting taking a nap. Your child might cry and yell for you, or simply roll around in the crib or bed, sit up and talk to himself, sing, or play with his blankie—anything but sleep. If he is simply hanging out in the crib or bed, that's okay. There's no reason to do anything, and you can let him lie down or play quietly for an hour. This is still a rest time for his brain and body, and it's important to keep this routine and pattern in place and allow him the space and time to sleep when he's ready again—maybe tomorrow, or maybe two weeks from now. If you hold the naptime in place, your toddler will most likely come around to sleeping again.

Keep naptime consistent. If your child's naptime moves around every day, it's not enlisting the forces of his circadian rhythms, which crave regularity. Just as with bedtime routines, your naptime routine should be clear every day—just a shortened version of your bedtime routine. Remember that anything can be part of your routine as long as it helps your toddler to wind down. Be sure to keep the routine the same every day. A toddler's nap routine might be:

Reading a few books

Changing diaper or using the potty

Turning down the lights

Singing one song

JONAH'S TEMPORARY "NAP STRIKE"

Andrea: Because of the Sleep Wave, Jonah was an incredibly good sleeper/napper. But then, around 2, he just stopped napping. I knew this couldn't be a good thing for him, or for me. I believed that napping was vital to him being the happy, easygoing kid that he was. Julie advised that this "nap strike" was completely normal and, most important, temporary, and that I should continue his nap routine, even if he didn't sleep. For one week—no naps, and then as quickly as they had ended, they started again. And he napped beautifully until 4 years old. I'm so glad I had this info and encouragement, because so many of my mom friends mistakenly dropped their child's nap at this point, when their kid was just taking a little nap hiatus.

230 · The Happy Sleeper

If the Reverse Sleep Wave is working for your little one at bed-time, start by trying to use it at naptime as well. However, if your toddler truly begins to cry after getting in her crib or bed for nap, do your Sleep Wave checks for naptime. The form these checks take will depend on if your child is in a crib or bed, and what she does when you leave the room, so read the Sleep Wave section to decide on your plan. If your toddler continues to cry or protest for 30 to 45 minutes or so after you put her down, you can go into her room and say, "Okay, naptime is over," get her up, and try again tomorrow. Remember that most children are at least 3 or 4 before they truly don't need to nap, so don't take your child's protesting at naptime as evidence that she doesn't need to sleep until she's at least this age and also meets the above criteria for dropping her nap.

Even after your child stops falling asleep at naptime, it's good to keep a regular "rest time" to unwind and relax. Kids are active and constantly stimulated during the day, so having a rest time allows them a quiet and peaceful break. This means that if your child has stopped falling asleep and you're quite certain that she's no longer going to take a nap, you'll still lower the lights, do your naptime routine, and allow her time in her bed with a few books. You might even set a timer for 30 to 40 minutes of rest time.

As children near the end of the napping age, they often start falling asleep later and later in the evening (maybe 8:00 p.m. or later). However, once you know that your child is no longer falling asleep at naptime, you'll want to move his bedtime earlier again, as early as 7:00 p.m. In fact, when your child stops napping, you may find that he sleeps virtually the same amount in a 24-hour period—it's just that it's all nighttime sleep now.

Moving from Crib to Big Bed

When to Move from Crib to Bed

The age at which parents move their little one from the safety and limits of a crib to a toddler or twin bed varies. Some little mini gymnasts can launch themselves from the crib at an early age and take us by surprise. Other toddlers stay happily in their cribs until age 3 or even older.

Moving to a bed is an exciting transition for both parents and kids, but we recommend that you don't jump into it too soon. Most children make the move at around age 2½ or 3 (although some make the move earlier if they start climbing out of their cribs). By age 3, kids are more likely to have the necessary impulse control and understand the concept of staying in bed all night. As a general rule, if your toddler is sleeping well in her crib, don't fix something that isn't broken! We know a lot of parents who moved a 2-year-old to the big bed only to have a little escape artist a few months down the road.

That said, safety is always number one, so if you even suspect that your child is close to climbing out, it's a very good idea to either move her immediately (depending on her age) or, if she's still under 2 years old, make sure the mattress is at the lowest level and try putting cushions (couch cushions work well) around her crib at night, just in case.

How to Move from Crib to Bed

When you first move your child to a bed, to prevent her from rolling out, you can use a crib that converts to a toddler bed, a twin bed against the wall with a railing on the outside, or a mattress on the floor (you can always add the frame later on if you're using a twin mattress).

If you haven't already, be sure that the room is 100 percent child-proof before getting the new bed. Find a way to make the new bed feel cozy with sides, similar to the crib. You can use bed rails, pillows, or rows of stuffed animals. Expect the transition to take a week or two for most toddlers. It's a big change!

- Keep the transition clear by removing the crib from your child's room. We know quite a few toddlers who struggled with this transition because their crib was in sight and they felt quite torn, understandably.

CRIB-BED CONFUSION

Bronwyn: Our 2-year-old, Henry, had been happy in his big-boy bed for about a month when all of a sudden he was all tears and panic over bedtime. Henry was asking to return to his old crib, still assembled in his bedroom. My husband and I thought that we were empowering Henry by allowing him the choice of whether or not to return to his crib. In the end, letting him choose where to sleep was too heavy a responsibility—he needed to be confident that his parents were in charge. Henry said good-bye to his crib,

briefly mourned his loss, and from then on we no longer had the
drama connected to his new bed.

- If possible, put the new bed in the same spot as the crib. Keep some familiar blankets and bedding from the crib.

- Prepare your child for the move by rehearsing with her stuffed animals, during daytime play, what it will look like. Have the animals go through the bedtime routine and sing the songs. Let her lead this play if she will—it will help her to feel in charge. If you're using the Reverse Sleep Wave, this is a good time to rehearse how it will go.

- Keep your bedtime routine consistent and include a new book about transitioning to the big bed. You could buy one or make a simple one.

- Help your child relate to this transition by pointing out children he knows who have moved to a big bed. Ask his grandparents to tell him about when you moved to a big bed or tell him yourself.

- If you're moving your toddler to a bed in preparation for a new baby, be sure to do so at least several months in advance so he doesn't feel that the baby has taken his place.

Some kids take to this new arrangement very well. Others have a honeymoon period of excitement, in which they stay in their bed beautifully, but after the novelty has worn off, they start getting up at bedtime or in the middle of the night.

The first night that your child starts sleeping in the big bed, use the Reverse Sleep Wave (page 205) to help him adjust; you can keep these 5-minute check-ons in place for months, or years. As long as the checks are short and sweet, they are a nice way for your older child to transition to sleep.

If your little one is having a hard time with the freedom of the bed and keeps popping up, it can be helpful to install a sturdy baby gate for safety and to create the feeling of an expanded crib. If your child is a climber, get one that either has vertical slats or has a flat surface (the goal is that there is nowhere for a foothold). In this case, once you've gotten her comfortable in her new bed, you can use the Reverse Sleep Wave or the regular Sleep Wave to help her learn the pattern of sleeping all night in this exciting, wide-open sleep space.

Nightmares and Night Terrors

Nightmares

Nightmares are normal and common for little kids. In the preschool years, bad dreams begin (or become obvious to parents) because:

1. Kids have advancing cognitive skills and powers of imagination.

2. It's still hard for little kids to distinguish reality from fantasy, so dreams can feel very real.

3. Little kids have language and can tell us about their bad dreams.

4. Kids know that bad things can happen. As children get older, they're exposed to ideas and stories that let them know that bad events are possible. This is why many kids have anxious dreams about being left or not being able to find Mom or Dad.

Having scary dreams is a fact of life for many little ones—it's not realistic to expect them to go away completely. Your goal as a parent is to help soothe your child and calm her down after a nightmare, while also helping her feel comfortable and confident in her room and stay in charge of self-soothing back to sleep.

Respond and Soothe

If your child cries and is afraid after a nightmare, go to her and do whatever is needed to calm her down. Some kids just need your presence beside them and a stroke on the back, whereas others might need you to pick them up and hold them until they're calm. (Don't add a feeding of milk at night to comfort your child, though, as she doesn't need this soothing association in the middle of the night. If she needs a drink, put a sippy cup of water next to her bed at bedtime.) Let your child know that you're right there and that she's in her room with all the same toys, books, animals, and so forth that she always has during the day. Dreams can feel very real (you probably know this from your own experience), and especially for young kids. In fact, your child may *insist* that something bad truly happened and it wasn't a dream. In this case, just let her tell the story and express her feelings, rather than trying to convince her it didn't really happen. Remind her of where she is and that everything is okay.

Talk About Bad Dream Strategies

During the day or at bedtime, talk to your child about ways that she can comfort herself and feel better after a nightmare. The point of these techniques is to empower your child. You want her to feel confident and in charge of her fears as much as possible. There are lots of choices here, so try a few to see what works or create your own. For example:

- At bedtime, give her stuffed animal "extra hugs and kisses" that she can access on her own after bedtime, anytime she needs them. Say this clearly as part of bedtime routine, for example: *I'm giving teddy 10 kisses that are just for you, if you need them tonight.*

- Tell your child that flipping her body to the other side or flipping the pillow over will "change the channel" on the bad dream. If she doesn't like the dream she's having, she can use this technique to change it. This gives her a concrete way to feel in control.

- During the day have your child practice closing her eyes and imagining a happy or comforting image or story. You can talk about replacing bad thoughts with good ones, or coach her in how to envision a good story in her mind while falling asleep or after a bad dream.

- Initially, when you teach your child to flip her body, her channel, or replace bad dreams with good ones, she might say, "It doesn't work! The bad stories just come back!" Respond with something like, "That's okay. It takes practice. It's okay to have scary thoughts. Just say 'no thanks' to them and move your mind to a different story." Help her come up with a few good stories, like thinking about a holiday or a fun family trip.

· Some people use a dream catcher (a special object in the bedroom meant to ward off bad dreams) to help their child feel comfortable falling asleep. Attach the dream catcher somewhere close to the bed, but don't have it loose in the bed (you want it to be reassuring, but not something your child can lose or has to fuss with).

DASHIELL'S BAD-DREAM TECHNIQUE

Heather: When my son Dashiell was 5, he was having occasional nightmares. I taught him how to flip his body over to feel better, but he came up with his own technique, which he told me about one morning: "Instead of flipping the pillow or your body, you have to think about flipping your mind. Sometimes flipping things outside your body doesn't work. But when you flip objects inside your body and in your brain, it could help. Like if I had a bad dream it would be pointing toward me, and the good dream is pointing to the room. You think, think, think and then you can flip your mind around so the good dream is toward you now." He also told me that this technique works for "small or medium" bad dreams. For large bad dreams, he needs Mom or Dad.

Help Your Child Feel Comfortable in Her Room

Spend a little time in the dark in your child's room, talking about how shadows are created, what light and dark really are, playing with light sticks or flashlights, and pointing out how the objects in her room are the same even when it's nighttime. Make sure she has a lovey or stuffed animal she likes. Try using a nightlight to see if this helps with fears of the dark, although some children feel more afraid when they wake up and see the dark objects and shadows that are created by nightlights. Find what works best.

If your child is afraid of the dark, let her simply express these fears and be curious about them, rather than just telling her there's nothing to be afraid of. For example, if your child says there's a monster in the closet, start by asking her to tell you what it looks like, sounds like, and does. Ask her what she thinks about this monster. Once you've listened to her answers or gleaned them from her manner and expression, empathize. Let her know you understand how she feels and that you remember feeling like that when you were her age. When you've acknowledged her fear, you can tell her that monsters aren't real but only exist in our imaginations, like dogs who can talk or teapots that sing. Some children will show you exactly how they need to process their fears by becoming somewhat fascinated by things like monsters and wanting to read books or look at pictures of them and talk about them a lot, usually with Mom or Dad right there for protection! This "leaning in" to what they're afraid of helps them to tame their fears by naming them and getting to know them better. Our tendency as parents is to immediately distract or dismiss fears, but that rarely helps kids to move forward.

GETTING COMFORTABLE IN THE DARK

Ali: When my girls Cienna and Rylee were almost 3, there was a period when they were afraid of the dark. I filled a box with glow-in-the-dark toys, flashlights, glow-stick jewelry, and glow-in-the-dark books and stickers. We'd have glow-in-the-dark parties, playing with all of these toys. We also would play with the flashlights and make shadows on the wall. This helped them to understand the concept of shadows and eliminated their fear of shadows. Our girls got to a place where they were excited to turn off the lights and were no longer afraid of the dark.

Return to Your Bed

It's very tempting to stay in your child's room until she's fully asleep or bring her into your room after a nightmare. There's nothing wrong with doing this occasionally, but if it becomes a habit, *you are way more likely to start hearing from your child every night.* This isn't good for her sleep, or yours. Comfort your child until you can see that she's calm, remind her that you're down the hall, review her self-soothing strategies, and gently walk out of the room. Most children return to sleep after this, especially if they know that you sleeping with them, or climbing in bed with you, is not an option.

If your child says she will not stay in bed, cries when you leave, or climbs out of bed to follow, tell her that you'll check on her in 5 minutes and use your Reverse Sleep Wave to do so. Make sure to review all of your strategies for calming down after a bad dream with her, both during the day and at night.

Process the Fears

You can talk about fears of the dark and bad dreams during the day. Just keep in mind that although dreams can feel very intense, they can also slip from memory very quickly (think about how infrequently you remember your own dreams). If your child is willing to talk about or draw pictures of dreams during the day, that's great (you could open the conversation by talking about your own dreams, too, kids love to hear us talk about our experiences). But if she doesn't remember or doesn't want to talk about it, don't press. Just review soothing strategies before bed again that night.

Avoid Scary TV Shows and Movies

We live in a world where scary media is absolutely everywhere, even often in the middle of a children's film. Little children should never watch truly scary shows or movies, despite how common they are. Also, if your child is scared of a scene or portion of a movie or show, respect his fear and fast-forward or help him leave the room during the scary part. Little kids are too young to grasp the difference between made-up scary and real scary. These images and themes can definitely contribute to nightmares.

Night Terrors

Night terrors are different from nightmares. A *nightmare* is a scary dream that typically happens during REM (rapid eye movement) sleep, and often during the last half of the night (when the most REM sleep occurs). During a nightmare, your child can wake up, cry, call for you, be afraid, and tell you what happened in the dream or why she's upset. After some time, with your comfort, your child calms down. Kids often remember the event the next morning (even if they don't remember the dream itself).

Night terrors (also called confusional arousals or sleep terrors) are periods in which your child cries, whines, yells, and can move around in her bed, even with her eyes open, but she is not fully awake. Night terrors can be very disturbing for parents because a child having a night terror seems incredibly upset and fearful, but is inconsolable and doesn't wake up. This can last a few minutes or sometimes a longer period, after which the child often goes back to sleep without ever fully waking up at all. Even if your child does wake up, she probably won't remember the episode in the morning.

Night terrors happen in the transition out of deep sleep (non-REM sleep) and usually at the end of the child's first sleep cycle—that is, in the first couple of hours after bedtime. Since a night terror doesn't occur in REM sleep, it's not a bad dream; it's more like your child is in a dissociated state, caught between a deep sleep and wakefulness. In fact, brain activity during a night terror suggests that the brain is in different states of waking and sleeping simultaneously.

It can be really upsetting to see your child having a night terror, especially if you don't know what's happening. Your instinct is to hug, hold, or try to wake your child up. This usually doesn't work, though (in fact, you might find it makes it worse). If that's the case, just sit next to your child, stay with him through the episode, and make sure he doesn't hurt himself, for example, by falling out of bed.

Generally night terrors aren't something to worry about. They're thought to have a genetic component, so they can run in families.

Sleep deprivation or irregular sleeping schedules may also trigger episodes of night terrors in kids who are predisposed. Sleep apnea (a disorder in which obstructed breathing causes a person to wake up briefly but repeatedly throughout the night) can also be a trigger for night terrors. Night terrors usually resolve on their own, but it's a good idea to mention them to your pediatrician if they happen frequently.

NIGHTMARES	NIGHT TERRORS
Last half of the night	First half of the night
Occur in REM sleep	Occur in non-REM (deep) sleep
Child is awake	Child isn't fully awake
Child can usually be calmed down	Child can't be consoled
Child usually remembers the next morning	Child doesn't remember the episode

Bumps in the Road for Toddlers

Life will sometimes throw your child's sleep off course for a bit. As you read through this section, notice these four steps emerging as a common theme when dealing with sleep regression or, ideally, heading it off before it begins.

1. Prepare your child for the change.

2. Only tackle one big change at a time (if you can help it).

3. Add 10 to 15 minutes to your calming bedtime routine.

4. Your child needs you to hold on to the steps of the Sleep Wave.

Starting a New School

This can be a big transition for many kids and can temporarily affect their sleep. Do all that you can to ease the transition for your child. Visit her school with her so that she grows accustomed to the new people and setting. Playact "schooltime" at home with her stuffed animals. Make her a personalized little book (or use a website where they make it for you) describing her new schedule and activities and, most important, make sure to have her connect with a particular teacher or classmate at the school. Don't plan to make any big changes in sleep or anything else while she is transitioning to school.

She may need 15 to 20 minutes of extra book and cuddle time during your bedtime routine for a week or two as she copes with all the change, so start a little earlier than usual. You can include a book about starting school, tell her stories about when you experienced the same thing, or discuss her ups and downs from the day. You may also find her taking a little longer to fall asleep, or waking more often at night. This is normal and temporary. Stick to your Sleep Wave strategies, do your 5-minute checks if she's crying, and she will be back on track before you know it. It's common for parents to revert to lying down with their child until she is asleep or bringing her into the parents' bed, but resist doing either of these. What your child needs from you during a big change is to hold on to the predict-able structure of how bedtime unfolds. The undoing of them can be daunting and the lack of sleep that comes as a result will make it even harder for your child to adapt to her new school.

New Baby on the Way

No doubt this is one of the most significant transitions for your child. Imagine that your spouse came home one day and you introduced him to your new second husband (or wife) and told him he would love this new mate of yours and to play nicely with him! Not easy for many little ones to adapt smoothly. Create a photo book for your child about his own birth and infanthood, put some of his baby photos around the house where he can see them, get a realistic baby doll and show him how you took care of him, read lots of books about what a new baby is like, and share the plan with him for what will happen when the birth takes place (let him choose some elements of the plan, like which pjs or books to pack for the new baby, as well as for his routine at home). You get the idea—there's much you can do to prepare and you will tailor it for your child's age and personality.

Read Chapter 6 for bedtime routines and tips with multiple children.

Steps 2, 3, and 4 are essentially identical to the way you would approach starting a new school, above.

HELPING A TODDLER ADJUST TO NEW BABY

Jennifer: Thanks to the Sleep Wave, Morton had been sleeping 10 to 11 hours through the night since he was 4 months old. He was 12 months old when we brought home baby Mack. Starting the first night his brother was at home, Morton began waking at 2:00 a.m. with screams and crying that lasted 2 to 3 hours. This went on for five to six weeks. We started spending extra quality time with Morton, and I also spent an extra 5 to 10 minutes with him in his room just before helping him into his crib. It helped us all and put a stop to the early morning waking.

Moving

Moving can be exciting, but it is also a stressful time for the whole family. Preparing your child will include maintaining as much familiarity as possible, while helping her adapt to all of the inevitable new stuff. Visit the new home a few times, if possible, and spend some fun time playing there. Make her a book about moving day, with photos of her old and new home and room. Talk about how it may feel to move and how you will feel sad to say good-bye to the old home. Let her know that it's normal to miss the old and feel excited about the new at the same time. Pack a special moving carton for her (have her help if she's old enough) with everything she'll need and want right away. This may include her bedding, curtains, pjs, favorite toys and stuffed animals, special books, and anything else in her bedroom that will make the new room feel familiar. Let her witness a bit of the move (when the truck arrives and a few minutes of the move on both ends), but, if possible, have someone care for her during the bulk of the move. When she arrives at the new home, either have her room already set up or, if she's old enough, have her help a bit. Spend some time playing and lounging in her new room so it begins to feel comfy and familiar to her. If she is sad or cries about missing her old home, empathize and let her know it's normal to feel this way.

Again, steps 2, 3, and 4 are essentially identical to the above scenarios. You'll find a way to tailor them to your family's unique needs.

Company in the House

How fun to have Grandma and Grandpa or a favorite bunch of cousins come to visit! But where will everyone sleep and what will this mean for all of your meticulous work on bedtime, consistency, and structure? Preparing for company will depend on many things, including your space, your child's temperament (flexibility), and what activities you'll all be doing. It's good for kids to flex and adapt to change, within reason. This may mean having cousins sleep in their room with them or moving their crib to an office or hallway so someone can use their room. Try to choose the plan with as little disruption as possible and, above all, avoid resorting to the most difficult sleep associations to undo, such as lying down with your child until she falls asleep. If the best sleeping arrangements are for your child to sleep in your bed, tell her that this is a special time, mark how many days it will be on the calendar, and count down those days until the transition back to normal sleep (in her own bed). If your child has a history of difficulty sleeping on her own, it's a good idea to avoid bringing her into your bed at all; in this case, find another setup so that it doesn't confuse her and make her sleep regress. Try to minimize disruptions in routines and bedtimes. Your visitors can take part in reading books and singing songs, and once your little one is sleeping, you can enjoy some grown-up conversation. Many parents love the idea of holding the naptime structure, as this also gives them a chance to bow out for a little break and rest.

Review steps 2 to 4 above for adjusting back to your normal routine after your company has departed.

☆ TROUBLESHOOTING ☆

My child is potty training. What should I do for sleep?

Wily little toddlers, how well they can sense a chink in our armor! Many parents have told us that while they can set limits on more sips of water or just one more book or song, when it comes to "I gotta go potty," all of their resolve goes out the window and bedtime often extends into an endless parade of trips to the potty.

For most children, including the last trip to the potty as part of the "last call for stuff" is the most effective approach to a smooth bedtime. After "last call," on goes the pull-up diaper and into bed until morning. Once your child is reliably waking up dry in the morning (make a pee trip first thing), you can move to cotton training pants (with a plastic cover and/or waterproof pad on the bed as well) and eventually to big girl or boy underpants. It's perfectly fine to have your child wearing underwear and using the potty during the day, but wearing a diaper or pull-up at night until he reliably wakes up dry (that could be a year or more later than when he finishes daytime potty training).

Occasionally we hear of a child who is allowed to get up during the evening or night to potty and does just fine, going right back to sleep. Other parents wake their child up to use the potty right before they themselves go to bed at 10:00 or 11:00 p.m. If either of these approaches works, without disrupting or decreasing sleep for anyone, it's perfectly fine. However, in our experience most toddlers and young children don't fit this description and will either get up over and over at bedtime or be incredibly unhappy if we try to wake them to use the potty in the middle of the night.

My child climbed out of the crib. What do I do?

Read "Moving from Crib to Big Bed" on page 230.

My child was sleeping well and now he's not. What do I do?

It is indeed shocking how quickly your toddler and older child's good sleep patterns can be thrown off course. For example, you take a trip where the family is all sleeping in the same room, in a different time zone, or in a place where any crying would disrupt others (or all three!); your little one gets sick and then has a hard time going back to the usual sleep pattern; a nightmare interrupts your toddler's sleep and you bring her into your bed; or any significant transition happens, like a new caretaker, parents separate or divorce, company comes to visit, child spends the night with grandparents, and so forth. After any of these common life events, your child may very well develop a new set of unhelpful sleep associations.

The two most common unhelpful sleep associations are the parent lying down in the child's room until she falls asleep, and bringing the child into the parents' bed to sleep.

Do your best during any of the above disruptions to not regress any more than absolutely necessary. Unhelpful sleep associations develop almost instantly for little kids. Knowing this will motivate you to avoid them if possible.

The less you resort to overhelping, the easier to get back on track once the disruption is over. If you have regressed all the way to the point where your child now expects you to either stay in her room until she falls asleep or bring her into your bed at any point during the night, don't worry. Go back to the Sleep Wave and Reverse Sleep Wave, and recommit to the consistent plan.

My child comes into our bed at 5:00 a.m. every morning. Is that a problem?

We always say that there is no one right way to sleep. Ask yourself, (1) Is everyone sleeping well? and (2) Is everyone okay with this plan? Is it working for the family?

If the answers are yes, than you don't need to change a thing. Some families sleep a full night with their kids coming into bed early in the morning because both kids and grown-ups easily fall back to sleep (or, even better, parents never wake up to begin with). If your child comes into your bed, and you are sleeping 7 to 8 hours and your child is sleeping 11 (or his full sleep requirement), you're good to go. If your early morning bed companion disrupts sleep for one or more in the family, then review the "waking too early" steps on page 224.

Will one night in our bed set us back in terms of good sleep habits?

This really depends on your child. Some kids can sleep in their parents' bed (when traveling, if having a nightmare, or with visitors in the house) and then go straight back to sleeping in their own room. It's best to be consistent during a period when you're *changing* a sleep pattern and establishing independent sleep. After this, lots of families enjoy cuddling up together (although the proclivity for rolling and perpendicular sleeping make kids not the best bed partners).

My child will only nap in her stroller. Is that okay?

It's not likely that your child will sleep as long or have as good-quality sleep in her stroller or car seat as she would in her bed. Review the section on naps and use the Sleep Wave checks to respond to her if she cries when you put her down for a nap. Remember that a consistent nap schedule and short nap routine are important to help prepare and cue your child's body for sleep.

Should we take the paci away from our 2½-year-old daughter? My dentist says we should but it really helps her sleep.

It's true that by this age, ending paci use is best for your child's teeth. The good news is that your child needs the paci for sleep less than you think. She's "used to" having it but doesn't really "need" it. Choose a day when you pack up all the pacis to "send them to a younger baby." Empathize that saying good-bye to them is hard and help her choose a new stuffed animal or cozy pj's to add to her self-soothing repertoire. You may have a few bumpy nights, but stick to your sleep plan and she will adapt.

6.

Special Circumstances

Co-Sleeping and Bed Sharing

The term "co-sleeping" means to sleep in close proximity to your baby—either in a co-sleeper, bassinet, or crib in your bedroom. Having your baby in close proximity is the American Academy of Pediatrics recommended way for your newborn to sleep.

"Bed sharing" or having a "family bed" means that you share a sleep surface with your baby or child. Interestingly, most families don't identify themselves as bed sharing, but in our experience (and research backs us up here), having baby in bed with parents is incredibly common. So many families do it, but people don't usually talk about it. This is probably because advice on bed sharing tends to be polarized—either being fully supported and endorsed as the best practice, or presented as an unsafe "no-no."

Here we'll offer you a reasonable, well-rounded look at the question of bed sharing and either help you do it in the safest, most sleep-conducive way, or figure out how to transition to independent sleep if you wish.

BABIES SLEEP WITH THEIR PARENTS FOR DIFFERENT REASONS:

- Parents plan to share a bed with their baby for an extended period of time, or as long as everyone is getting enough sleep.

- Parents plan to share a bed for the first 3 to 4 months or so, and then move baby into her own crib and room.

- Parents plan to put baby down in her crib, in her own room at bedtime and then bring her into the parents' bed during the night. An older child might move himself to the parents' room in the middle of the night or early morning and finish sleeping there.

- Parents don't have a clear plan but find themselves bringing their baby or older child into their bed because nothing else seems to be working.

In the first three scenarios, parents are making the choice to share a bed, while in the last scenario bed sharing is a reaction to a sleep issue.

When people ask for our advice on their sleep arrangements, we start by asking two questions: (1) Is everyone sleeping well, including both parents and baby? and (2) Is everyone in the family happy with the arrangement? If the answer to both is *yes*, there's no reason to change a thing, as long as all safety rules are being carefully followed. Especially in the newborn months, having your baby in the bed can be convenient for feeding and actually help everyone sleep (and let's face it, some babies are like heat-seeking missiles bent on proximity). There are valid concerns and downsides to sharing a sleep surface with your child, though. Here is an overview of the pros and cons to sharing a bed.

THE BENEFITS OF HAVING BABY IN YOUR BED:

- **Breast-feeding:** More frequent arousals (see below), Mom's smell, and close proximity mean that nursing gets a boost when Mom and baby are sleeping together. Sharing a bed or having your baby in a co-sleeper also means that you don't have to get out of bed to nurse your baby throughout the night.

- **Physiological benefits:** Some studies have shown that Mom and baby sleep is altered slightly when sleeping in close proximity. For example, babies have less deep sleep and more frequent arousals when they're close to Mom—both of which may be protective against SIDS.

- **Bonding:** Having baby next to you feels good to some parents, especially those who may not feel like they have enough time with their baby during the day.

- **It's not forever:** Whether or not your baby tucks in with you in the first months of life doesn't mean anything about her future sleep habits. If bed sharing works for you, don't worry that you'll be sleeping with your elementary schooler. It's true that changing a sleep pattern can take work, especially if your child is older and more aware, but if you're consistent, you can absolutely do it.

BENEFITS OF BABY SLEEPING ON HER OWN:

- **Safety:** The biggest consideration when it comes to sharing a bed is your baby's safety, which is why the American Academy of Pediatrics recommends sharing a room with your newborn, but not a sleep surface. In our experience, many people who don't plan to have their baby in bed end up this way unintentionally—and these families are less likely to fully research or understand the safety information for bed sharing (whereas people who plan to share a bed often investigate this topic in preparation). If you are bed sharing (whether you mean to or not!), it's very important to read all of the current safety information very thoroughly and follow all recommendations. See resources in the citations at the end of the book. These are a good place to start your research.

- **Parents' sleep quality**: Your baby spends less time in deep sleep when you're right next to her, and you might, too. Some parents (especially moms) don't sleep as soundly with baby nearby, and babies can be noisy! If this is the case, you might decide to move your baby to another sleep surface in the same room, or transition her to another room when you're ready. Your sleep and your partner's are very important.

- **Grown-up time**: If you're sleeping with your baby, will you and your partner have alone time in the evenings? It can be hard to foster self-soothing in a baby who is sharing a bed, so many parents start to either keep baby up until they go to bed, or lie down with their child until she's asleep (dozing off themselves in the process). Having grown-up time at night is a good idea, so you might consider putting your baby down in a crib for the first portion of the evening and bringing her into your bed if she wakes up in the middle of the night.

Many parents worry that if they share a bed with their baby, the baby will have a hard time learning to sleep independently. It's true that your older baby or toddler might have feelings about moving to her own bed (or she may welcome the idea—you never know), but as with all aspects of sleep, if you're confident and consistent, she will make the transition just fine.

Improving Sleep When You're Bed Sharing

This section is for families who are choosing to share a bed for all or part of the night.

0 to 4 Months

All of the concepts in Chapter 3 for helping babies move gradually toward self-soothing can also be applied when sharing a bed. For example, to use the Soothing Ladder with your bed-sharing baby, you'll try shushing, patting, jiggling, replacing the pacifier, and other steps on the ladder before picking her up and feeding her when she wakes. In addition, the following strategies for improving self-soothing (which also happen to be the most crucial ones for all little sleepers) apply but need a little more explanation when sharing sleep.

Put Your Baby down Awake

Look for opportunities to practice putting your baby down awake at least once a day. When sharing sleep, this often involves ending a feeding, whether breast or bottle, before baby falls asleep. Watch closely, and when slow swallows turn to quick flutters, take your baby gently off the breast or bottle and let him finish falling asleep. Even if you've been nursing all the way to sleep for a while, you can shift to this approach. When you first do this, it's often necessary to put your baby back on and off the breast or bottle over and over, until he finally falls asleep without it. Each time you try this method, the number of repetitions should decrease. It can be pretty tricky, as it requires you to stay awake and pay attention to the feeding.

Discern Your Baby's Sounds

If baby is fussing, whining, grunting, or squawking, resist the urge to swoop in. Babies can be very noisy on their way to self-soothing. This is especially difficult when the little noisemaker is right there next to you. It's a natural impulse to immediately start patting or shushing. As hard as it is, practice playing possum and see if your baby can fall back to sleep without your help. Every time she does, she is strengthening this ability.

Don't Overhelp

If your baby wakes up at night, be curious about the least intrusive thing you can do to settle her (see "The Soothing Ladder Method," page 62). Resist responding right away and stay curious about what, over time, your baby may be capable of. Last night, he may have needed that pat, pat, pat, whereas tonight he may fall back to sleep without it. Don't let baby cry for long, though. For the first 4 months, we don't recommend letting your baby cry for more than roughly 1 minute.

5 Months to 2 Years

The Sleep Wave, described in Chapter 4, can be applied when your baby is going to sleep in her crib or co-sleeper for naps, at initial bedtime, and during the first stretch of the night, while you're still up and before you bring her into your bed (your baby should not be put to bed alone in your bed). What's harder is keeping the pattern consistent when your baby wakes during the night in bed with you.

You can also choose to use the gradual weaning formula (see page 149), to wean from some or all night feedings. This is challenging with baby in your bed, but it's possible and can improve sleep significantly. If Mom is nursing, it's helpful that she wear a nursing top of some kind, so that the milk supply can be "put away" once the feed is over or once it is completely weaned.

If you continue to bed share once your baby can move around and roll, it's important to ensure that she doesn't fall out of bed, whether you're there in the bed with her or not. Options include bed rails and putting your mattress on the floor with a rug or carpet around the edges. It's also key to never have any crevices where your baby could get trapped, between the bed and the wall, headboard, or anything. Don't use pillows or anything soft to form a barrier to keep your baby from falling out of the bed. Make sure to do your own research and find the best resources for safe bed sharing.

Moving Your Child to Her Own Room

If you decide that you want your baby or child to start sleeping independently, you can make this change by following a consistent plan. Based on your child's age and personality, this process will be different; some will have more trouble getting used to the new setup, while others may even sleep better and welcome the space at night.

Moving a Baby

1. Make sure that you've read the Healthy Sleep Habits section for your baby's age and put these building blocks in place.

2. The first step is to help your baby get comfortable in his room. Spend time playing there and make sure that your

baby is familiar with his room. Ideally, he can even spend a little alone time napping or playing in his crib during the day.

3. Start the move gradually, by putting your baby down for his first stretch of nighttime sleep in his own room. For a week or two, you might decide to bring him into bed after the first waking. Gradually, see if you can put him down again in his crib in the middle of the night, after feeding or soothing him. For a while you may end up with your baby in bed with you by the time morning comes. With this gradual approach, though, your baby is growing familiar with his room and practicing self-soothing. Eventually, you may have to use the Sleep Wave to help your baby over the last hump of sleeping independently.

MOVING LITTLE ROUX TO HER OWN ROOM

Kelly: Sweet, peaceful bed sharing when Roux was a young baby had shifted to sleepless nights for all of us as she became an alert older baby who woke frequently during the night. By the time she was about 6 months, I was bleary-eyed and barely functioning from sleep deprivation. It was time to move her into her own room. I wasn't ready to wean, and I didn't mind having her join us at some point in the night (as we gradually got her used to her own room)—I just wanted her to start by learning how to fall asleep on her own. Establishing that pattern was a big victory. We've all been sleeping better and I still get lots of cuddles in during the day!

Moving a Toddler

If you're moving a toddler or older child into his own room, there are a few options:

1. Make sure you've read the Healthy Sleep Habits section for your child's age and put these building blocks in place.

2. Start by getting your child used to playing and spending time in his bedroom. Create positive associations and maybe even do some shadow play with flashlights or glow sticks in the dark. Make sure to do at least the last several steps of his bedtime routine (child-led play, books, and songs, for example) in his room, while gradually dimming the lights.

3. Try using the Reverse Sleep Wave (page 205) to help your child fall asleep independently in his own room at bedtime—you may be surprised by what he's capable of.

4. The process for moving your toddler can be the same as with a baby: Have your child nap in his own room, or start the night in his own room, and then for a week, transfer him to your bed if he wakes up. This is a better idea than letting your child fall asleep in your bed and then transferring him while asleep (don't bait and switch—your child should go to bed as a conscious participant). After one to two weeks, if your child is still waking up in the night, you can use the Sleep Wave as presented in Chapter 3 or 4 (depending on his age) to help him return to sleep on his own and sleep independently for the full night.

5. Another choice is to gradually wean your child out of your room. This looks much like "The Gradual Parent Wean" (page 220), only *your child* is the one inching out of *your* room. It will work best with a verbal child. Making it very gradual is most effective.

6. Make sure that no matter what approach you choose, you acknowledge your child's progress and new ability. "Hey, you slept in your room last night! How was that?" or say to your partner at breakfast (so your child can hear), "Did you notice that Max fell asleep last night in his room? When I checked in on him, he looked pretty cozy!" Also make sure that your child has a blankie, lovey, or stuffed animal he likes, as well as a quiet, dark, comfortable bedroom.

Daylight Saving Time

Love it or dread it, daylight saving time is one of those facts of life that we have to adjust to. There are different ways to approach daylight saving time.

Jump Right to the New Time

You can have your child simply jump to the new time. This often works just fine for older kids, who might feel a little groggy for a few days while they adjust. If you're doing it this way and the time is *springing forward*, your child may go to bed a little later according to the new time on Sunday night (after the time change) because his body won't yet be tired. Wake your child at his usual waking time on

Monday, according to the new time, so that his body starts the adjustment. That night he will most likely be able to fall asleep at his regular bedtime. If the time is *falling back*, you can just put your child to bed at the time according to the clock on Sunday night and he will most likely be very tired.

Another approach is to anticipate the change and help your baby gradually shift to the new time.

Shifting Your Baby Gradually

(QUICK SUMMARY):

- **Spring forward:** What used to be 6:00 p.m. will now be 7:00 p.m., so your child won't quite be ready for sleep at his usual bedtime. For a few days before the change, adjust sleep times a little *earlier* each day in anticipation.

- **Fall back:** What used to be 8:00 p.m. will now be 7:00 p.m., so your child will be sleepy before it's bedtime. Adjust sleep times a little *later* each day in anticipation.

STEPS FOR SHIFTING YOUR BABY GRADUALLY:

1. **Start by assessing your baby's current sleep schedule** and figuring out what the time change will mean.
   - If your baby's schedule is just where you want it, you'll help her adjust to the new time.
   - If your baby's current schedule is off and the time change will help (for example, it's fall and you want him to go to

bed an hour earlier or it's spring and you want her to go to bed an hour later), you're in luck. You will be able to shift your baby immediately to the new time. It will still be very important to pay attention to blocking out daylight and keeping bedtime and naptime routines consistent.

- If your baby's schedule is off in a direction where the time change will make it even worse, adjust slowly to the new time and then continue gradually until you've reached the desired bedtime. One of the most daunting scenarios is when it's fall and your baby is already waking up way too early in the a.m.

2. **Decide the rate of adjustment** ideal for your individual child. Babies tend to have a harder time with the change, while some older kids can jump to the new time the way we do. If your baby is easygoing and flexible, you can choose the faster (20 minutes per day) adjustment. If your baby is more sensitive to change, you can choose the slower adjustment (10 minutes per day).

SPRING FORWARD

- Depending on the rate of adjustment you've chosen, you can start three, four, or six days before the time change. You will start your bedtime routine and put your baby to sleep 20, 15, or 10 minutes *earlier* each day. You will do the same for naps, if your baby has a nap schedule. If not, continue to use the "span of awake time or 90-minute" method (see page 73) for naps. It will take you three, four, or six days to reach the 1-hour mark, depending on how gradually you shift.

- If your baby hasn't completely adjusted by the time daylight saving time arrives, just continue the adjustment during the next week.

FALL BACK:

- Depending on the rate of adjustment you've chosen, you can start three, four, or six days before the time change. You will start your bedtime routine and put your baby to sleep 20, 15, or 10 minutes *later* each day. It will take you three, four, or six days to reach the 1-hour mark, depending on how gradually you shift.

- If your baby hasn't completely adjusted by the time daylight saving time arrives, just continue the adjustment during the next week.

3. **Remember routines and environment.** Keep bedtime and naptime routines in place and predicable. All that effort and consistency will pay off now, as these cues help your baby adjust to the new time. Also make baby's room very dark. Light creeping in earlier in the morning or lingering into the summer evening can add to baby's challenge to adjust to the new time.

Travel and Time Zone Changes

Generally, it's parents who get anxious about travel and how it will affect baby's sleep. But remember that babies don't know that travel can be stressful—they're just living in the moment and enjoying the new sights. Depending on the age and sensitivity of your little one, in addition to the location and length of your travel, there are many things you can do to smooth the way to optimal sleep during your trip.

Travel and Sleep

- Bring your baby's familiar sheet, lovey, pj's, and anything else that will remind him of his sleep environment at home. This will become more important the older he gets.

- Bring dark trash bags and painter's tape to put over the windows of the place your baby will be sleeping. If you're staying with friends or family, ask your hosts if they have what you need to make the room sleep conducive (dark curtains or blankets to cover windows, or a fan if your baby is used to this), and ideally have this set up before you arrive if you're arriving at night.

- Bring a carrier or sling on board an airplane. Your baby may need you to walk the aisles with her to fall asleep.

- Many parents use a portable crib (Pack 'n Play) as baby's bed away from home. Put it up at home and maybe even use

it once or twice so baby is familiar with this alternate sleep/
play place.

- Find as quiet and dark a spot as you can for baby's sleeping spot. A mom once told us she put her baby's bed in a large closet in her hotel room and her baby slept better than she ever had! You can use a large bathroom as well.

- Do everything possible to maintain your curious stance and give your baby some space, at the same time knowing that it's normal for sleep to regress during travel. Be prepared to put the Sleep Wave back into place, if need be, once you get home. The biggest mistake we see is that the overhelping associations, which began during travel, continue once the family is back home.

- Should you use the Sleep Wave while you're traveling? Use your judgment about this. If you think that your baby or child is familiar enough with the surroundings and her sleeping space (one reason it helps to bring a familiar portable crib, her loveys, and so forth), you can use your 5-minute checks to respond to her if she cries. Just be extra sensitive about this and know that she may need a little warm-up time in the new environment before she can be expected to sleep independently. That might mean playing in the room for a while, doing a rehearsal with stuffed animals, or talking through the routine with your child. If your child is over 2 years old, you may also want to use the Reverse Sleep Wave (page 205).

Time Zone Changes

- **If the trip is under a week**, you may never need to shift your baby or child to the new time. For example, if you're traveling from California to New York, your baby's internal clock will tell her it's her normal 7:00 p.m. bedtime when the New York clock says 10:00 p.m. If that works for you and it's a short trip, you might want to just keep her on that time. Use blankets, blackout fabric, or garbage bags to cover the windows and block early morning light.

- **If the trip is longer, or has a big time zone change**, shift your baby gradually to the new time. Use daylight to stimulate and reset her internal clock. In general, babies adjust at least as quickly as we do to such a significant change, which is about a day for every hour of time difference. Give yourselves time to adjust at the beginning of a big trip and try not to plan major activities right away. As soon as you arrive back home, begin to shift back to your normal schedule.

Multiple Children or Close Living Quarters

Using the Sleep Wave When You Have Multiple Children

If you're using the Sleep Wave and you have multiple kids or limited space in your home, it brings up some logistical issues.

If your children share a room and you want to work on sleep with one or both of them, you can opt to temporarily move one baby or child to a new sleeping space. For example, if you have a 3-year-old and a 7-month-old in a two-bedroom home, you might be wondering how to let your 7-month-old practice falling asleep without disrupting his sibling too much. There are lots of creative solutions to this issue. For example:

- Move your older child into your room temporarily, while you use the Sleep Wave so that baby can learn to fall asleep independently and/or sleep through the night in the kids' room. This could mean moving your child onto a mattress on the floor in your room. Once your baby is sleeping well, move your older child back. Make sure to let her know (and periodically remind her, even estimate it on the calendar!) that this is a temporary adventure and that she'll soon be sleeping in her room again.

- Move your baby somewhere else in the house while you use the Sleep Wave. We've seen families do this in many ways, for example, by converting a walk-in closet (make sure there are no shelves above your baby with items that could fall), using a screen in the parents' bedroom to divide the space, or keeping baby in the hallway or even in a large bathroom temporarily. These options aren't optimal, of course, because your baby is learning to sleep in a different environment than the one she will be in long-term, but it will still help her practice self-soothing, and she will now sleep better when you put the two kids back together.

If you have one child but don't have an extra bedroom, you can also opt to set up another place in the house, such as a large closet or a screen dividing the bedroom or living room, while you're working on sleep (or as a permanent solution—babies don't mind small spaces, as long as they are safe and get enough ventilation). You can also have one or both partners sleep in the living room while implementing the Sleep Wave in your room. Separating baby from parents works well when you're using the Sleep Wave, because by 4 to 5 months most babies are very aware of and activated by parents' presence. Being in the same room makes it much harder for baby to learn the new pattern (Mom or Dad responding, but baby is responsible for the soothing now). This is often especially difficult during that dreaded 5:00 a.m. wakening, when most babies have a hard time anyway.

If you temporarily move out of your room, once your baby has practice with falling asleep independently and sleeping through the night, she's more likely to do this when you move back into your room again. When you move back into your room, be ready to do some 5-minute checks if your baby really cries, because your presence sleeping in the room again may disrupt her sleep initially. It's always possible for babies to share rooms with parents (of course, it's a perfectly natural way to sleep), but it does mean being very consistent with the Sleep Wave, and it takes some getting used to for both you and your baby.

If you're worried about noise, you can let your neighbors or other family members know that your baby is practicing falling asleep and that there may be a few nights in which they hear some protesting and crying (earplugs and a basket of goodies couldn't hurt). Explain this in advance. Use white noise, such as a low fan, for siblings if they need it.

Bedtime Tips for Multiple Children

Especially when you have a young baby and a toddler or older child, it can feel confusing to know what to do before bed to accommodate the needs of all kids. The dinner-to-bedtime hours are often the most challenging—it's normal to feel like chaos, frustration, and exhaustion rule at this time of day.

In the beginning, one or the other child may seem to get the short end of the stick—either you're spending all of your time attending to your baby and you're missing your older child, or your older child's routine is very set, and you feel like your baby doesn't get a proper bedtime routine. It's tricky to meet both kids' needs. In the beginning, you may have to keep your baby's routine very simple, and tote her along with you while you take care of your older child. As she gets toward 6 to 7 months, you will be able to do both bedtime routines more or less in sync. Happily, a baby and older kid can actually do well with the same bedtime, around 7:30 p.m.

EXAMPLE OF ROUTINE FOR BABY AND OLDER CHILD TOGETHER

· Bathe both kids (if you can manage this safely—otherwise, bathe one at a time or one child at a different time of day).
· Put pajamas on both baby and child.
· Set your older child up with a book in bed while you feed your baby (if this is hard, make a bedtime chart, so that your older child knows the routine well, and use a lot of positive

encouragement). If you have a young toddler, set him up with an engaging toy.
· Take baby to her room, sing song, place her in bed.
· Come back to your older child and finish story time, give kisses, and say good night.

Heather: When my son was a baby, his bedtime routine was a long, carefully crafted affair of bath, infant massage, multiple books, and songs. But when my daughter was born, we didn't have time for this Cadillac of routines focused only on her. I'd give her a bath along with her brother, put her pajamas on, feed her, sing her one song, and put her in the crib. Amazingly, I realized one night that every time I walked into the bedroom with her and turned the doorknob, just so, while saying "good night" softly to the rest of the house, she started to yawn—every night, almost on command! One night when my dad was over, I even asked him to step inside the door and watch. Sure enough, on cue, she yawned. He couldn't believe it. Her "routine" was my entering the room, saying the same words in a calm tone, turning the doorknob, turning on the fan, and closing the blinds in the room. The point is that you don't need an extravagant routine for it to be a powerful one.

TIPS TO KEEP IN MIND FOR YOUR FAMILY BEDTIME
ROUTINE:

1. **Plan, plan, plan.** The key to smooth, peaceful, and predictable bedtime is *planning*. Start your bedtime routine at the
   same time every night, and keep it very consistent—this
   works with your children's internal clocks and helps everyone in the family know exactly what to expect night to
   night. Make a chart, or a list (you may want to make a
   quick list every day, if you have a lot of naps and schedules
   to juggle). Naps and sleep are much more erratic with a
   newborn, but as your baby's sleep times become regular,
   your routine will, too. A picture chart for your older child
   of the steps involved in the bedtime routine can be helpful
   (see page 201).

2. **Be creative. Engage your little and big helpers.** There are
   lots of possibilities for how to approach bedtime, depending on ages, temperaments, and who you have there to help
   you. If your partner is there during bedtime, it's an opportunity for each parent to share a little one-on-one time
   with each child. If you're flying solo, you may put some
   novel toys or a cardboard box in your toddler's play yard
   while you put the baby down or have baby on a play mat or
   bouncy chair while you get your toddler out of the tub and
   into pj's. You can wear your baby or even nurse her while
   you read a book, sing a song, and say good night to your
   toddler. Or, you can have your toddler "help" you sing the

last song and say night night softly to baby (most toddlers would like it to be in this order, but they have to stay quiet and calm during the baby's routine). Along the way, prepare your kids for the steps to come.

It may seem like the easiest solution, but try to avoid having your toddler watch TV or use another electronic device during this time (except, of course, do what you need to when you have a newborn in the house). Remember that becoming competent, significant, and included members of the family are primary needs of kids. It's an opportunity for your children to practice resourcefulness and patience as they wait to get their needs met. Stay curious—think, "What will happen if we *don't* turn on the TV?" You may be surprised at your little one's ability to rise to the occasion.

3. **Your children are sensitive to your emotional state.** Take good care of yourself so that you can be as present and calm as is humanly possible. Start the bedtime routine early so you're not rushing, dim the lights, put on music, and add another step in your routine that you really enjoy, like taking a walk around the block together after dinner. You could even start your routine with a creative deep-breathing game for you and the kids. As your children grow and mature, you will create routines that are sweet and effective. You may even find yourself looking forward to bedtime routines.

Twins and More

When many of us see a new parent with twins, our jaws literally drop. Having one child feels overwhelming as it is; it's hard to imagine doubling it. How you adjust your sleep approach with twins will depend on several things.

- Are they identical or fraternal?

- What level of outside help will you have?

- Is your partner available for feedings during the night?

Scheduling Rules

Establish a shared feeding and napping schedule. This is in contrast to the approach of on-demand feeding and unpredictable sleep schedules for newborn singletons.

1. **Eat together.** Babies who feed at the same times, day and night, are likely to sleep at the same times. If you're breastfeeding and super-skilled at it, you may be able to feed your twins at the same time, using the football hold (this one takes patience and practice). Other options are breastfeeding one baby while holding the bottle for the other or feeding both from bottles. Of course, ideally, you're not alone and have helping arms to hold and feed one of your babies.

2. **Snooze together.** Put your babies down for naps at the same time. Identical twins tend to coordinate their schedules more easily than fraternal twins. Either way, as they grow and mature, they will be able to nap at the same time if you get them in a regular rhythm, which will allow you to have crucial time to rest and regroup before the next round. This also applies to sharing a bedtime routine and a set bedtime.

3. **Wake baby up?** It's so rare that we recommend waking a baby, but many twin parents swear that you have to break this rule to create the above-mentioned coordination of sleep times. With this approach, you wake whomever is still sleeping at the end of a nap, so that both babies will be ready to go down together for the next nap or bedtime. This can also apply to morning wake-up time. In order to keep the first nap on schedule, many twin parents will wake their babies at a certain time, say between 6:00 and 7:00 a.m., ideally at least 11 hours after bedtime.

RULES AND WHEN TO BREAK THEM, FROM A TWIN EXPERT AND TWIN MOM HERSELF

Molly: Even if it seems ridiculously hard, most twin parents do keep their babies on the same schedule, which gives them some routine and predictability. We veered from this rule when we let Charlie, our better sleeper, nap a little longer, so that Will could have some one-on-one time with us. Plus, one cranky baby was easier than two cranky babies! My twins are 5 now and I've blocked out so much from when they were babies. I can't say it enough: It's really hard. Get all the help you possibly can!

One Crib or Two?

Sleep safety recommendations say to have your newborns sleep in your room, in a co-sleeper or crib, for the first 3 to 4 months. Don't use a bassinet or Moses basket because twins can become overheated if they're lying too close together. Twins can sleep together, side by side, on their backs in the same crib, until one of them can roll or move around. At that point, to be completely safe, they should be moved to separate cribs, ideally where they can see and hear each other, which is soothing and reassuring to them. You may worry that they'll disrupt each other, but twins have an uncanny way of co-regulating, despite the frequent awakenings and cries.

Will It Ever Get Better?

Twins can be a tad behind on sleep development due to being born early. Rest assured that you can gradually hand over more and more of the soothing to your babies until they become independent sleepers. Just as with singletons, the key is to develop a curious stance rather than getting stuck overhelping. Sometimes twins end up being great sleepers because their parents are extra motivated to keep schedules very clear and regular.

Can I Use the Sleep Wave with Twins?

Absolutely! If your twins are 5 months (adjusted age if premature) or older and still not falling asleep on their own, the Sleep Wave (page 122) is your ticket. Assuming your plan is to have both children sleep in the same room, in most cases it will help to separate them temporarily as you implement the Sleep Wave. Wait until they are both falling asleep independently to put them back in the same room together. We've had parents come up with creative solutions for separating their twins while implementing the Sleep Wave: one crib in the living room behind a screen, hallway, bathroom, or closet, while the other is in their bedroom. It is also possible to try to implement the Sleep Wave with both children in the same room, especially if they are used to tuning each other out and progress quickly with falling asleep independently. If you find that they are frequently disrupting each other, you can switch to separate rooms for a few nights.

When to Forget the Schedule

Some parents, especially those with fraternal twins, prefer to follow each baby's cues around feeds and sleep times. In these cases, there is often one baby who is sleeping better and longer than the other. A plus is that parents have more opportunities to give each baby some much-needed individual attention. This approach is also easier to adopt if you have a nanny or family member with you so you can tag team.

TWINS PROGRESSING DIFFERENTLY

Jill (mom of fraternal twins): In the early months, my daughter Hayden was a better sleeper than her sister, Logan. So my husband and I each chose a baby to care for every night. We would alternate. That way, we each had nights where we got a little more precious sleep and the girls were able to show us how their sleep progressed differently. I couldn't have done it this way without my husband right there by my side.

Call in Your Village!

If it's one thing all parents of twins and multiples say, it's to *get lots of help*! Whether it's your partner, a hired nanny, Grandma, or friends, you will need frequent and regular helpers there with you to share duties and give you a break sometimes. Sadly, in our society, the norm is still for moms to feel that they're supposed to do everything by themselves. We don't believe this is true or natural, even with only one baby. Only you know how much and what type of help you need, and often people wait for your cue to pitch in, so don't be afraid to take the lead requesting and creating your team of helpers.

Working with Child Care Providers

Sleep at Day Care and Preschool

If your baby is in day care, start by asking the caregivers how they normally put the babies to sleep. What are the routines and schedules? If they rock, feed, or hold the babies until asleep, you'll need to explore with them if they're willing to do naptime the way you do at home. Most places will work with you as much as they are able. Things will inevitably be a little different at home versus at day care, but that's okay. It is a completely separate environment, so your baby quickly learns the difference between the two.

Preschool teachers are unlikely to rock or feed your toddler before nap, but they should be attentive to when he needs help getting settled, especially at the beginning. The high side of sleeping at preschool is that the routines are very set, and the expectations clear. Kids aren't as invested in dragging out the process of going to sleep, because they see the rest of their peers getting their mats and blankets and following a structured set of steps. Some nappers will have an easier time falling asleep at preschool because of the group dynamic and the consistency.

Your baby's nap schedule at day care may be different than at home. This can work just fine. You'll have to see how your baby does with a schedule that is different in two environments. For example, your 18-month-old may still take two naps at home, but at day care she does well with one nap (and gets to be part of the daytime activities with other children). Especially when your baby is at a transition phase with naps (somewhere in between three and two naps, or two and one nap), she may have days when she takes one more nap, and that's okay. Eventually her nap schedule will be the same at home and at child care.

Working with Child Care Providers at Home: Babysitters, Nannies, Grandparents, and More

When you're working on sleep, consistency across all caregivers will be a huge plus to your baby. Some babysitters or nannies will go to heroic efforts to get your baby to sleep without fussing or protesting, including rocking, holding, stroller rides, etc. They are trying to show you what an attentive caregiver they are. But if your baby or child is learning the Sleep Wave, it's important to communicate very clearly with all caregivers *exactly* what you want them to do at bedtime, naptime, and in the event that your baby protests or wakes up. Here are some tips for creating consistency for the Sleep Wave in the home.

An interesting tendency we've seen is how often parents report that their baby or toddler goes down awake with no problem for anyone who's not Mom or Dad. Tricky little ones! This is great information for you that your baby is completely capable.

- Share the concept of the Sleep Wave with anyone in your home who puts your baby down for a nap or at bedtime. Explain it in enough depth to get them on board. Have them read sections of this book or look at the Sleep Wave Planner in the Appendix.

- Tell them the steps of the Sleep Wave and create a "handout" for them to refer to over time. Include the basic steps, your script (which they should use word for word), and your mantras.

- Have them "shadow" you several times as you go through all of the steps of the bedtime or naptime routine and then continuing to the Sleep Wave. If your baby is already falling asleep quite well on her own, you will have to describe and show them what to do, just in case she wakes unexpectedly.

- Make sure that they have a reliable timer for the 5-minute checks.

- Make sure that they are able to reach you for the first several times, in case they need clarification or support.

- If your toddler or child is responding well to the Reverse Sleep Wave, share with them exactly how that works and what it looks like.

Going Back to Work

This is a tremendous adjustment for both you and your baby, whenever it happens. It's normal for moms and dads to have many difficult feelings around the loss of time together and concern about how everyone will adjust. On top of this emotional roller coaster is the challenge of the logistics and juggling of who goes where, when, who will care for your baby, and how in the world you will get everything done.

Sleep can easily get derailed during this time. If you plan ahead and take steps to hold on to the progress you've already made sleepwise, you'll end up with more quality awake time with your baby in the long run. Here are some tips:

- If you plan to implement the Sleep Wave, do so at least two weeks *before* you go back to work *or* a month or more *after*, not during; one big transition at a time is plenty for the whole family.

- If you need to shift your baby's bedtime later, due to your work schedule, try to minimize this, even if it means that one parent won't see baby until morning playtime. Your baby needs at least eleven hours of sleep at night.

- You may find that you're short on time at the end of the workday. It's fine to go straight into your bedtime routine as soon as you get home. This time should be soothing and pleasurable for both of you. Dim the lights, put on some comfy clothes, and choose books and songs that you really love.

- Some moms choose to keep a nighttime feeding in place, so that they can fit in a little extra bonding time. This can work very well, especially if you're nursing and concerned about maintaining your milk supply. Just be sure not to start adding in more feedings later in the night as time goes on.

- Do everything in your power not to regress if your baby is already falling asleep on his own. Stick to the Sleep Wave (and Reverse Sleep Wave at bedtime if using it), expect a few bumps during this time, and know that your baby will go back to what he has proven to you he can do.

Single Parenting

This job of caring for a baby or young child is daunting enough with two parents in the home. For those of you doing it on your own, it's nearly impossible to fathom. We humans are social creatures and depend on each other to thrive. With this in mind, and with the knowledge that babies benefit from having many caring adults love and tend to them, finding regular, dependable support (whether it's from family, friends, or hired help) will be key to you finding the balance that you and your baby need. Needless to say, good sleep for you will be an absolute necessity.

- Organize your team. Whether it's family, friends, or nannies, the time you spend putting helpers into place will make all the difference in the world. We all need "our village" and single parents need this even more so.

- Using the sleep strategies in this book will be crucial to give you the time and energy you will need in this tremendously demanding role. You will likely be sleep deprived for the first several months, but getting sleep on track as soon as possible will help enormously.

- Keep sleep consistent across caregivers. Keep your team in the loop and make sure that their pattern of response is the same as yours. This will help your baby feel safe and know what to expect, which will also ensure that his sleep doesn't regress. If Grandma rocks him to sleep and the nanny feeds him to sleep, you're going to have a much harder time putting him into his bed awake.

- Despite all that is on your plate, be sure to carve out a little bit of time, just for you, a few times a week at least. Take a walk, take a hot bath, or have coffee with a friend. You need some balance and a chance to refuel.

- Try to find a new parents' group in your area. Not only will you have support and understanding from your new friends, you may be able to share some child care. We need each other.

7.

Parent Sleep

"I'm a parent—I'm not supposed to be well rested."

A mom of two little kids said this to us once. It's a sentiment we hear from parents all the time. This lovely mom—a working parent with a toddler and preschooler—was fully committed to helping her children sleep well, but her own sleep was a low priority. Her sleep needs were squeezed by work and family; after her kids were asleep, she was at her computer until 11:30 p.m., went to bed at midnight, and was up at 6:30 a.m. to get the day started. She felt drowsy and less productive at work, and it was hard to motivate to exercise or see friends.

This is a widespread problem. Parents are sleep deprived, but they either don't know it or they don't think they can change it. There's a myth out there that poor sleep is an occupational hazard of parenthood and that you just need to tough it out because it comes with the territory. We hear parents joke that they'll sleep 10 years from now!

THE RISKS OF POOR PARENT SLEEP

· You're moody and have low energy.

· There are safety risks: 37 percent of adults say they've fallen asleep at the wheel.

· You're less creative and make poorer decisions and more errors.

· There are health risks, such as weight gain, hypertension, and heart disease.

Don't accept poor sleep as a way of life. Of course the first months with your baby will change your sleep drastically (if your baby is under 5 months, read "Parent Sleep" on page 93). But in the long

Did you know that when you're sleep-deprived, parts of your brain are still asleep?

term, you absolutely can be a well-rested parent (no, this is not an oxymoron)! Most adults need 7 to 8 hours of sleep every night to function at their best (research indicates fewer than 5 percent of adults are "short sleepers," who need only 6 hours of sleep or less). Even moderate sleep deprivation mimics the effects of ingesting alcohol beyond the legal driving limits—you don't want to go about work and family life that way!

The House That Values Sleep

Your sleep habits—good or bad—have a trickle-down effect on the rest of the family. Think beyond just solving immediate sleep issues to how you're affecting your child's relationship to sleep. This relationship is created in the moments, big and small, that make up every day. You've seen the way your child models your behavior in many arenas? Sleep is no different. If she sees you taking care of yourself and valuing your sleep (along with healthy eating and exercise), it's a worldview that will rub off on her.

Especially once your child is at least 2 years old, both show and tell her that you value your own self-care and sleep. This can take many forms:

- **Model healthy sleep habits** (see below).

- **Have conversations about sleep.** Tell your child that grown-ups need about 8 hours of sleep, and kids need about 11 to 12 hours at night because their brains and bodies are growing so much. Notice with your child how it feels when we don't sleep enough, and how great we feel when we do sleep. Explain that the brain works faster and better with great sleep, whereas when we don't sleep well, our mind feels a little cloudy.

- **Take care of your own bedroom.** Design it in a way that makes you happy, clear out clutter, make your bed, and talk about how your bedroom is a cozy, calm place that you love. When your child is old enough, have her make her bed or help you do it.

How Parents Can Get the Best Sleep

We meet plenty of parents who don't sleep well, even after a baby or child is sleeping through the night. For most of these parents, following sleep advice and making behavioral changes in sleep habits and schedules will help.

In this chapter, we'll troubleshoot the most common sleep issues for parents and give you tangible advice for fixing your sleep with the same care that you dedicate to your children's sleep needs. If you have a newborn, this section will be helpful, but please also see "Parent Sleep: Help in the First 4 Months," in Chapter 3, page 93.

Note: If you try to make changes to your routines and habits and still find yourself sleeping poorly or feeling tired, it's important to talk to your doctor because it could be related to a sleep disorder or another health concern.

My Baby Sleeps but I Don't!

If your baby's sleep has just started to improve, you might notice that you still wake up when she used to. Your mind is on high alert, still expecting to be needed during the night and ready for action. For most parents this goes away and they start sleeping continuously after their body has adjusted.

On the other hand, a lot of parents (especially moms) tell us that they feel very sensitive to noise at night and ready to jump at all times. This, unfortunately, is a natural part of parenthood for some of us. We're constantly living with the knowledge that our kids *might* need us (even long after they've started sleeping well), and it makes our brains more activated. It's a good evolutionary strategy to keep us on our toes, but it makes for some restless nights. If this is the case for you, try to protect your sleep as much as possible and help yourself relax. This might include turning down or off the baby monitor so that you only hear when your baby really needs you, wearing earplugs if your partner can be on duty, using a white noise machine or fan in your room, and practicing relaxation exercises to fall asleep (see Appendix, page 318).

Sleep Tips for Parents

These are sleep strategies for parents. Many of these are based on gold standard recommendations for achieving good sleep for *all* adults, but the advice we give you here is tailored to parents specifically.

1. **Adjust your schedule.** Especially if you're a night person or someone who used to occasionally sleep in, aligning your

sleep with a child's can be hard, but it's really important. Your child's early wake-up time (whether it's 6:00 a.m. or 7:30 a.m.) is now a fixed point, around which most parents need to adjust their own sleep. You need 7 to 8 hours of sleep (it helps to know exactly how much is optimal for you), so if you know you're going to be awake at 6:00 a.m., you'll need to be in bed by 10:00 or 11:00 p.m.

This may sound like an obvious calculation, but you can't imagine how many parents we meet who go to bed late every night (or at least a few nights a week), wake up with their child, and then wonder why they're exhausted! Remember that your sleep needs are *actual* sleep time, not just the time you're in bed, so if you need 8 hours of sleep and it takes you 15 minutes to fall asleep, you'll want to get into bed 8 hours and 15 minutes before your child's wake-up time. When you don't do this, you carry small— but growing—amounts of "sleep debt" with you.

Don't cut this calculation too close! Now that you're a parent, you never know what's going to happen in the middle of the night—someone could have a nightmare, or wake up coughing and need you. If you get 8 hours of sleep on a regular basis, you'll be okay if you have a night of 6 hours because you have to attend to a sick baby. If you're always cutting it close or skimping on sleep, those tough nights will hit you much harder.

Your downtime is important, but . . . A lot of parents tell us that they stay awake too late because they relish their downtime after the kids go to bed—they want time to spend with each other, or time to work, watch TV, eat dinner, or read. Having time to yourself is really important, but the best way to go about this is to put your child to bed early. If your baby is in bed at 7:30 p.m. and wakes up at 6:30 a.m., this gives you at least 2 hours after her bedtime before you need to think about getting ready for bed yourself.

A consistent schedule is important. Your body is happiest when you go to bed at the same time every night, even on the weekends. Too many parents miss hours of sleep during the week and hope to make it up over the weekend, but it's very hard for your body to adjust this way and it can make you feel more tired. It's much better to sleep consistently than to think about paying your sleep debt back at a later date.

2. **Avoid alcohol before bedtime.** What do you mean, alcohol helps me fall asleep! We hear this a lot, because drinking in the evenings is a common habit for parents, especially after a long day of taking care of babies or juggling work and family responsibilities.

   Yes, alcohol is a sedative, but it can disrupt sleep during the night. Consuming alcohol before bed can cause a person to have more light sleep and wake up more in the second half of the night. This is like a "rebound effect" that occurs after the effects of alcohol have worn off. REM sleep and slow-wave sleep change under the effects of alcohol, as do core body temperature and the action of certain neurotransmitters.

   Not surprisingly, drinking leads to reduced alertness the next day and more difficult doing things that require dividing your attention (like parenting). This has been shown in many studies; for example, pilots who drank alcohol between 6:00 and 9:00 p.m. were significantly impaired when they were tested on a flight simulator 14 hours later (with no alcohol left in their system). We know that you're probably not flying an aircraft tomorrow, but you still need your wits about you!

Of course this doesn't mean that you should avoid drinking altogether. It's only if you notice that you're waking up in the night after drinking, or you're feeling tired the next day even though you thought you got enough sleep. Just take note of how alcohol affects you.

3. **Turn off the screens.** One of the biggest sleep stealers for parents is working, browsing, or chatting on an electronic device like a laptop or phone close to bedtime. Many of these emit blue light, which affects circadian rhythms and suppresses the release of melatonin, making it harder to fall asleep once you climb in bed (see Chapter 8).

   Social media, work, e-mails, and online research can really suck you in. It's incredibly easy (and very common for many adults and teens) to stay up late because their mind is still engaged and can't relax. If you read a stressful message or story before bed, or feel compelled to keep researching a topic or working on a project, it can wind you up and really make it harder to sleep.

   This is why we recommend *shutting down electronics at least an hour before bedtime.* If your bedtime is 10:00 p.m., make it a rule that at 9:00 p.m. your close-range electronic gadgets all go off. Don't check messages, work, or browse on your computer after this time. If you can't sleep, try not to reach for one of these gadgets—read a print book or use a reader with no backlight.

4. **Exercise.** Exercising during the day is known to improve sleep quality. If you have a regular workout routine, that's great. If you're home with your baby, see if you can take a walk every day—getting some sunlight during the day will help with sleep as well.

5. **Your routine.** Yes, grown-ups need bedtime routines, too! Having wind-down time that follows the same pattern every night cues your brain to shift gears and get ready for sleep. Eat a light snack. Don't have a conversation about finances or other sources of stress for at least a couple of hours before sleep. Turn off electronics 1 hour before bed. Protect this time and know that you have to allow your body time to unwind.

SAMPLE BEDTIME ROUTINE

7:30 p.m.—Baby is asleep—yay!

9:00 p.m.—Read a book, have a light snack of toast with honey and sip chamomile tea. Dim the lights in the house.

10:00 p.m.—Get in bed. If you have a hard time falling asleep, practice relaxation breathing or another mindfulness exercise (see the Appendix).

6. **Your bedroom.** We've met a lot of parents who put careful thought into arranging and furnishing their child's bedroom, only to forget about their own. You need a comfortable sleeping place, too. It helps your sleep to have a bedroom that feels welcoming, visually pleasing, and calm. Make sure you have:

- A comfortable mattress, pillows, and sheets; test out each before you buy

- Cool and fresh air (open the windows during the day if possible)

- Darkening shades or curtains to block out early morning sunlight

- A calm space, without piles of paper, computers, a treadmill (yes, we've seen plenty!), bills, or other work-related materials

  The best practice is to not have a television in your bedroom, although we've met well-rested families who do. The issue with television is that it can cause you to stay up too late, or to doze off while watching and wake back up again to turn it off and resettle. Assess whether having a TV in your room is disrupting your sleep and remember it has to work for both partners.

7. **Rotate sleep-in mornings.** A consistent schedule for weekdays and weekends is best. But if parents have "sleep debt" accumulated from the week, switching off each morning on the weekend, so that one person sleeps in (even if it's

just an hour) on Saturday and one sleeps in on Sunday, is a strategy that works well.

8. **Associate your bedroom and sleep.** If you can't fall asleep after 20 minutes or so, get up and move to another place in the house where you can read a book or do something else that is relaxing. If you spend a lot of time awake in your bed, your body will start to associate that place with being awake.

9. **Nap smart.** Naps have major upsides and downsides, so you have to evaluate how they work for you. A nap can really help if you're tired during the day, and they're especially needed when your baby is really young. The best naps are short and early (late afternoon naps can interfere with nighttime sleep). If you sleep only 6 hours at night and you can consistently nap during the day, that might be just fine—it's the "siesta" mentality. However, if you nap during the day, it will be harder to fall asleep at night because a nap relieves the "sleep drive" (Chapter 8). This causes you to go to bed later and perpetuates the cycle of not getting enough nighttime sleep. Even a 10-minute doze on the couch in the early evening can make it harder to fall asleep at bedtime. If this is the case, try not to nap at all and to go to bed earlier.

We all have a natural low-energy point in the day (usually the mid-afternoon, around 2:00 or 3:00 p.m) because of our circadian rhythms. Around this time, many adults feel drowsy—this is often attributed to post-lunch sleepiness, but it is actually a lull in between two peaks of alertness in the circadian system. After this window of drowsiness has passed (even if you don't nap during it), you usually become more alert again in the evening.

Maybe it's not surprising that parents need much of the same sleep advice babies do (well, except for the parts about earplugs and alcohol). After all, babies are just small people! We all need a regular bedtime; a consistent, calming routine; no screen time before bed; and fresh air and exercise during the day. We're all wired to sleep well, as long as we don't get in our own way.

8.
What Is Sleep?

Falling asleep, staying peacefully asleep, long and healthy naps—all are rooted in your child's biology. When you understand a few basic principles of how sleep works, you can use this knowledge to help your child sleep better at any age.

In this chapter, we'll take you through the basics of sleep science so you can:

1. Understand the underlying mechanisms of sleep.

2. Use this understanding to set your child's sleep schedule and improve naps and nighttime sleep.

Just like language or motor skills, sleep matures over the first years of your child's life. The biology of newborn sleep is distinct from older baby sleep, which is different from preschool sleep . . . and so on. As your child grows, the patterns and physiology of her sleep will change—knowing what's going on in her brain and body will make you better able to support her sleep development.

The Two Processes That Regulate Sleep

You've probably watched your newborn baby flicker awake and drift off again almost instantly and randomly throughout the day. This switch from sleep to wake to sleep again is controlled by a basic brain mechanism that acts much like a seesaw, moving your newborn in and out of sleep through the day and night.

As she grows, two main processes begin to regulate her sleep (and continue to do so for her life): the *homeostatic sleep drive* and the *circadian system*. The sleep drive is like pressure that builds the longer you're awake, and then releases while you sleep. The circadian system is made up of internally driven rhythms that are approximately 24 hours in length. You'll see here how these systems interact and influence when and how long your child sleeps, and how *the best sleep will happen when the two are coordinated.*

The Homeostatic Sleep Drive

The homeostatic sleep drive is very simple to understand: The longer you're awake, the greater the drive toward sleeping. For adults, after a day of being awake, the pressure is great enough that you become drowsy and fall asleep (or if you didn't get enough nighttime sleep, the sleep drive might be more intense and allow you to nap). The sleep drive in babies and children is very strong and builds quickly.

The sleep drive has a powerful influence over your baby's nap schedule because babies and toddlers build up pressure to sleep over just a short amount of time. If they don't nap sufficiently, they can become irritable, less capable of learning, and more resistant to falling asleep. Napping relieves this pressure.

This is why your baby is often ready for sleep after 60 to 90 minutes of being awake, and your toddler after 2 to 3 hours. Parents are sometimes astounded that their baby could sleep for 12 hours, be awake for 60 minutes, and fall asleep again. But even with a good night of sleep, the sleep drive quickly builds during the daytime hours.

PRACTICAL TAKEAWAYS

- Don't be surprised by your baby's need for frequent naps— sleep drive builds very quickly in babies and young children. Be aware of your baby's optimal *awake span* between sleeps. Put your young baby down to sleep after each 90-minute span of awake time during the day.

- Even a short nap (10 minutes or less) reduces the sleep drive. Keep this in mind when your child sleeps in the car or stroller—it can make it harder for her to fall asleep for a regular nap, since the sleep drive has already been relieved. With a toddler or older child, taking a brief nap in the late afternoon can make it harder to fall asleep at bedtime.

- Napping continues to be very important for children until around the end of preschool, in part because their sleep drive is strong. If children don't nap, they are less able to regulate emotions, learn, and think creatively.

The Circadian System and the Internal Clock

If the sleep drive were acting alone, you would get progressively sleepier and sleepier over the course of the day. That's not the whole story, though. The other system regulating your child's sleep (and your own) begins with a powerful internal clock, nestled in the brain. This clock is a biological pacemaker that controls the circadian rhythms (roughly 24-hour cycles), allowing us to anticipate the light-dark pattern of day and night. It's the same type of clock that causes a morning glory to open with the sunlight or birds to sing in the morning.

The internal clock sends us messages throughout the 24-hour day, influencing our sleep-wake pattern and many other biological processes. As night falls, body temperature begins to go down and levels of the drowsy-making chemical melatonin rise in preparation for sleep. Toward morning, the activating chemical cortisol rises. During the daytime, the circadian system opposes the sleep drive with activating signals (so that you don't just get sleepier as the day goes on). There are two peaks in alertness in the day, one in the morning and one in the early evening. In between these two peaks is when most adults feel a little drowsy, usually in the mid-afternoon. This is when children who nap once a day take their nap. At bedtime, alerting signals from the circadian system are withdrawn, sleep drive takes over, and the circadian system helps us stay asleep, even as the sleep drive becomes less strong as the night goes on.

When your child wakes up in the morning—experiencing the first rays of sunlight and starting to eat and play—it's akin to pressing "start" on her internal clock. From this point forward, when she's drowsy for her first nap and when she's ready for bed later that evening will be influenced by when this start button was pressed. Your child's rhythm is also influenced by regularity. Going to bed at the same time every night, waking up at the same time every morning, and napping on roughly the same schedule every day keeps the circadian system in sync and helps her be alert and drowsy at the proper times.

What Time Your Child Is Alert and What Time She's Drowsy

The circadian system naturally makes your child alert or drowsy at different points during the day. Interestingly, the drive toward sleep is quite high in the morning at your child's wake time, and it continues to be high for another few hours (for example, from 6:00 to 9:00 a.m. for a child who normally wakes up at 6:00 a.m.). This is called the *circadian sleep maintenance zone*, and it's why babies and young children can easily nap soon after waking up.

At the other end of the day, there is a *wake maintenance zone*, also known as the "forbidden zone" for sleep. This is a period a few hours before your child's regular bedtime, when it's harder for her to fall

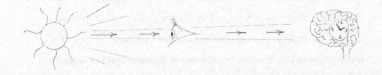

The circadian system: Light picked up by the eye travels along the optic nerve to a tiny cluster of cells in the brain's hypothalamus, called the suprachiasmatic nucleus (SCN). This process keeps us on a 24-hour rhythm and influences factors such as when melatonin (sometimes called the "hormone of darkness") rises in the evening to make us drowsy, when we feel alert and productive, when we're hungry, our mood, body temperature, and more. The SCN is the master clock that controls circadian rhythms, as well as the other clocks in cells throughout the body, so they're all in sync.

asleep. This is a second wind, a time when your child's circadian system is making her more alert (in order to counteract the homeostatic sleep drive). If you notice that your child seems sleepy in the afternoon but around dinnertime miraculously gets her energy back, this is the forbidden zone in action, winning out over the sleep drive. If your child has a regular bedtime with a calming routine and dim lighting, her circadian system will withdraw its alerting signals and she'll become drowsy at that bedtime—now the two forces are working together. Since the circadian system drives alertness a few hours before bed, this may be why babies usually have a longer period of awake time at the end of the day, and why they tend to take shorter naps or be a little fussy in the late afternoon.

The internal clock is accurate, but it doesn't keep to exactly 24 hours on its own (the average clock length for adults is 24.2 hours). Therefore, we have to reset it each day and keep it at 24 hours with exposure to sunlight in the day and darkness at night; this process is called "entrainment." The internal clock has to be somewhat flexible because the length of the day changes with the seasons (a clock set to wake you with the sun in April would get you up well past sunrise in May). That is why it's built so that it can be constantly readjusted (entrained) by external cues. All this is vitally important when it comes to understanding sleep patterns that can be very precise (your baby wakes up almost on cue), yet subject to getting out of sync when external cues (lights on at night, too much activity by other family members, and so forth) are changed.

WHEN THE INTERNAL CLOCK DEVELOPS

A fetus does have a rudimentary circadian system and shows daily rhythms (for example, in heart rate and activity levels) sometime in the second trimester. But this is thanks to the signals of Mom's hormones (such as cortisol and melatonin), not the baby's own internal clock.

When your baby enters the world (and is no longer influenced by Mom's hormones), he loses his sense of day and night. A newborn's circadian system on its own is immature. Brand-new babies tend to sleep on and off without much of a day-night pattern; their sleep is fragmented. But every day after he enters the world, your baby's sense of a daily rhythm continues to develop (research suggests that even a newborn's circadian system is sensitive to light). At about 6 weeks, infants start to have an increase in evening melatonin (which makes

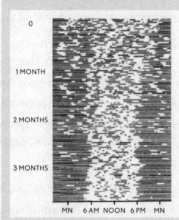

Rest-activity pattern of a newborn. Dark bars represent sleep. Adapted with permission from Rivkees et al.

304 · The Happy Sleeper

them drowsy), and at this age most infants are more active and awake during the day than they are at night.

By around 2 to 3 months of age, babies have more pronounced rhythms of sleeping and waking and their natural sleep onset is more or less coupled to sunset (this is why we encourage you to put your baby to bed early). They also now have a circadian pattern of core body temperature—this is important because low body temperature at night is a natural component of sleep. All these factors are good news for sleep development, and as time goes on, your baby continues to consolidate sleep at night and be awake for longer periods during the day.

Artificial Light, Electronic Gadgets, and Sleep

Modern life is not very sleep friendly! While our bodies are naturally programmed to sleep as night falls, artificial lights keep us awake and entertained much later.

Light suppresses melatonin, a chemical that normally rises as we become drowsy and ready for sleep. In particular, short-wavelength light (which appears as blue and is emitted by many electronic screens) is the most disruptive to sleep—this kind of light has been shown to suppress melatonin and delay sleep onset. If there are bright household lights or your family watches screens and electronic gadgets up close in the hours close to bedtime, it can make it harder for you to become drowsy. Artificial light can affect sleep in people of all ages.

PRACTICAL TAKEAWAYS

• You can't rush the development of your newborn's circadian rhythms. Regular sleep takes time (roughly 4 to 6 months) because your baby's nervous system is naturally maturing. You can help the process along by exposing her to indirect sun in the day and keeping light and activity low at night.

• Your child is exquisitely attuned to light cues. Use this to help him set his body's clock by getting up at roughly the same time every morning, napping at the same time, and going to bed at the same time every night.

• Get out and exercise during the day.

• Manage artificial light in the evenings so that you don't confuse your child's biological clock and suppress melatonin. Dim the indoor lights 60 minutes before bed, keep your child from using electronic devices such as tablets and computers before bed, and keep electronics out of your child's room. If you have a nightlight, make sure it's very dim and ideally use a red bulb (red light does not have the strong affect on circadian rhythms that blue light does). Don't turn on bathroom lights in the night; use a nightlight in the bathroom instead.

• Put your child to bed early—this is the way her body is naturally programmed.

• Block early morning sun rays with darkening shades or curtains.

Sleep Cycles, REM Sleep, and Non-REM Sleep

You've probably heard of REM (rapid eye movement) and non-REM sleep before. It takes time for children to develop these clearly defined sleep stages. Your child's "sleep architecture" will be similar to an adult's at around age 3 or 4 (see below for a description of the adult sleep cycle).

WHILE YOUNG BABIES SLEEP, THEY MOVE THROUGH STAGES DESCRIBED AS

- **Active** (the precursor to REM sleep) in which babies twitch and make sounds and facial expressions.

- **Quiet** (the precursor to non-REM sleep). During quiet sleep, your baby's breathing is regular and his body is very still. This is a deep sleep. Mature non-REM sleep has distinct stages, but it takes roughly 6 to 8 months for your baby to develop these.

Baby Sleep Is Active

Roughly 50 percent of a newborn's sleep is active, and little babies can move directly into active sleep (whereas children and adults move through non-REM sleep before entering REM). This is why if your baby falls asleep on your lap, you might see her eyes flutter, mouth grimace, and arms and legs twitch when she does so—she's more easily roused while in this type of sleep. In adults, muscle movement is inhibited during REM sleep (thankfully, so we do not act out our dreams), but this full motor inhibition takes time to develop, so babies move their arms and legs quite a bit. This active sleep can last for 20 minutes or more before your baby transitions into quiet, or deep sleep. Active sleep (or what is eventually called REM sleep) slowly decreases until roughly age 3, when it makes up 20 percent of sleep (as in adults).

Sleep Cycles Are Shorter

Infant sleep cycles are roughly 60 minutes—it's not until around school age that your child's sleep cycles will become 90 minutes, like an adult's.

Babies Are Noisy Sleepers

Does it sound as if there's a tiny dinosaur in the room? In active, or REM, sleep, newborns can be quite mobile and vocal. Young babies have a natural tendency to twitch a lot during REM sleep, and they can move their arms and legs, breathe irregularly, and make all kinds of funny sounds. This is sometimes strange or concerning to parents, but it's normal for your baby to make sounds at night, and it's important to know that it doesn't always mean that you need to help her or pick her up. In fact, learning to discern your baby's sounds at night is really important to her ability to develop self-soothing skills. If your baby snores, gasps, or snorts a lot while sleeping, this is important information for your pediatrician, so he or she can rule out sleep disorders like sleep apnea.

DO BABIES DREAM?

Babies spend a huge amount of time in REM sleep (the stage of sleep when dreaming occurs in older children and adults). Newborns spend about 16 hours asleep each day and roughly 50 percent of that time in REM sleep—that's a lot of potential dreaming time! Some think that babies do dream, with simple images and experiences (a dog barking, a twirling mobile, a nipple). Others believe that dreaming develops over the years as the brain matures and that, as children grow, their dreams become more complex and rich with thoughts and feelings.

DID YOU KNOW?

Every species sleeps, but we've evolved and adapted our own best ways to do so. In a pack of sleeping ducks, the ones on the outside will sleep with only half of their brains so they can keep watch for the rest. Dolphins and whales are also known to put half the brain to sleep at once.

ADULT SLEEP
Adults Cycle Through Four Stages of Sleep

Stage 1. Eyes closed, you're at the threshold between wakefulness and sleep. You can easily be awakened in this stage—if you are, you may not know you were asleep at all. Sometimes people have the sensation of falling (this is called a "myoclonic jerk," or a "sleep start").

Stage 2. This is light sleep, in which your heart rate begins to slow and body temperature begins to go down.

Slow wave sleep. Now you're in deep sleep. Your blood pressure and heart rate go down and your breathing slows. It's harder to wake you up. A lot of deep sleep happens in the first part of the night.

REM. Roughly 90 minutes after falling asleep, your brain becomes active, but voluntary muscle movements are inhibited. Brain waves are faster and less organized than in non-REM sleep and the eyes scan back and forth under the lids. REM is the stage in which most dreams occur. As the night progresses, you experience more REM sleep (this is why you're more likely to dream toward morning and why most kids' nightmares happen in the second half of the night).

Appendix

Creating Your Child's Sleep Schedule

Use this information as a reference to help you set your baby or child's sleep schedule.

1. Sleep Needs

AGE	NAPS	TOTAL NAP HOURS PER DAY	TOTAL NIGHTTIME HOURS OF SLEEP	TOTAL SLEEP IN 24 HOURS
0 to 4 weeks	Varied, many	7-9	7-9	16-18
1 to 2 months	3-5	5-7	8-10	15-16
3 to 5 months	3-4	3-5	9½-12	14-15
6 to 8 months	3	3-4	10-12	14-15
9 to 11 months	2	2½-4	11-12	14-15
12-15 months	2	2-3½	11-12	13-15
16-23 months	1-2	1-2	11-12	12-14
2-3 years	1	1-2	11	12-13
3-4 years	0-1	0-1½	11-11½	11-13
4-6 years	0	0	10½-12	10½-12

2. How Many Naps Does My Child Need?

5 months: three naps (if baby catnaps, she may even take four naps/day)

9 months: two naps

15 to 20 months: one nap

3 to 5 years: Most children stop napping

3. Span of Awake Time Between Sleeps

The optimal amount of time they are able to stay awake based on their sleep drive:

5 to 6 months	1½–2½ hours (sometimes with one 3-hour span in the afternoon)
9 months	3–3½ hours
15 to 20 months	4 to 5 hours (depending on the length of nap)

4. Nap Schedule Examples

0 TO 5 OR 6 MONTHS OLD
(USE SPAN OF AWAKE TIME)

6 TO 9 MONTHS OLD (THREE NAPS)

	EXAMPLE 1	EXAMPLE 2
Bedtime	7:00 p.m.	7:30 p.m.
Wake time	6:00 a.m.	6:30 a.m.
First Nap	7:30 a.m.	8:30 a.m.
Second Nap	12:00 p.m.	12:30 p.m.
Third Nap	3:00 p.m.	3:30 p.m.

9 TO 15-20 MONTHS OLD (TWO NAPS)

	EXAMPLE 1	EXAMPLE 2
Bedtime	7:00 p.m.	7:30 p.m.
Wake time	6:00 a.m.	6:30 a.m.
First Nap	9:00 a.m.	9:30 a.m.
Second Nap	2:00 p.m.	2:30 p.m.

15 TO 20 MONTHS TO 2 TO 3 YEARS (ONE NAP)

	EXAMPLE 1	EXAMPLE 2
Bedtime	7:00 p.m.	7:30 p.m.
Wake time	6:00 a.m.	6:30 a.m.
Nap	11:30 a.m.	12:30 p.m.

3 TO 5 YEARS (ONE NAP)

	EXAMPLE 1	EXAMPLE 2
Bedtime	7:00 p.m.	7:30 p.m.
Wake time	6:00 a.m.	7:00 a.m.
Nap	12:30 p.m.	1:00 p.m.

Sleep Progress Chart

In this chart, record the time baby goes to bed, as well as the time of any night wakings, how long you feed (if feeding or weaning), how long protesting and crying lasts with Sleep Wave checks, and what the outcome is (for example, baby self-soothes to sleep). If you're consistent with checks, you will see progress over time. Start with bedtime on Day 1, continue with naps on Day 2, and now you're on your way!

For a printable Sleep Progress Chart with multiple days, go to www.thehappysleeper.com.

DAY 1–NIGHT

EVENT	TIME	AMOUNT FED (IF APPLICABLE)	PROTESTED FOR	OUTCOME/ NOTES
Bedtime				
Night Waking 1				
Night Waking 2				

EVENT	TIME	AMOUNT FED (IF APPLICABLE)	PROTESTED FOR	OUTCOME/ NOTES
Night Waking 3				
Night Waking 4				
Night Waking 5				
Wake Up				

DAY 2–DAY

EVENT	TIME	PROTESTED FOR	OUTCOME/ NOTES
Nap 1			
Nap 2			
Nap 3			

DAY 2–NIGHT

EVENT	TIME	AMOUNT FED (IF APPLICABLE)	PROTESTED FOR	OUTCOME/ NOTES
Bedtime				
Night Waking 1				
Night Waking 2				

EVENT	TIME	AMOUNT FED (IF APPLICABLE)	PROTESTED FOR	OUTCOME/ NOTES
Night Waking 3				
Night Waking 4				
Night Waking 5				
Wake Up				

Sleep Wave Planner

Here you can make notes for your sleep plan. For a downloadable version, go to www.thehappysleeper.com

1. CURRENT SLEEP SCHEDULE

Timeline for nights: including waking, feedings, length or amount of feeding.

| _____ |

Bedtime   Wake

Timeline for days: including naptimes and feeding.

| _____ |

Wake   Bedtime

2. NEW SLEEP SCHEDULE

BEDTIME	WAKE TIME	NAP	NAP	NAP

For babies under 5 to 6 months, use the *span of awake time* to know when to nap, rather than setting a schedule based on time of day.

3. HEALTHY SLEEP HABITS

New bedtime routine

New nap routine

SLEEP ASSOCIATIONS

HELPFUL	UNHELPFUL
Paci/thumb	Feeding
Lovey	Bouncing/rocking
Tummy time/rolling	Car/carrier
White noise	Other
Other	

How does baby/child fall asleep?
Where does baby/child sleep?
Room environment checklist: Dark, cool, comfortable mattress, fitted sheets, lovey, moving air, and/or white noise?
Parents' Goals for Sleep

Script for Sleep Wave—Use for Night and Naps and Keep Consistent

_____

_____

_____

Weaning—Decrease Thirty Seconds or ½ Ounce Every Other Night

_____

_____

_____

Mantras (see pages 136–7 for examples)

_____

_____

_____

_____

FINAL REMINDERS

Check-in with script every 5 minutes if crying, stay extremely consistent, don't soothe during checks, and stay very calm and confident.

Mindfulness Exercises for Parents

You're knee-deep in dishes, running a bath, reviewing your mental checklist for tomorrow, and maybe even manning the needs of multiple kids at once—and now we're asking you to be attuned?

Sounds like a tall order, but we have a well-researched tool in our corner that will help make this possible: mindfulness, or the practice of being aware and present. Mindfulness techniques are at the leading edge of research, showing powerful effects on health (lowering blood pressure, boosting the immune system, improving mood, and more). Only recently have we been able to understand from a brain science perspective why and how mindfulness helps us in so many ways. The research on the power of mindfulness is so compelling, it only makes sense to learn about it and apply it to your life as a parent. It's your direct route to attunement.

If you're a busy parent (is there any other type?), the idea of being in a "calm, curious place" may sound impossible. But modern exercises for growing mindfulness don't require you to sit cross-legged and still. They are portable, and any activity can be used for meditation. Let us introduce you to the Kitchen Sink meditation because, if you're like us, you spend a good amount of time there. Yes, you heard us. We're going to help you strengthen neural connections while you're rinsing those sippy cups.

It's very easy. The next time you're washing dishes, focus on the feel of the water on your hands, the sound of the water flowing, and the warmth and suds. Be in the simplicity of what is happening, only in this one moment. Direct your mind away from your to-do list, your worries, what is stressing you, and toward the sensations in your environment. It takes repetition. At first your mind might wander over and over. The more you do it, though, the better you become at it. This is like a mental muscle, so you have to practice.

There are many ways to meditate. The key is finding the ones that work best for you. The goal of meditating is to practice it every day, even for just a few minutes, so that when you need it, you can draw on those strengthened brain pathways to make a new, thoughtful, more aware choice. Keep it simple, work it into your daily routines, and you'll be surprised to find your awareness naturally increasing.

Here are some doable ways for parents to meditate. During each of these, inhale and exhale through your nose.

Bed Meditation (Before anyone knows you're awake!) Sit up, focus on the air moving in and out of your lungs. Cool on the inhale, warmer on the exhale.

Body Scan On each breath, check in with a body part, working from the top of your head to the tips of your toes. On each exhale, relax that part. Notice where you hold the most tension and repeat those areas a few times.

Relaxation Breathing Focus on your breathing. Lengthen your inhales and exhales. Notice your chest and tummy expand on the inhale. On the exhale, feel everything release. Let gravity help you let go.

Walking Meditation Focus on the pressure you feel on the sole of each foot as you walk, what you see, or the sounds you hear in the distance. Just let the sensations enter your awareness.

Push the Pause Button At a challenging moment, practice pausing. Do nothing. See what it feels like to not react automatically.

Eating Meditation Focus on a bit of food, the taste, the textures, the aroma. Let the sensations enter your awareness. Jon Kabat-Zinn has a famous meditation on eating a raisin. This one can completely change the way you enjoy food!

Sleep Meditations for Parents

Belly Breathing Lie on your back with your hands flat on your belly just below your waist. Focus on the rise and fall of your hands over your belly as you take long, slow breaths in and out through your nose. Try to gradually lengthen your breath and take as long to exhale as you do to inhale. If you find yourself thinking about your to-do list or your worries, gently bring your attention back to your breath and your hands rising and falling on your belly. You may have to direct your attention back many times, and that's okay.

Breathing Meditation Inhale to the count of 8, hold for 4 counts, and then exhale, letting everything go. Feel a complete release on the exhale and sink into it for 2 to 3 counts. Repeat this until you fall asleep. Keep your mind's attention focused on your breathing and gently refocus your attention if it wanders.

Peaceful Place Bring your attention to an image of a place or scene you find calming. It can be anything: your favorite beach or vacation spot, clouds in the sky, the steps of a dance routine, mentally decorating your home, lying on the ground and looking up into tree branches; it's very individual. The idea is that if you really explore this scene in your mind, it directs and focuses your attention and leaves no room for planning, worrying, ruminating, or other mental activities that might be keeping you up. Gradually you'll feel your body and mind relax.

Body Scan Slow down your breathing and, on each exhale, focus on and release completely one small body part. Start at the top of your head and release every part of your face, neck, shoulders, arms, torso, pelvic area, and legs, all the way down to your toes. Feel your muscles in each body part relax and let gravity release them down into your mattress. If you're still awake when you get to your toes, start at the top of your head again. You can repeat body parts that hold the most tension, such as your eyelids, forehead, jaw, shoulders, chest, and belly.

Acknowledgments

Our hearts are bursting with gratitude; many thanks are in order.

This book would have been entirely impossible had it not been for the vision and all out enthusiasm of our lovely and super-sharp editor, Sara Carder. She "got" us and our ideas right from the start, and was always rooting us on. It would have been just as impossible without Michelle Tessler, our brilliant agent who has been a pillar of support and tremendous ideas all along. They were both fantastically patient and caring with us as they held our hands on this wonderful journey.

Many formidable sleep and child development experts reviewed material for this book. Thank you to **Mark S. Blumberg, Ph.D.**, Editor-in-Chief of *Behavioral Neuroscience*; **David M. Cloud**, CEO of the National Sleep Foundation; **Sujay Kansagra, MD**, Director, Pediatric Neurology Sleep Medicine Program at Duke University Medical Center; **Scott Rivkees, MD**, Chairman of Pediatrics at the University of Florida College of Medicine; **Nanci Yuan, MD**, Director, Sleep Center at Stanford University; and **Yael Wapinski, MD**, pediatrician. We had the unique honor of consulting with the breastfeeding gurus Wendy Haldeman and Corky Harvey, founders of the unparalleled Pump Station and Nurtury, who taught us many crucial things about breastfeeding that truly take this book to a new level. Owner Cheryl Petran has also been incredibly supportive, for which we are grateful.

The dear, bright-spirited mommies in our Wright Mommy and Me groups, along with our sleep consult families—in all their new parent vulnerability—have been the most incredible teachers. Their honest discussion of the mind-bending effects of sleep deprivation, and understandable confusion over how to make it better, is what made us certain that the topic of baby sleep needed some real rethinking.

From Heather: My friends and family have been cheering me on every step of the way while writing this book. A special thank you for reading and giving me notes: Laurel Garber, Rob Garber, Ben Hansford, Madeline Holler, Brynn Karwas, Tootsie Olan, Mary Posatko, Justine Osborne, Amanda Salvado, Gillian Turgeon, and Robert Turgeon. A huge squeeze to Summer Drew, the beautiful photographer for our book cover and website.

Thank you to my husband, who knows my voice best, who gives me pivotal notes and is so enthusiastic about my writing, he wants all my sentences to end in an exclamation point! Your support for me, and every time you came home beaming with a marked-up draft in hand, has made this book possible. Thank you to my mom and dad, both scientists, who love and support me always, have been the biggest influences on my writing (*if you can, say it with fewer words*), and read everything I give them with the attention of a high-stakes grant proposal. I love you beyond words. My two kids, Dashiell and Eloise, who have the most beautiful faces and big hearts (thank you, Dashiell for your great ideas—many 5-year-olds will benefit from your bad dream–fighting techniques!) You two sweet little people are the reason I started writing about this topic, and you're the source of all the inspiration and joy that has come ever since.

From Julie: I need to thank my precious village; I couldn't have done this without you. Sleep can be a polarizing topic—little did I know how much support would be bestowed on me from so many lovely people.

Words cannot describe how exceptionally talented and passionate my Wright Mommy and Me group leaders are, nor how their belief in this way of thinking about sleep and attachment, along with their support for this book, have been truly life changing for me.

My teachers, professors, colleagues, and most exceptionally, my mentor, Dan Siegel, MD, whose brilliant work and concepts formed the basis for explaining how an integrated way of understanding attachment, creates space for little ones to develop optimally and master new skills, while continuing to feel safe and loved. I am forever indebted to his passion and generous spirit.

I have such an insane wealth of friends who have cheered me on as this book took shape, I could never name them all here but they include friends from my childhood, my ballet class, my book club, my Culver City community and my life. You know who you are and I love you so much! A special thanks goes to Michael Sheehy, who has always believed in me.

The dearest of the dear are my Pump Station ladies, Carol, Judy, Kate, Rita, Linda Yadira, Dinora, Norma, Rosie, and many more. Your warm smiles and unfailing kindness to me will always be remembered.

I never thought I could write a book, but my family never doubted it. My parents and siblings (Stephen, David, and Susan) are the epitome of unconditional love and belief in me. The ringleader of this clan is my biggest fan, highest standard setter, and most loving presence in my life: my mom, Dorothy Wright. She also happens to be a pediatrician and the devoted mom of four who doesn't remember exactly how she got all of us to sleep! My dear beloved father, A. William Wright, who died ten years ago, was a very thoughtful and curious thinker, a neurologist. I know he would have loved the exciting field of interpersonal neurobiology, which informs the marriage of brain science and human experience in a book like ours. I'm also extremely fortunate to have the gift of my fabulously lovable and curious son, Jack, who was my best teacher and inspiration. His quiet belief and pride in me, along with his gentle spirited drawings are priceless beyond my wildest dreams.

Citations

References are in the order in which they appear in the chapters.

CHAPTER ONE: THE HAPPY SLEEPER

Effects of sleep on language, attention, emotional control, and cognition

Gomez, R. L., Bootzin, R. L., & Nadel, L. (2006). Naps Promote Abstraction in Language Learning Infants. *Psychological Science*, 17(8), 670–674.

Sadeh, A., Gruber R., Raviv, A. (2003). The Effects of Sleep Restriction and Extension on School-Age Children: What a Difference an Hour Makes. *Child Development*, 74(2), 444–455.

Touchette, E. et al. (2007). Associations between sleep duration patterns and behavioral/cognitive functioning at school entry. *Sleep*, 30(9), 1213–1219.

Children's sleep patterns and parents sleep

2004 National Sleep Foundation Sleep in America Poll, Children and Sleep.

Kids and caffeine

Branum, A. M. et al. (2014). Trends in Caffeine Intake Among US Children and Adolescents. *Pediatrics*, 133(3), 386–393.

Sleep troubles persist

Byars, K. C. et al. (2012). Prevalence, patterns, and persistence of sleep problems in the first 3 years of life. *Pediatrics*, 129(2), 276–284.

Naturally short sleepers

He, Y. et al. (2009). The transcriptional repressor DEC2 regulates sleep length in mammals. *Science*, 325 (5942), 866–870.

Stanford sleep studies and parent's sleep deprivation

Dement. *The Promise of Sleep*. New York: Dell, 2000.

Learning and academic success

Gomez, R. et al. (2011). Learning, memory, and sleep in children. *Sleep Medicine Clinics*, 6, 45–57.

Gruber, R. et al. (2012). Impact of sleep extension and restriction on children's emotional lability and impulsivity. *Pediatrics*, 130(5), 1155–1161.

Touchette, E. et al. (2007). Associations between sleep duration patterns and behavioral/cognitive functioning at school entry. *Sleep*, 30(9), 1213–1219.

Behavior and emotions
Golan, N. et al. (2004). Sleep disorders and daytime sleepiness in children with attention deficit/hyperactivity disorder. *Sleep*, 27(2), 261–266.
Cortese, S. et al. (2006). Sleep and alertness in children with attention deficit/hyperactivity disorder. *Sleep*, 29(4), 504–511.
Paavonen, E. et al. (2009). Short sleep duration and behavioral symptoms of attention deficit/hyperactivity disorder in healthy 7 to 8 year old children. *Pediatrics*, 123(5), 857–864.

Health
Landhuis, C. E. et al. (2008). Childhood sleep time and long term risk for obesity: A 32-year prospective birth cohort study. *Pediatrics*, 122(5), 955–960.
Cappuccio, F. P. et al. (2008). Meta-analysis of short sleep duration and obesity in children and adults. *Sleep*, 31(5), 619–626.
Hart, C. et al. (2013). Changes in children's sleep duration on food intake, weight, and leptin. *Pediatrics*, 132(6), 1473–1480.

Parent's life
Van Dongen, et al. (2003). The cumulative costs of additional wakefulness. *Sleep*, 26(2), 117–126.
2002 National Sleep Foundation Sleep in America Poll, Adult Sleep Habits.
2005 National Sleep Foundation Sleep in America Poll, Adult Sleep Habits and Styles.
DrowsyDriving.org http://drowsydriving.org/about/facts-and-stats/

CHAPTER 2: THE HAPPY SLEEPER APPROACH

Attachment and Attunement
Siegel, D. *Parenting From the Inside Out*. New York: Tarcher/Penguin, 2003.
———. *Pocket Guide to Interpersonal Neurobiology: An Integrative Handbook of the Mind*. New York: W. W. Norton & Co., 2012.

Babies are like little scientists
Gopnik, A., Meltzoff, A., Kuhl, P. *The Scientist in the Crib: What Early Learning Tells Us About the Mind*. New York: William Morrow, 2000.

The Development of Infant Memory
Rovee-Collier, C. (1999). *Current Directions in Psychological Science*, 8 (3), 80–85.

CHAPTER 3: BABY (0 TO 4 MONTHS)

Safe Sleeping Guidelines
American Academy of Pediatrics, healthychildren.org

The vestibular sense
Eliot, L. *What's Going on in There?* New York: Bantam, 2000.

CHAPTER 4: BABY + TODDLER (5 MONTHS TO 2 YEARS)

Self soothing and going into bed awake
Burnham, M. M. et al. (2002). Nighttime sleep-wake patterns and self-soothing from birth to one year of age: a longitudinal intervention study. *Journal of Child Psychology and Psychiatry*, 43(6), 713–725.
2004 National Sleep Foundation in America Poll, Children and Sleep.
Touchette et al. (2005). Factors associated with fragmented sleep at night across early childhood. *JAMA Pediatrics*, 159(3).

Artificial light and circadian rhythms
Lockley, S.W., Brainard G.C., Czeisler, C.A. (2003). High sensitivity of the human circadian melatonin rhythm to resetting by short wavelength light. *Journal of Clinical Endocrinology and Metabolism*, 88(9), 4502–5.
Rahman, S. A. et al. (2011). Spectral modulation attenuates molecular, endocrine, and neurobehavioral disruption induced by nocturnal light exposure. *American Journal of Physiology*, 300(3), 518–527.

Breastfeeding and breastfeeding benefits
Lawrence & Lawrence. *Breastfeeding: A Guide for the Medical Professional* (7th ed.). Philadelphia: Saunders, 2010.
Walker, M. *Breastfeeding Management for the Clinician: Using the Evidence* (2nd ed.). Sudbury, MA: Jones & Bartlett Learning, 2009.

Formula, solids, and sleep
Montgomery-Downs, H. E. (2010). Infant feeding methods and maternal sleep and daytime functioning. *Pediatrics*, 126(6), 1562–68.

Sleep training
Price, M. H. et al. (2012). Five-year follow up of harms and benefits of behavioral infant sleep intervention: randomized trial. *Pediatrics*, 130(4), 643–651.

CHAPTER 5: CHILD SLEEP (2 TO 6 YEARS)

Bedtimes, cognitive performance, and behavior
Kelly, Y. et al. (2013). Time for bed: associations with cognitive performance in 7-year-

old children: a longitudinal population-based study. *Journal of Epidemiology & Community Health.*

Kelly, Y. et al. (2013). Changes in bedtime schedules and behavioral difficulties in 7 year old children. *Pediatrics,* 132(5) 1184–93.

Nightmares and night terrors

Sheldon, H. et al. *Principles and Practice of Pediatric Sleep Medicine* (2nd ed.). Philadelphia: Saunders, 2014.

CHAPTER 6: SPECIAL CIRCUMSTANCES

Co-sleeping

Mosko, S. et al. (1997). Infant Arousals During Mother-Infant Bed Sharing: Implications for Infant Sleep and Sudden Infant Death Syndrome Research. *Pediatrics,* 100(5), 841–849.

Bed sharing and safety

http://cosleeping.nd.edu/safe-co-sleeping-guidelines/

http://www.askdrsears.com/topics/health-concerns/sleep-problems/sleep-safety/safe-co-sleeping-habits

CHAPTER 7: PARENT SLEEP

Van Dongen et al. (2003). The cumulative cost of additional wakefulness. *Sleep,* 26(2), 117–126.

National Sleep Foundation: Healthy Sleep Tips.

Ebrahim et al. (2013). Alcohol and sleep: effects on normal sleep. *Alcoholism: Clinical & Experimental Research,* 37(4), 539–49.

CHAPTER 8: WHAT IS SLEEP?

Sleep development

Sheldon, H. et al (2014). *Principles and Practice of Pediatric Sleep Medicine* (2nd ed.). Philadelphia: Saunders, 2014.

Artificial light and circadian rhythms

Lockley, S. W., Brainard G. C., Czeisler, C. A. (2003). High sensitivity of the human circadian melatonin rhythm to resetting by short wavelength light. *Journal of Clinical Endocrinology and Metabolism,* 88(9), 4502–5.

Rahman, S. A. et al. (2011). Spectral modulation attenuates molecular, endocrine, and neurobehavioral disruption induced by nocturnal light exposure. *American Journal of Physiology,* 300(3), 518–527.

Gronfier C., et al. (2003). Efficacy of a single sequence of intermittent bright light pulses for delaying circadian phase in humans. *American Journal of Physiology*, 287(1), 174–181.

Figure: Rest-activity pattern of a newborn
Rivkees, S. A. (2003). Developing Circadian Rhythmicity in Infants. *Pediatrics*, 112(2), 377.

Animal sleep
Rattenborg, N. C. et al. (1999). Half-awake to the risk of predation. *Nature*, 397, 397–398.

APPENDIX

Easy Mindfulness Meditations
Kabat-Zinn, J. *Wherever You Go, There You Are: Mindfulness Meditation In Everyday Life*. New York: Hyperion, 2009.

Index

Author Bio

Heather Turgeon, MFT, is a psychotherapist who writes about child development and parenting. Her writing has appeared on *Babble* (as the long-running Science of Kids column), *Salon*, *The Daily Beast*, and others, and she has covered the topic of sleep for many outlets, including as a science writer for the National Sleep Foundation. Heather lives in Los Angeles with her husband and two little ones—both of whom are happy sleepers.

Julie Wright, MFT, is one of Los Angeles's best-known parenting group leaders and has taught thousands of moms in her popular Wright Mommy and Me groups at the celebrated Pump Station & Nurtury. Julie is a psychotherapist whose work focuses on empathic, mindful parenting, attachment, and sleep. She has specialized training and experience in the 0 to 3 years, interning at Cedars Sinai Early Childhood Center and LA Child Guidance Clinic. Julie lives in Los Angeles with her son, and visits her East Coast family often.

Also by the authors

Now Say This

The Right Words to Solve
Every Parenting Dilemma

The 3-Step Approach to Effective Communication

BABY TO
SCHOOL AGE

Heather Turgeon, MFT,
and Julie Wright, MFT

AUTHORS OF
The Happy Sleeper

Parents have the best intentions to be patient and loving,
but in the heat of the moment, they too often find
themselves feeling helpless, desperate, and so frustrated
that they resort to yelling, threatening, bribing, or caving.
Now Say This solves the dilemma: how can you be
empathic and effective at once?